# Who's Who
# in American Poetry
# 2021

*Frances L. Kalapodis*

## John T. Eber Sr.
### MANAGING EDITOR

A publication of

## Eber & Wein Publishing
### Pennsylvania

Who's Who in American Poetry: Vol. 2

Library of Congress
Cataloging in Publication Data

ISBN 978-1-60880-702-4

Proudly manufactured in the United States of America by

# Eber & Wein Publishing

Pennsylvania

# Who's Who
# in American Poetry

# I'm Standing

I'm standing in my truth,
that the color of my skin does not define me.
I'm standing in my truth,
that no matter what anybody says I matter.
I'm standing in my truth,
that I can do anything I put my mind to.
I'm standing in my truth,
that my background made me who I am today.
I'm standing in my truth,
that your judgment of me will not change my character.
I'm standing in my truth,
that accepting myself comes before accepting others.
I'm standing in my truth,
that my place in this world means something.
I'm standing in my truth,
that I am loved and cherished.
I'm standing in my truth,
Are you standing in yours?

Chevelyn Tafushia Curtis
*Arnoldsville, GA*

[Hometown] *I grew up in Athens, GA* [Ed] *high school diploma* [Occ] *gallery guide at an art museum*
[Hobbies] *read, spend time with my family, and write* [GA] *I haven't reached it yet.*

## The Face in the Mirror

The face in the mirror.
Who is she?
There is a face in the mirror looking back at me.
A stranger in the mirror staring right through me.
With eyes as soft as silk.
With a face as warm as a quilt.
And a heart as big as all outdoors,
Full of nothing more than love.
There is a face in the mirror looking back at me.
A stranger in the mirror staring right through me.
The image of a lady with a lonely heart.
The image of a lady standing in the dark.
The image of a lady who wants to
love only one.
But the haunting image in the mirror
came to be only me
There is a face in *my* mirror looking back at me.
A stranger in *my* mirror staring right through me.
Who is she?
Only me. Just me.

Monica Lynn
*Wixom, MI*

[Hometown] *Detroit, MI* [Ed] *master hair stylist and educator with Farouk Systems* [Occ]
*cosmetologist, educator* [Hobbies] *fishing, music, boating, bicycling, camping, traveling*

*My greatest achievements are my family—my kids Randall, Desireé, and Christopher, and grandkids Alyse, Damar, RaSHay, LaNay, Kira, Serenity, Bryce, and Elias. I love them more than words can ever say. And working with kids in homeless shelters and being able to bring a smile to their faces*

## Picture Window

As the Pandemic is reaching everyone
I watch life through the safety
of a picture window
Clouds expand with mist turning
everything gray
Soothing sounds of traffic flowing
Dark trees and red brick buildings
Outlined against the
turbulent sky
Raindrops slowly slide down
the glass pane

As night envelopes me I face again
stressful night terrors
Dreams of being hopelessly lost
on a train to nowhere
Waking up to half remembered dreams
soon forgotten forever
Fatigue as we fight this virus with
Overwhelming isolating anxiety
as night and day blend to
a new normal
life of terror

Barbara M. Cohen
*Fairport, NY*

[Hometown] *Fairport, NY* [Ed] *BFA Massachusetts College of Art* [Occ] *retired* [Hobbies] *writing, poetry, drawing, pictures, reading, cooking and baking* [GA] *having my poems published*

*The years have been difficult dealing with the coronavirus, but becoming more introspective has been a surprising plus to the isolation of quarantine. Now, fully vaccinated, like many others, I'm timidly re-entering a former life I only vaguely remember. This poem "Picture Window" is a reminder of the push and pull of life living in a pandemic.*

## Mr. Rogers, Mr. Jackson, and That Awesome Mr. Beck

When our starter starts to struggle
So you think he may be hexed
Just replace him with the trio
That makes batters nervous wrecks
That set of fearsome firemen
Will have those hitters vexed
Mr. Rogers, Mr. Jackson and that awesome Mr. Beck
When we lead by just a run
And the game's been neck and neck
We can call on those three stoppers
Those three aces in our deck
Those Giant mow-'em-downers
Loved a bushel and a peck
Mr. Rogers, Mr. Jackson and that awesome Mr. Beck
If our starters never finish
Might we say, "Oh what the heck?"
Who cares who gets the victory
When all four have thrown that spec
We'll rejoice in having hurlers
Whose arms are so high tech
Mr. Rogers, Mr. Jackson and that awesome Mr. Beck

Jim Alfred Healey
Aptos, CA

*I'm an eighty-four-year-old baseball fan. In 1986, I won the Willie McCovey Hall of Fame contest. The prize was an all expense paid trip to Cooperstown to see him enshrined. For twenty-five years I played senior softball and was on a seventy-year-old team that won the world series. I now play tennis, golf and pickle ball and I belong to the Sons of the Desert and the Society of American Magicians. On my car license frame it says Route 66 Road Scholar.*

## A Note Beside the Bed

I awake one winter morning
to find a note beside my bed
That you have decided it's
over and want to be alone instead.
You said you once loved me,
but that feeling is now gone.
All the years we were together
of all we did in time. It's
over in a moment with a note
beside the bed.

Jean Cast
*Greenlawn, NY*

## God Blessing to You and Your Sweet Little Family

There is a friend for little children
above the blue sky,
and friend Who never changes,
Whose love will never die.
Our earthly friends may fail
us and change with changing gears.
This Friend is always worthy
of that dear name He bears.
Jesus Christ my Lord and Saviour.

Alice M. Clark
*Burlington, NC*

## If I Was

If I was a singer
What would I sing
I'd sing about our love
And what you mean to me

If I was a writer
What would I write
I'd write about our good times
And how we've always said our good nights

If I was a builder
What would I build
I'd build a house of love
And with love it would be filled

If I was a sower
What would I sow
I'd sow a great harvest
And love it would grow

If I was pilot
Where would I fly
I'd be flying high in the sky with a banner behind
And it would read about our love for you and I

To my wife of fifty-two years

Russ Burleson
*Little Rock, AR*

[Hometown] *Little Rock, AR* [Occ] *retired* [Hobbies] *spending time with my wife* [GA] *accepting Jesus Christ as my Savior, a marriage for almost fifty-three years to the love of my life*

## A Missionary's Story

I listened as the speaker told his story.
He spoke of huts with paper-thin walls made of mud
And small sticks woven together, thatched roofs over
Dirt floors. The small square structures were called
"kay-pay" which meant home for mountainous people of
Haiti living near the Dominican border.
Family children living in the kay-pay are given
Chores early in the life as "Bale-kay" which meant
Keeping the dirt floor swept clean.
Children are often left at home alone while parents go
To sell homemade wares to obtain food money.
When this occurs the oldest of the children is chosen
To care for siblings to include feeding and bedding
Even though the chosen one may only be seven years old.
The missionary continued, "I have noticed the clothes
Of the children are old, dirty and need repair. When
The girls' dresses are out-grown the tops are turned
Down and worn like a skirt with a t-shirt for a top.
There are no shoes to wear so their feet become
Encrusted with mud and sometimes also have dried blood.
He ended his story mentioning the dirt cookies eaten
When they had no food. Haiti is in crisis. Help us.

Mable M. Guiney
*Fort Walton Beach, FL*

[Hometown] *Fort Walton Beach, FL* [Ed] *BS education, post-graduate work* [Occ] *public school teacher* [Hobbies] *reading, quilting, crochet, crafts and making jewelry* [GA] *graduating army boot camp at the age of 34 / USAR-SFC rank E-7*
*I was born in Norfolk, VA in April of 1943. Soon after birth our family moved to southwestern West Virginia to live in the Tug River Valley where one side of the valley was in West Virginia and the other side in Kentucky. Tug River was our swimming site in summer. I completed high school and began working for the Cleveland Trust Bank for several years. Later I enrolled at Evangel College in Springfield, MO graduated with a BS degree in education and taught in public schools before joining the USAR. Meantime I married a college classmate.*

## Ode to People in Pain

I'm in pain, but feeling fine
asking how I'm doing is no crime
my body wracked with pain is no shame,
the rheumatologist is not to blame.
My twisted body has given me fame.
My prayers to God, to the Great Divine,
has kept my pain at a low level whine.
My hands won't fit in any glove,
it takes five minutes to shove, shove, shove.
My feet won't fit in any shoe
I do end up feeling tired and blue!
I walk crooked everywhere I go,
I should thank God for every day, I know!
I won't bother you anymore about my pain,
crying to myself to sleep gives me no shame.
The sun comes up, the sun goes down,
I won't spend my life always wearing a frown!

Sylvia Weakley
Etlan, VA

[Hometown] *Etlan* [Ed] *nursing assistant* [Occ] *caregiver* [Hobbies] *singing, dancing, gardening, playing chess* [GA] *giving my heart to the Lord and Savior, Jesus Christ*

*I love taking care of my granddaughter, Paetyn, and my mother, Sylvia Shultz. What inspired me to write this poem was seeing people struggle, trying to live in pain, and still end up smiling anyways! Most of us, including me, depend on God for strength to get through he day, still loving and serving our Lord and Savior, Jesus Christ! A friend named David also inspired me, talking to him and seeing what he has to deal with every day.*

# A Pandemic Year Haiku Review March 2020–March 2021

A CCRC:
IL, AL, HCC.
Premier Cadbury.

Senior citizens
Confined to their apartments:
No social meetings.

The dining room closed.
All meals brought to apartments.
Singles eat alone.

No activities
Permitted in the complex:
Lobby is vacant.

Bus transportation
For doctor visits only:
Other trips canceled.

How long will it last,
This "shelter-in-place" routine?
No one seems to know.

Craig E. Burgess
*Cherry Hill, NJ*

[Hometown] *Audubon, NJ* [Ed] *MS in foreign languages* [Occ] *high school Spanish teacher* [Hobbies] *travel, photography, poetry* [GA] *civilian humanitarian award from the Chapel of Four Chaplains After teaching Spanish for twenty-six years, I became a writer and historian. I served as liaison to the US Navy for twenty-five years and wrote a patriotic history on one of Audubon's three Congressional Medal of Honor recipients. After being diagnosed with a rare blood cancer, which resulted in two cornea transplants, I moved from my lifelong home in Audubon to a continuing care retirement community (CCRC) in August of 2017 and currently serve as president of the Premier Cadbury Residents' Association. My poem was inspired by how the senior citizens in my retirement home suffered during the COVID-19 pandemic.*

## Pain Afflicted and Inflicted

We start to die when we are born
The end depends on the beginning
We can't change the world, nor are we expected to
but we can change the mood of our location
Better to take on a challenge
while prepared and confident,
than to risk succumbing to it unexpectedly
The whole world is full of demons
We just have to exorcize them out
Just because we don't hear something
doesn't mean it wasn't said
There is body language, body gestures
facial expressions, and sign language
We can seem to unite during solace
but not during solemn
No one can see their reflection in running
water, only in still water
Ensure that those you love know it because
once you or them are gone, no matter how
loudly it is screamed, it wouldn't be heard
The heart has no traction
Even if we could empathize
the pain wouldn't be comparable
except through biopsy of a broken heart

Kendrick Williams
*Fort Worth, TX*

[Hometown] *Birmingham* [Ed] *graduate student in health informatics* [Occ] *healthcare* [Hobbies]
*cooking, writing, research* [GA] *winning past poetry contests*

*My pen name is Mindpollution since I try to influence readers to view things differently. I am a graduate
student in health informatics currently.*

## A German Shepherd Ponders Life

What will I do, what shall I be
If every opportunity were opened to me
Will I wear a badge and serve only the best
Will I pass all my training and stellar each test
I have passed my puppyhood; now I ponder my fears
What will I do in my remaining years
Will my life matter to someone each day
Will I be homeless, unwanted and live as a stray
Will I die on a highway with no one to care
Or will a soldier not die because I was there
Will I go to a shelter to be put to sleep
Or will I have a family to be mine to keep
Will my name be immortal on a monument wall
With all heroes like me who took the big fall
Will I partner a cop, will I go to war
Why was I born, what am I for
Choose me to serve and protect
That role I can fill
I cannot select
That is your will.

Barbara Ann Snow
*Bronson, FL*

*I was born in Framingham, MA eighty-one years ago. My lifetime career was in regulating and protecting animals in non-profit humane societies and municipal animal regulation agencies. Following retirement I took a volunteer position with the US War Dogs Association, and I now direct the southern chapter. I attended college for two years and received much credited training in my profession. I love to bead and create jewelry for non-profits, visit friends, and be connected with my church. I am most proud of helping to pass a dog fight felony bill in Louisiana.*

## God's Cozy Love

When troubles or hard times come,
I'm wrapped in God's cozy love!
When I'm sick or others around me are sick,
I'm wrapped in God's cozy love,
And I'm able to share his love with them!
When I sin or do wrong things,
Because Jesus died for me,
I'm wrapped in God's forgiving love!
When no one is around,
Jesus is always there,
I'm wrapped in God's cozy love!
When I'm not heard,
Jesus hears my prayers,
I'm wrapped in God's cozy love!
When I don't have work or do have work,
I'm wrapped in God's cozy love!
When I have little or much to share,
I'm wrapped in God's cozy love!
When I need help or care,
I'm wrapped in God's cozy love!
God's love is always around me!

Angela Christine Michael
Mesa, AZ

[Hometown] *Mesa, AZ* [Ed] *high school, some correspondence writing courses* [Occ] *housekeeping Christian care home* [Hobbies] *writing, reading, listening to music, arts, and crafts* [GA] *sharing God's love with others*

*I have some learning challenges; still God is always helping me and looking out for me!*

## Still a Successful Woman

You called me every evil name in the book
But a woman of God
Fooled by your lustful demon that kept me around!
You kicked me when I was down
I nurtured you like a loving spouse
To even visiting you in the jailhouse
Like a beast pulling domestic violence on me!
You kicked me when I was down
Does my intelligence upset you?
Why is your jealousy deadly as sin?
Cause I walk with a mean strut
Standing firm under pressure and never cracked up!
Did you want to see me successful?
Why are you a wolf in sheep clothing?
I was fuel to your soul, attached you to my bankroll!
You kicked me when I was down
I had to let go of being mistreated,
keeping God first before men
Protected because I'm one of God's chosen
And still a successful woman

Vonda Howard
*Milwaukee, WI*

## God! God! God!

God! God! God!
Of the red, white and blue.
Teach each of us to recognize
All blessings come from You!
Were You not our Founding Cornerstone?
Did we not claim our rights from You?
Your name is on our money.
In court, we use it too.
So why do You suppose
Some cringe and wring their hands
When the rest of us rejoice aloud
"God bless us and our land!"

Mary Elizabeth Santomauro
*Stagecoach, NV*

[Hometown] *Stagecoach* [Ed] *high school and some college* [Occ] *retired* [Hobbies] *freelance writer, yard work* [GA] *gave birth to 3 boys and 2 girls*

*America needs to come back to God if we want to survive!*

## Yesterday's Dream

Yesterday's dream
Fills the pages of my mind
Edge worn, verses faded
Yet I search for what I created
Oh let the wavering dream
Blow away
So my heart can release
The joy of God's fulfillment
In each day

Jo Worthington
Lakeland, FL

[Hometown] *Baltimore, MD* [Ed] *master of divinity* [Hobbies] *books and discovering God's creatures and His wonders in nature* [GA] *years work at the hospital in Long Island, NY*

*This poem slipped out of my heart. I knew God had a plan for my life. I began to run trying to fulfill His purpose. Then suddenly change came slowing my steps. A new journey entered where through His word I now walk. It took me into a relationship with God that I had never known. Dreams will fade, His fulfillment will last for eternity.*

## Forever Changed

Have you heard the news?

A virus, unlike any other disease,
from half a world away,
has changed our lives forever,
So now without delay,
together we must prepare for it to stay.

Losing those we hold so dear,
there's no escape, only fear.
How many lives must end?
Let us not pretend we do not see the tears.

Young, old, strong, frail, bold and meek,
must not forget but believe
in all we've learned to share and teach,
seeking answers to put our minds at ease.

We are told out of the darkness comes the light,
sadness will turn to laughter
if only we can love each other
every day and every night.

Yes, we are the news.

Renette JoAn Colwell
*Prescott, AZ*

[Hometown] *Carrington, ND* [Ed] *federal judicial courts and several attorneys* [Occ] *retired paralegal*
[Hobbies] *reading, traveling, writing short stories and poetry* [GA] *being a published author*

*I have been writing for over fifty-five years and it gives me such peace of mind in this chaotic world. I feel so blessed to have so many friends and family supporting my writing achievements. My husband and I now live and love our life in Prescott, AZ.*

## Society—Not My Cup of Tea

So let's talk. Let's talk about the world. Of
ethics and dreams, of morals, religion, reality, and
who has what things.
We claim we all want the same
but we turn our backs on others just to entertain.
Whispering lies that spread like radiation to a fast
burning flame. And we think we've got game.
Large or small, as a community our faith should
be strong banding together when life gets hard or
things go wrong.
For no man is an island unto himself,
so put that pride you have on the top shelf
and open up your hearts as well as your hands and
have faith in yourself as well as in man.
Stop listening to the lies you're being
told and search for true wisdom; it's worth more
than any fool's gold.
Now don't pick up that stone
and cast it at me just because I can see that which
you cannot see.
Knowledge and wisdom are powerful
things. Just like sleep rejuvenates all the
mind can bring.
Courage isn't faith alone, and it's not
enough, when you walk that long dark walk home.

Ruby D. Santa
*Philadelphia, PA*

[Hometown] *the old country Saint Augustine, FL* [Ed] *graduate of many fields* [Occ] *have more than my share* [Hobbies] *too numerous to name* [GA] *to this day it's still the birth of my children*

*I'm grateful for the many things life has to offer. Good or bad it's a world filled with wonder.*

## Once Upon a Dream

Once upon a dream I wandered in a world supreme, free from hate,
Free from greed, free from poverty for those in need.
Disease was gone, no plagues to greet us with each new dawn.
A dream you say! That's all it was, just a fleeting fantasy
of something that could never be.
Don't be so fast to say never, for who is it that makes up the
hate and the greed and other oppressions that make this world
A troubled place?
It's you and I and everyone who turns a blind eye to all the
Injustice we see on our streets today.
I pray that some day our world will be like my dream.
With God's help, I truly think it can.
I was inspired to write this poem by thinking that each of us
Should look into our hearts and minds to make this world a better place.

James Harwood
*Spencer, WI*

[Hometown] *Spencer, WI* [Ed] *high school, military* [Occ] *carpentry* [Hobbies] *poetry, vintage electronics, old radios, juke boxes* [GA] *wonderful family—six children, many friends*

*I was born a year after the end of WWII; a baby boomer I became. Raised on a farm in central Wisconsin. Went to a one-room country school and on to high school in a little town of Loyal, WI where I was fortunate enough to have an English teacher we affectionately called Mrs. B. She taught us to love prose and poetry, which has stayed with me to this day. After high school I served in the US Army during the Vietnam conflict. Returning home I got married and raised a wonderful family of six children.*

## The Night Has Come

The days are long with no end in sight
I waited patiently for you to come
I am in captivity; the chains are shackled tight
I cried out but there was no one to hear my call
I am in darkness
There is not a gleam of light
No one to find me
I am lost and alone
Abandoned and enslaved
Waiting to be freed
Where are you?
Why can't you hear me?
Do you know that I am gone?
Will you ever find me?
I hear the voices of the night
I am in a state of insanity
The haunting, the setting, the creaking of old boards
I am afraid, still in the corner of my imprisoned mind
There is nothing to do but wait
Surrender to the night
At last, the long night has ended
I am free to face another day.

Susanne Sylvia Young
*Feasterville Trevose, PA*

[Hometown] *Feasterville Trevose, PA* [Ed] *master's degree with distinction in secondary and special education; BA in speech and language pathology and audiology* [Occ] *speech therapist* [Hobbies] *writing, gardening, and interior design* [GA] *I am an ordained minister, which avails me to help others and live selflessly.*

# Moral Fabric, Golden Rule

Did I use my mind?
Did I seek what I
Came to find?
Was I too kind?
Was I left behind?

Did I use my voice?
Did I make the wrong
Or right choice?
Make it down the
Narrow trail
Did I ultimately fail?

Did I draw water
From the well?
Did I ring the
Moral bell?
Only time will tell
If virtue will sell

Andrea Soller
*Zanesville, OH*

## Creative Destruction

The lust that forces women to give birth—
External, male, and often linked to love—
Can orchestrate a symphony on Earth,
An overture of DNA, above

The normal life that normal people do,
And yet it's utter chaos through and through.
Creation is a kind of breakthrough force
That shatters silly, stolid points of view.

It makes us craft a wholly different course
From what we always had been taught is true.
So too is greed an engine of desire,
A hunger always yearning to acquire.

Both lust and greed can bring us paradise,
But for that pleasure—Oh, how high a price!

Neal Arvid Donner
*Los Angeles, CA*

[Hometown] *Wernigerode, Germany* [Ed] *PhD* [Occ] *teaching violin* [Hobbies] *staying healthy* [GA] *my little grandson*

*I was lucky to have good parents.*

## Jeff

From your flat rooftop, hiding behind a peak
We slingshot water balloons
From a place they cannot see
We crouch, we laugh, as people look around
They go about
And make their way back home

As the summer sun quickly begins to go down
The moon takes over to shine bright on this town

We are young and the warm night is our age
The stars provide us company that keep our secret safe

Nestled closely on your couch
As we both hold open and share a book
We read together our horoscopes
And might give each other that look

You are my friend and this alluring night is ours
I could be yours, but I'm being a coward
I am fighting this feeling as you confess yours to me
I don't respond, knowing that hurts you deeply

We crouch, we laugh, I want to stick around
Instead I leave
And make my way back home

Patricia Richter
*New Berlin, WI*

[Hometown] *Eagle, WI* [Ed] *associate degree in fashion marketing* [Occ] *floral designer* [Hobbies]
*Barbie collecting, journaling, cleaning, decorating and dancing* [GA] *never giving up or losing hope
because everything always seems to work out!*
*I met Jeff during the summer of 1997 and we spent several fun evenings hanging out, rollerblading, going to
parties, and softball games and enjoyed most of our time together alone getting to know one another. He had
given me a framed song lyric sheet of "Can't Fight This Feeling" by REO Speedwagon and a very sweet letter
explaining how he felt about me. I wasn't ready for a new relationship, but I really did like him. I went back
to school. He moved away. It has been twenty-four years, and I wish I had given him a chance.*

### Forever and a Day

The golden years are the
vintage years
and life is in full bloom!
Our lives have reached that point
in time.
These are the words that I
want to say.

I'm so glad you came into
my life.
You're my lover.
You're my friend.
And if tomorrow should be
forever,
there still is one day left.
As my promise was to love
you—forever and a day.

Florence C. Tibbs
*Las Vegas, NV*

*My husband and I have known each other since 1942. We married June 3, 1948. We have six married children and twenty-four single and married grandchildren. We have fourteen great-grandchildren. Life has been wonderful! I'm a retired church organist and pianist. All my life my husband and I have been active in church work. We've traveled to all countries except South America. Thankful and love to you.*

# Hope

Hope is such a precious commodity!
Sometimes it's almost impossible to find!

Hope is still real!
Hold on to it
When it comes by and don't let go!

Maxine Harville
*Bay Minette, AL*

[Hometown] *Bay Minette* [Ed] *finished 12th grade* [Occ] *working at Vanity Fair* [Hobbies] *oil painting* [GA] *writing poems*

*I hope this will help others to know that our Heavenly Father still cares for us!*

## Madness

I bet you didn't know someone could love you this much.
I can't get these memories out of my mind.
I try so hard to let go, the madness is invading my mind.
I need to know if it's real love or just my madness keeping it alive.
I finally see the light. I realize what you need.
I'm not expecting you to care.
But for me it was for real.
As the madness is hell, the madness was the deal.

Dorothy Ann McFarlane
*Maynard, MA*

## "Poems Are on Aisle 52, Right Next to the Thesaurus Three-packs"

"Welcome to the back of the line,
a short one I'm sure you won't find;
I should have called this in from home.
While looking at signs of distress
and watching the long lines compress,
I like to spend time on my phone.

"I guess it is worth a day trip
to fill up a small cargo ship,
there is no need to come often.
I'm always buying way too much
of all kinds of different stuff,
I hear this place sells a coffin.

"Ten pounds of shrimp, gallons of juice,
a wheel of cheese, four pairs of shoes,
and a tin of three dozen tarts.
You can see this thing's way too full,
tough for any oxen to pull;
maybe next time I'll get two carts.

"Did you try the samples back there?
I ate without concern or care,
plenty for lunch so you would think.
Most would say I've gotten my fill,
after check-out you'll see me still,
in line for a hot dog and drink."

Ian M. W. Norman
*Mobile, AL*

## The Joy of Being a Mother

Four precious children God gave me,
Being a mom was amazingly fun you see.
For we played, we laughed and did many things together,
I'll treasure those times we had forever.

Oh, the wonderful joy of being a mother,
If I could live life over, I'd choose no other.
Such precious memories I have of those years.
My heart just wants to shed joyous tears.

Ah, how the years flew by so fast,
My heart holds wonderful memories of the past.
We have our children at home for what seems a short while,
So, I prayed I could let each one go with a smile.

Each child moved on when they were grown,
For God only gave them to me on loan.
Then these children had to walk out into a life unknown,
Ah, but because God loves you, you need never be alone.

Jeannie Gladson
*Medford, OR*

[Hometown] *St. Petersburg, FL* [Ed] *high school, some college classes* [Occ] *superior court clerk* [Hobbies] *knitting, sewing, adult coloring pages* [GA] *leading Operation Christmas Child in my church and going on a trip to Ghana*

*I am eighty-eight years old! Many years ago I had four children under seven years old and I loved being a stay-at-home mom. I treasure these years as some of the best years of my life. After they were grown, I had a neighbor who called to offer me a job as a municipal court clerk. I amazingly took the job and five years later I moved up to the superior court for fifteen years before retiring. I praise God for blessing me for so many years. He gave me a wonderful life!*

## Golden Wings

On the golden wings of an archangel
I fly ever so high up in the sky.
Soaring like an eagle ever so high
As I will always be wondering why.
More awesome fun than you could know;
Only God knows where I will go.
God sent a golden archangel for me to ride
To show me what Heaven really looks like
Of which I never would want to hide.
On the golden wings of an archangel that's me
As I learn what my future will be.
Heaven is an awesome wondrous site to see.
On the golden wings of an archangel I fly.
Then the archangel whispered to me
God will take good care of your needs
So honey just let your troubles be.
On the golden wings of an archangel is me.
My spirit is truly one of a kind and free.
So now I am living in my prime
And everything will be just fine.
I am not just a simple human being;
I'm a spiritual being, living a human experience
Letting that special spirit inside me "soar"
On the golden wings of an archangel, I fly.

Deanna Maria Bacon
*Colona, IL*

## I Made This for You

I made this for you
My granddaughter said
As she handed me her drawing
Of a stick man holding hands
With a little stick girl floating above
A field of green with orange dots,
A stick tree lounging beside.

After all these years those stick hands
still clench firmly, those stick smiles
Are just as carefree and loving, the world
Is green and the flowers bright as always
And even with all that has happened
In our lives, we are yet the stick figures
And the vision of a child's imagination.

Joel Byron Belland
*Kiel, WI*

[Hometown] *Zenda, WI* [Ed] *master's in English from the University of Nebraska* [Occ] *English teacher*

*For me, it's all about family. We have only bits and scraps, like this poem, from the past to cling to while passing on into the future. We can only hope that our future continues and we are remembered by our family to come. God's grace and blessings on us all.*

## Confidence

Do not disturb confidence
with doubt.
It is a long journey
deep through the depths
of demise.
Weighted by the heavy dense nothingness that binds all,
there is a light accompanying darkness,
flickering the constant cheerful choice.
That helping hand firmly perpetual,
respecting desires in its higher ethereal humbling mode.
The given instinct to change in grace
the outcome of a lifetime
and the rhythm of a soul.

Suzy Rubi
*Dorado, PR*

[Hometown] *Doardo, Puerto Rico*

## Forgiveness

The life of love
 Lives
The Son of the Father
 Gives
The Lord of our life
 Makes
The sword of the soul
 Takes
The gift of the word
 Is alive
It's those who know
 Who survive

Sandy Adams
*New Smyrna Beach, FL*

*The language of life offers clear conclusions for the opportunity of personal emotional growth.  I hope my compilations assist others peace of mind.*

## A Daydream of Yesteryear

The amusement park was the very best.
There was peace and the world was at rest.

When I got off the trolley and entered the park,
The music and laughter became a big spark.

Clowns, clowns were everywhere,
Tossing their juggling balls into the air.

Then there was the caterpillar ride—
When the cover flipped over you were tucked inside.

There's the hot dog stand—"I'll have one please.
I like lots of mustard and a little cheese."

The merry-go-round, ferris wheel and swings—
These are my favorite things.

Oh! There's a roar coming from the lion's den—
He's saying "Thank you for visiting—we'll see you again."

The trolley is calling it soon will be dark.
Time to get ready to leave the park.

Mary Warholak
*Chinchilla, PA*

[Hometown] *Chinchilla, PA* [Ed] *Marywood College* [Occ] *housewife, mother, gold leaf artist* [Hobbies] *painting (portraits, still life), gold leaf church restoration* [GA] *gold leaf restorations at St. Nicholas Ukranian Oath Cathedral in Chicago, IL*

*Ticket, cashier, theater secretary for many organizations. Three wonderful children, great husband who was in the Korean War, died in 1989. Received a full scholarship for art from Syracuse. Studied art at Marywood University, Albert Ondush, Leon Valenchese. I worked at the Seranto Dry Goods, The Globe Store, Sprague and Henwood, Scranton Public Library, Third National Bank, and Abington Players. My biggest accomplishment was becoming a gold leaf artist. I did work from east coast to Midwest where I worked in the greatest cathedral in the free world, St. Nicholas in Chicago, as well as St. Michaels and St. Vladimirs in Scranton, PA. I am eighty-eight years old.*

## Craving Silence

Why does the silence seem so difficult to find?
How can one be chorded to the peacefulness of the mind
in this daily, fast-paced, society?
All the activity and movement unable it is impossible to unwind.
What happened to the art of silence?
In the silence the answers to questions might appear.
With all the hustle and bustle, interference of the daily grind—
how does one take or make the time to hear?
Tuning into nature, listening to the birds chirping,
coming into spring…
It's almost a thing of the past, for some, and doesn't mean a thing.
Television volume, traffic moving, cell phones and iPods,
how can one hear a thing of—beauty?
For a few moments there is silence—all ceased for a few seconds…
deep breathes, inhale and savor.
Those seconds cannot alter your behavior—minuscule.
Pen to paper jotting down the memory of those moments—
soundlessness,
left questioning why it doesn't occur enough,
back to a reality that has no quality.
Universe speeding up, time disappearing in the blink of an eye
Church bells echo in the distance—
followed with the shrilling sirens of
fire engines and ambulances speeding by.

Nancy L. Cox
*Denver, CO*

*Born and raised in Cleveland, OH. Moved to Denver, CO in 1995. I've always been artistic—crafts, poetry, art/drawing. I was a professional astrologer for twenty years, touched base with the metaphysical world. Picked up my writing again in 2007, took a couple writing courses. My genres are poetry and short stories. Two unfinished novels and notebooks full of poetry and short stories I've composed. I have thirteen self-published poems. My goal is to publish an anthology of my poetry one day. So many distractions—not enough silence/quiet time to think or concentrate.*

## Global Victory

We will be victorious
When not one more gun is picked up
Not one more bomb is dropped
Or one more word of hate is spoken.
Victory will come
When there is no reason to pick up a gun
Because there are no more oppressors.

Suki R. Kaplan
*Manchester, CT*

[Hometown] *New York City* [Ed] *master's degree* [Occ] *retired* [Hobbies] *writing* [GA] *raising two children as a solo mother (my late husband passed away when my children were starting elementary school)*

*Suki Kaplan grew up in New York and after receiving her master's degree in performing arts at the Strasbourg, France campus of Schiller International College; she was a three-union thespian for thirteen years. After she married and had two children, she taught in a private school where the lesson plans from her Young Travelers class became the inspiration for her first published children's book,* Around the World with Littlest Cat, Across the Great Pond. *Presently, she is working on her rough draft of a novel whose story is based on a personal life experience.*

## Silent Scare

Walking to make your leave
No way to truly believe
With the slam of the door
I'm on my knees punching the floor
Hand stretched all the way out
Throat so horse I can't even shout
Darkness that fills with a silent scream
Pain that causes rips at my seam
Body overwhelmed, becoming numb
This is it and the time has come
The feel of cold steel in my hand
Punching my ticket to the promise land
My life is ready to be unbound
In my hand is the final round
Suddenly, the darkness has disappeared
With sunshine, my eyes become cleared
Breath in my lungs feeling tied
Until I see you laying by my side
Tears down my cheeks from my silent scare
We must remember to wake from the nightmare

Joseph Walter Hawkins Jr.
*Saint Joseph, MO*

[Hometown] *Rushville, MO*

### Sista

Mary, Mary, Sister stylin' with class
Lots of flare with a dash of sass
How does your garden grow?
Six lovely flowers all in a row
Every lass delicate and fair of face
All so blessed with regal grace
Tending and nurturing them into blooms
Like the essence of fine perfume
Marigolds, larkspurs, mums adorning one space
Violets, daisies, lilies in a special place
Each with the strength of a warrior, so brave
Their hearts full of kindness and generosity save
Creative and bright, their talents galore
You have created these gems and more
Spunky and ornery their nature can be
Humor and joy for the world to see
Each one different, yet alike in every measure
Thank you Sista' for these amazing treasures

Ruth Frances Angle
*Huntingdon, PA*

*This poem is dedicated to my loving sister and her precious daughters.*

## The Letter

You are gone.
The sound of taps still
ringing in my head.
It doesn't matter if I am up and awake
or lying in my bed.
The gun volleys are loud and stinging
clearer than any songbirds singing.
I reach for your hand but it's not there
I look for your smile with a blind stare.
Sorting through clothes you will no longer wear
please give me the strength from somewhere.
I discover a letter you wrote to me
tucked away in a file for me to eventually see.
You told me you loved me, I was one of a kind
peace now has a chance to enter my mind.
Others have said grief takes time and
things will get better
I beg to differ,
my life has a chance now
because of your letter.

Linda Marie Coppola
*Seminole, FL*

[Hometown] *Seminole, FL* [Ed] *business and fitness* [Occ] *retired* [Hobbies] *poetry, yoga, and senior fitness* [GA] *raising three beautiful daughters*

*This poem is dedicated to my husband and veteran Vincent Michael. I have written poems for him since we met and I miss him dearly. I am a retired entrepreneur and opened my first health club in Southern California. After thirty-three years I still teach a few classes. Life is precious and family the most.*

## You and Only You

You give me life
You bless my soul
You make me hole
When I am lost
You cradle me
By your grace
All that I am
Is by your
Deliverance and
Praise.

Sandra Neumann
*Peru, IL*

[Hometown] *Peru, IL* [Occ] *writing poetry* [Hobbies] *painting landscapes on canvas* [GA] *writing poetry for the world*

*If it wasn't for my great uncle who bought me a poetry book I don't think I would be writing poems till this day. So thank you, Great Uncle, for opening my eyes and seeing that there are beautiful people out in the world and glorious words to hear and read*

## Covid Time No More

We never have as much time as we think then they're gone and we say if only I told them how much I love them time comes and goes never knowing at what moment our hearts beat no more that overwhelming sadness And deep-rooted Grief that feeling and lost a loved one Tears Trickle down like rivers flowing swollen eyes tissues discarded Never ending-for those who accept him It's heaven others destiny below Covid time no more

Eufemia Dee Tatham
*Lancaster, CA*

[Hometown] *Los Angeles* [Ed] *Dr in religious studies* [Occ] *civil engineer* [Hobbies] *rock hound (gemologist)* [GA] *being able to communicate with others*

*What I see is time has changed the world and we are all affected in this massive change. Let us appreciate each other for we all bleed regardless of our color.*

# We Have a President

We have a president
He is number one
We've been waiting for this challenge
At last the time has come
To work without fear
To make America great
To take the lead
For the United States
He must plant seeds
To prove that he does rate
He is number one
In all of the states
Little seeds of understanding
Little seeds of trust
Little seeds of knowledge
To prove that we must
Take on a task
A big one indeed
To make life better
For everyone in need
This will only happen
If we work together
As a team
No matter what they weather

Kayla Kimball
*Blue Earth, MN*

[Hometown] *Blue Earth, MN* [Ed] *high school* [Occ] *electronics factory supervisor, retired* [Hobbies] *writing poetry, watching Minnesota Twins, Vikings, Timber Wolves*

*My poem was inspired by the new president Joe Biden's first one hundred days in office. I started writing poetry when I had to quit work and take care of my husband 24/7. When I would get him to bed at night, I needed to do something to take my mind off of the horrible day we had.*

39

# The Day the World Stood Still

On September 11, 2001,
The day had really just begun;
The first plane flew in under its own power
And struck the first World Trade tower.
A short time later, a plane came into view
And crashed into tower number two.
The searing blast, the smoke and flame,
Many innocent lives Death began to claim.
A plane crashed in Pennsylvania bound for Washington;
A plane struck the Pentagon before the madness was done.
As sirens wailed and alarms were sounded,
All across the US, every plane was grounded.
A short time later in Manhattan town,
Both twin towers came crumpling down.
The smoke, the dust, the loss of life,
Left us numb in our grief and strife.
The world stood still, we held our breath,
But there was no escape from this thing called Death.
To you innocent victims, we make this vow,
We'll avenge your deaths, someday, somehow.

James Mayou
*Mashpee, MA*

[Hometown] *Mashpee, MA* [Ed] *semi-retired* [Occ] *part-time grocery clerk* [Hobbies] *collecting baseball cards, karaoke, and writing poetry* [GA] *marrying my wife, Nancy*

*I wrote this poem twenty years ago. I was on duty with the 267th CCSQ at the time (an Air National Guard outfit). We witnessed, on TV, the second plane crashing into the tower in Manhattan. Within seventy-two hours we had assets headed overseas. My outfit was activated shortly thereafter. We were one of the first units to deploy. It is still on my mind even after twenty years.*

## A Thought Can Be Dissolve

A thought can be dissolved
Upon the tongue
Swallowed like saliva does
And never to be found
It ponders the mind
Torments the brain
Hammers the heart
Then goes secretly
With the soul

Barbara C. Singh
*Woodhaven, NY*

## Lip Burn

Too fast a first sip
Too early and too tired for this
Wait a bit, but this time don't trip
The aroma and flavor is like a gentle kiss
The key to a blissful morning beginning
Opens a door of possibly Columbian origin
Which develops gradually as the pot continues to boil
Hoping to gain a new perspective without too much toil
Looking forward to this day and great start
Enjoying my steaming java with no time to sit
Although it will be hard for this cup and I to part
Coffee lip burn is always worth it

Darryl Monteiro
*Fall River, MA*

### Nancy

There is a friend of mine I knew a long time ago
We worked together when things were busy
Then they got slow
She always dressed like she was in a show
So I gave her a name and she loved it just so
I always thought you were Fancy...Nancy
With that sparkle in your eye
Being positive all the while
Now you tell me you're dumpy, dumpy
Well in my eyes you're not

F - fun to be around
A - always positive
N - nice in every way
C - cool as a cucumber
Y - young at heart

N - never a harsh word
A - always brings out the best in people
N - nice to a fault
C - calm and collected
Y - yearning to please

To me you will always be Fancy...Nancy

Vera M. Meney
*Rochester, NY*

[Hometown] *Rochester, NY* [Ed] *financial specialist* [Occ] *retired* [Hobbies] *music*

*I live in the state of New York and love to read and write poetry. My growing up years were very happy. I used to work as a financial specialist, but have since retired. Someday I would like to write a book of poems. This poem is about Nancy, a friend I used to work with years ago.*

### America

You're the light in the
darkness. You're the color
in the rainbow. You're the
sparkle of a star. You're the
beauty of the rose. You're the
reason the poets write the prose.
　　I have found the reason
for my existence. I knew one day
I'd find. The mystery was cleared
up when I saw you for the
first time.
　　You're what we're all
looking for in this vast universe
when we can't find reason or
rhyme.

Virginia McCoy
*Marina Del Rey, CA*

[Hometown] *Marina Del Rey, CA* [Ed] *business college* [Occ] *general office, caregiver* [Hobbies]
*writing, collecting books* [GA] *working a movie premier and publishing*

*I grew up in Venice, CA. After school my friends and I would play on the beach. Our grammar school was
close by. One of my friends parents managed an apartment building on the boardwalk. We sometimes slept
in a vacant room and the sound of the waves put us to sleep. A blissful memory. I was born in Missouri but
we moved too California when I was six. I wrote the poem because it is how I feel about my country.*

## Imperfections

Judge me not,
For my mistakes differ from yours
But we are one in the same
Like the wind,
God also made
It's unique in its own way
For I cannot fathom the day
Where we will have compassion for one another
Love thy neighbor and thy brother
Peace, joy, and love
All in one
What a wonderful feeling
To activate the fruits of the Spirit
Distractions form in many ways
Judge not,
For I am perfectly imperfect
Just like you
We will be and do better
Holding one another accountable
Don't just say it
Actions prove it
Let's do this
Love God, yourself and others
Leave your fingerprints on the world

Latisha Coleman
*Springfield Gardens, NY*

[Hometown] *Queens, NY* [Ed] *Long Island University* [Occ] *social worker* [Hobbies] *spoken word, basketball* [GA] *writing a poetry book, producing a spoken word album*

*Latisha also known as "Mz. Conception" loves her gift of poetry. She can change the atmosphere wherever she is. Her deep messages go far beyond what's written. She loves delivering it to different people from all over the world. Thank you for taking the time to read or listen to her work.*

# Is God Speaking?

God is talking as never before! Through these connecting world events He's right at the door! COVID-19, killings in the street, George Floyd protests, Black Lives Matter, transition of our civil right's icons are signs of the shaking, the times that are hastening! Pull yourselves together, suit-up My people, I'm coming back for thee! The city known as Earth is not your permanent home. What is man that he should be above the angels? You have desecrated My land over which I left you in command! Get this, too! You have trodden down My people like a sharecropper plows his fields. No emotion, no compassion, no love; you've stomped 'um out like cockroaches under your heels! Yes, hear this, too! I need you to know, "You're all My creation, different colors and hues." What's this superior talk against blacks, browns, and Jews! I paid the price! My blood was spilled and sacrificed for E-V-E-R-Y man! I'm the author and owner of this universe, the stars, the heavens, and the land! My people, I want you to know, My word in the Bible is true and real! If you intend and care to reign with Me, I command and invite you to walk in I-N-T-E-G-R-I-T-Y! Faith, hope, and yes love must come along. These are absolute essentials to make Heaven your home!

Marlene Lewis
*Brooklyn, NY*

*"Is God Speaking?" is a poem and testament to the God I serve and to those who may agree with the words I have composed. Since COVID-19 all our lives are changed forever! Hopefully, all of us have become God-conscious, showing the agape or God-kind of love that is so needed in this world at this time! Now, as never before, Marvin Gaye's "What's Going On" is so applicable, as well as Dionne Warwick's song "What the World Needs Now."*

## Lying Beside You

Lying in your arms at night,
at the end of a perfect day,
feels like "coming home" to me,
safe and tender in every way.

Holding you and touching as we
move through the night's sleepy dance.

I know that our love is deep and real,
and not one of mirth or chance.

So if you ever wonder
if my love could go astray,

just think of us all entwined
at the end of a perfect day.

Carol A. Schlaepfer
*Lady Lake, FL*

[Hometown] *Lady Lake, FL* [Ed] *retired electronics designer* [Occ] *created manufacturing blueprints in aerospace (engineering)* [Hobbies] *writing, water color artist, activist* [GA] *living this long and still embracing life*

*I wrote this poem one morning upon awakening many years ago. The words just came as I reached for pen and paper. They flowed so easily as I remembered my new love and our wonderful easy way of moving through the night. Silence, sleep, touch, warmth, turn, touch again. Safe is a beautiful word. Waking with a full heart, feeling content, rested, happy. Savoring my thoughts and wishing they would stay forever.*

## 911 as the Eagle Soars

She was flying higher
As the smoke went
Down beside her
She knew there
Was something wrong
As the tears filled her eyes
She could hear the people cry
She was so scared and all alone
The buildings crashed
Down beside her
She took her wings
And flew even higher
She knew that
She had to get home
Whatever was going on
She knew she had to be strong
For the fire in the sky
Was blazing ever high
Her heart was beating faster
For she has seen the disaster
And longed to be free and home
Her spirits filled her power
And she flew now even harder
Until she was finally home
To her surprise
Her babies never died
And still
Tears filled her eyes...

Corena M. Elmer
*Elk River, MN*

*I wrote this poem several years ago and decided to release it on the twentieth anniversary of 9/11. The eagle gave me the inspiration, because she is our American symbol. She's both powerful and strong. I would like to dedicate this poem to all the heroes and their K9s who helped find victims in this terrible tragedy. And to the people who have lost loved ones—my heart pours out to you. Also, to all the men and women who have served, "God bless you."*

## The Portrait

I'm sitting in the silence of myself
Quietly trying to think calm
Peaceful within myself
Concentrate on being
Still and comfortable
Don't move that thought
Try to hear the silence
Breathe, relax, count each breath
Secure your feelings
Think of nothing but pleasantries
Rest your mind in this zone of tranquility
Brace a sense of contentment
Feel the spirit of your soul
Let it show on your face
Find yourself and don't let go
While the artist is painting

Daniel Valese
*Nutley, NJ*

[Hometown] *Nutley, NJ* [Ed] *high school graduate, public safety courses* [Occ] *retired policeman, realtor* [GA] *saved a young man from hanging himself, a miracle to find in time*

*The portrait artist Dominic Algieri named drawing, "Jersey Cowboy" to enter state art contest won third place for New Jersey then entered portrait into a second art competition in Passaic County, NJ and came in first place. I was the subject cowboy in the drawing, "The Portrait," and wrote thoughts about posing for the artists.*

## The Guimond Family Haiku

Kayden has the strength
To protect the ones he loves
The lion watches

Imagination
This is what fuels Julian
Gorillas love him

Alaric the Wolf
An Earth soul full of courage
He will lead the pack

She's Lila Stevie
Butterflies and wolves help her
The world adores her

Hannah is the owl
Beautiful and wise is she
Family comes first

Lucas J. Guimond
*Fort Edward, NY*

[Hometown] *South Glens Falls* [Ed] *SUNY Adirondack* [Occ] *patriarch* [Hobbies] *writing, investing, Marvel comics, gaming, mythology, religious thought & studies* [GA] *my family clan*

## Honey

The birds and the bees
come flying on the tree
the bird and bees so
they make me see
the birds and the bees
became a puzzle to me
a aves an insect how
do they match, the
birds and the bees
are looking at me.

Beverly A. Foster
*Pitcairn, PA*

## Through the Eyes of Love

As a child you are loved and taught to love others.
You are young and happy, not a care in the world.
As you grow you watch your parents and grandparents show you and teach you many things,
never thinking what is their life like, growing old.
They are always there for you.
Blessed with children of your own God gives you wisdom to teach them about love and life.
As a grandparent you open your door to loving little faces of smiles and laughter.
So much joy comes with the energy of their hugs and shining eyes of their love.

Roberta E. Drebes
*Quincy, IL*

## Journey

Crossing the ocean to distant lands
Chartered bussing through county roads

The earth orbits around the sun
Stars in motion we've just begun

The solar system is a part of the maze
Part of the galaxy, moving ablaze

Miles are measured in light years away
As I look outward from harbors bay

The best journey I can have
Is surrendering to Jesus all that I am

Harold Gardner
*Bagley, MN*

# I Hope It Is Over

In the sun I can now bask
No more wearing a mask
No more keeping my face hid
so I don't get or spread the COVID
I do my own shopping, not just write a list
Went back to see my dentist
Not stuck in the house watching the days pass
I can attend mass
I can visit family and friends
These are truly godsends
I've had all my shots of vaccine
I sanitize and keep everything clean
I hope it is over for good
But I still take every precaution like everyone should

Chester Williams
*Jewett City, CT*

[Hometown] *Jewett City, CT* [Ed] *tenth grade* [Occ] *trailer driver* [Hobbies] *sports, gambling* [GA]
*married the love of my life*

## Mama

My children
scatter like jacks
on hard concrete.
Bouncing the red
rubber ball,
I gather as many
as I can.

Kathy Cullen Langen
*Batavia, NY*

[Hometown] *Batavia* [Ed] *BA in English from SUNY at Buffalo and associate's degree in commercial art from Genesee Community College* [Occ] *retired* [Hobbies] *writing, spending time with my children* [GA] *completing 14 years of employment in the Central Library of Rochester and Monroe County*

*I was born in Buffalo, NY to Elanor and Matthew Cullen in 1946. I went to the university on a regents scholarship. I keep a journal and write regularly. I started writing poems in 1988.*

## Better Days Ahead

Somewhere, where smiles meet sun's Heaven,
There are better days ahead.
Somewhere, where whispers in lovers' moments meet warm winds of spring,
There are better days ahead.
Somewhere, where touches meet seams of passion,
And we enjoin in secrets of heart and body,
There are better nights that await us.
Somewhere, where the words from our voices meet
Invitations from heart and soul,
There are better times to follow.
Somewhere, where even when we're alone,
There is someone who loves us who waits for us,
In that place, our love calls home, better times await us.
Somewhere, where the horizon rises through the bedroom window,
To meet lovers awakening in their new dawn,
There are moments we will remember as precious secrets that are ours alone.
Somewhere, when every turn of our lives seems to come down to a kiss or an embrace,
In a lover's welcome home,
We will know as time wanders on,
All pasts are healed, all desires sealed,
All moments of love and happiness found and revealed.
Then, in the air, a warm breeze of certainty we know as sacred and sure,
Will tell our hearts pure, all that is past has been cured,
We will all know then we've endured,
We will all know then without fear,
There are better days ahead.

Greg Lane Bass
*Pleasant Prairie, WI*

*Greg L. Bass is a poet, author, and photographer. His poetic style results from studies of modern American poets such as Wagoner, Berry, Merwin, Neruda, Collins, and of course Frost. Bass influence also comes from in depth readings of John Muir and Aldo Leopold, leading, historic, and profound minds in environmental thought. Bass has also lived in Texas and wandered the Hill Country where he published*

## Passing Storm

After the storm is over
The world seems washed and renewed.
Trees stand still as a picture
As sun dances on morning dew.
What calm greets the new morning
After night storm pelted the earth.
The world turned so lush and green
As if given a Devine new birth.
Are we like that when we pass over?
All shiny, bright and new,
Pain and cares unremembered
Surrounded by a bright new view?
Perhaps here birds are our chorus
As if angels sent singing to earth,
Making me wonder if
The bright new morning
Is our miniature
heaven on earth.

Glena Joy Boston
*Lancaster, PA*

[Hometown] *Midwestern city* [Ed] *nursing degree* [Occ] *retired* [Hobbies] *traveling throughout the US and Europe, hot air ballooning with family* [GA] *making the world a better place around me in loving, laughter, and making those around me feel better*

*I wrote this after a passing storm. It had little effect around me other than to make me wonder about the storms and afterlife. I found out one area nearby had eighty trees fall down in our park of eighty acres. Poetry has been my expression throughout life's journey. It's served me through living and loss. I only have to read what my muse wants me to write to recall love, feelings and inspiration. It's become my diary of life, people and times as much as a photograph would.*

## Silent Elegy

Hot the sun beats down, searing my heart in two.
He is gone, and the sun beats down all around.
Where is the rain, the gentle rain
To make my tears to fall?
Where is the cooling water to quench my grief?
The sun beats down, and my heart shrivels inside
And is dried to nothingness.
My parched tongue emits no lamentation;
The tear ducts of my eyes burn shut.

Marian Postel Scott
*San Antonio, TX*

[Hometown] *Davenport, IA* [Ed] *BA in English* [Occ] *English teacher, housewife, mother, grandmother* [Hobbies] *writing poetry, being in plays/musicals* [GA] *marrying my wonderful husband*

*I am not sure why I originally wrote this poem. Obviously, I had just lost someone very dear and close to me. It is very appropriate for recent time; however, I did just lose my wonderful husband four months ago, so the poem seems to express exactly how I feel.*

## Praise and Power of a Woman

Soul of womanhood
Legend
Rich in imagination and warm at heart
The symbol of honor and human dignity
Almighty God has blessed her with beauty and power
Praise and power of a woman
The curves of the creeper
The roundness of the moon
The brightness of the sunrays
The velvet smoothness of the skin
The lightness of the flowers
Praise and praise of a woman
The modesty of the humble plant
The swiftness of the light
The vanity of the peacock
And the shrewdness of a business person
Praise and praise of a woman
The womanhood has a warmer, softer heart
And has devoted great
Sacrifice for raising a child against her career
Built good character and humanity in a child
Bravo for a woman, success at home
And a success in the business world
Praise and success of a woman

Bhupen V. Randeria
*Playa Del Rey, CA*

[Hometown] *Los Angeles, CA* [Occ] *chemical engineer* [Hobbies] *tennis, reading, composition—poems* [GA] *automatic advanced food processing, two gold medals in poultry*
*I started writing compositions as a hobby a few years ago but now it has become my passion and inspiration. By profession I am a food technologist and chemical engineer. I worked as a corporate technical director and high technical positions in few food industries in the United States. I have about twenty-nine scientific publications in leading scientific journals and I am a fellow of several international science societies. A few years ago I built a large food processing plant and adhesive plant in Mumbai, India. I have received several international awards, two gold medals, and one poet-of-the-year award. I have received two recording contracts for my two compositions "Time" and "Touch Me, Feel Me" from a leading label company in Memphis, TN.*

## Parents

I am so grateful for the parents I had.
They had their flaws, but they were my mom and dad.
Most people thought that my dad was too stern.
But protection for us was his main concern.
We did what he said and we understood why.
We avoided the pain of that "look in his eye."
We knew, if he said it, our safety was first,
Though the reasons for actions were never rehearsed.
Taking care of yourself was the name of the game.
Then there would be no one to blame.

Carol Ann Kaufman
*Portland, OR*

[Hometown] *Portland* [Ed] *Master of Education* [Occ] *teacher for deaf and blind students* [Hobbies] *growing flowers* [GA] *starting a non-profit for the students who needed to experience life outside of books I am so grateful for the parents I had and for my brothers and sisters also.*

## Mary at Home: Henry Street

Glad memories of you, Mary Sanders:
Your damasked table set with moss rose china
Polished silver gleaming in candlelight.
From your kitchen a parade of laden platters
Side dishes aplenty, hot rolls, too.
Feasting us, you gathered together
Your family, our friends—
Bill, L.C., Jim, Tim, Charlotte, Winnie, you—
Seven. Our magic number.
Dining in style, we laughed, teased, indulged.
An abundance of food and stories
With a final course of home-baked pie
And richly-brewed coffee. Such a time!
Later, guttering candles, a discreet yawn,
Genteel signs of an evening's end.
Good night, gracious Mary—sister, friend.
You fed our bodies, enriched our spirits.

James Ross Bailey
*Columbus, OH*

[Hometown] *Columbus, OH* [Ed] *Indiana University, doctorate in literature* [Occ] *teacher, college professor* [Hobbies] *gardening, cooking* [GA] *earning three college degrees*

*Reading and writing have always been my interests. I was a teacher of literature and writing for most of my life, and I know there is always more for me to learn.*

## America Weeps

America hangs her head in shame
She weeps for our many sins
For we the people are the nation
And our misdeeds she must bear
Old Glory hangs furled and limp
The Liberty Bell is rusted and still
And our peace light grows dim

We've broken our forefathers trust
Our honor lays trampled in the dust
Do our brave boys now die in vain
As the fight in a foreign land
Wake up my fellow men
Whatever your race or creed
And make this nation great again

Let's put down the violence
That has torn our land asunder
And left our towns in smoking ruins
Lets put America back on her pedestal
And pray that God will guide us
Through these dark days
And bring us again to peaceful ways

Evelyn Stonesifer
*Lecanto, FL*

[Hometown] *Lecanto, FL* [Occ] *retired* [Hobbies] *collect horse statues, coins, and stamps*

*I'm ninety-five soon to be ninety-six in June. I've had a full life and am thankful I can still get around and take care of my flowerbed and bonsai plants. I was born in Maryland and lived there 'til 1968 when my husband and I moved to Florida. I've been a great animal lover all my life with horses being my first love. Over the years many horses have come into our life the special ones being an appaloosa named Dancer and a miniature named Shorty.*

### Trapped in My Own Thoughts

"You're not pretty enough."
I have the biggest smile that lights up a room.
"You're not thin enough."
I have the shape of a teddy bear who
everyone wants to cuddle.
"You're too tall."
I have the height to oversee my future.
"Your head is too big."
I have the know yo change the world.
"Your nose is too wide."
I can smell my path that will lead me
toward success.
"Your ears are huge."
I can hear the sounds of greatness.
"Your hair is too kinky."
Every strand of hair tells a prominent
story about my life.
"Your feet are too gigantic."
My steps will continue my journey for
a lifetime.

Millette Roberson
*Katy, TX*

[Hometown] *Katy, TX* [Ed] *master's in education, bachelor of business administration, licensed presenter* [Occ] *teacher* [Hobbies] *reading, writing, and participating in running/walking marathons* [GA] *a co-author of Grand Canyon University Vomime*

*The poem depicts how understanding and embracing our differences will allow us to withstand others judgment.*

## Sharing Comes from the Heart

Building and encouragement comes from positive people who are gentle and kind-hearted who have words of wisdom from the heart. Sharing from the heart is the window of a persons eyes which comes from a positive person who shows that they care about someone. Life is good and what you make of it by sharing from the heart. Treat others the way  at you want to be treated by respect and sharing positive words with others that comes from your heart. Encouragement and building someone with positive words or lending a hand to help someone if they need it. Brighter and greater days are coming ahead is something wonderful to look forward to. Sharing from the heart with someone special you love and care about comes from the heart. Positive words from people who encourages other or lift them up with positive words that come from the heart makes people happy and fun to be around and confidence to be with and to trust. Sharing from the heart is a person who has a lot of joy and understanding that comes from the heart.

Rickey Ethridge
*Meridian, MS*

[Hometown] *Meridian, MS*  [Ed] *high school*  [Occ] *salesman, hotel and restaurant management, paralegal, nurses aid, book editing and accounting*  [Hobbies] *writing poems, playing guitar, singing music (lots of Elvis Presley)*

*I have a high school diploma and have worked in hotel and restaurant management, as a paralegal, and in civil litigation. I've been nationally accredited from Ashworth University. I have a nurse aide and bookkeeping/accounting degree from Dodd Institute. I love music, especially Elvis Presley. I love to write poetry. I've been doing this since February 2, 1971. I was eight years old and today I'm fifty-eight years old. I still love to do this. I like to play basketball. I like kickball, football and softball.*

## God in Disguise

The detective seeking out the culprit
turns out to be the culprit—
but does he know it,
can he show it.
It takes a hit, bit by bit
until the culprit shows up
if the detective has emptied his cup.
When the mask comes off—who is there
but the unseen wearer
and not the pall-bearer
outdated through use....
And so there is no excuse—
the Wearer of the mask
has performed its task
until the play is done
as we move under the sun
in a strange kind of fun.

Henry F. Mende
*New City, NY*

[Hometown] *Manhattan, NY* [Ed] *high school, art school, and army* [Occ] *artist, painter, musician, and writer* [Hobbies] *jazz keyboards* [GA] *cheerful disposition*

## Before Any Beginning

Before any beginning
The "Un-Beginning" *was.*
When there was only *void.*
Only the Un-Beginning *was!*

When all was *naught*
Only the "He *who is*"
The "Un-Beginning" *was!*

Blessed be He!

Nancy A. Priest
*Lake Leelanau, MI*

*Poetry has always been one of the loves of my life. I've studied the religions of the world searching for what I call "Bed-Rock," to find and comprehend the beginnings of what we call "faith" in God. Studying in Israel and volunteering at digs at Tel Dor and Ekron, I now consider myself a regular Philistine!*

## To My Love

I once was just a raging storm
Who walked alone and forlorn
I thought love was just a myth
As through my fingers it would drift
Then one day I saw your face
My world opened into a new place
You accepted me as I am and didn't ask me to change
You just enjoyed me, made me feel accepted not strange
For the first time I understood what love could be
You make me feel it ever so deeply
I now look forward to what the future might hold
When I am with you, I feel warm not cold
Your whole being is beautiful, light, and good
You make me feel hope, able to cope, ways that I should
You are my everything, my soulmate, my world
One day perhaps I will be forever your girl
I dream of the day when we become one
I hope perhaps I can give you a daughter or son
When we can have our happiest of life
Together we will tackle and conquer issues in life
I love you more than you will ever know
I can only try to find ways for it to show
I love your hugs and your kisses, too
I love everything, yes, everything about you
I hope you love me like I love you
Until our forever and past our I do's

Heather R. Worley
*Moclips, WA*

# Love Will Continue

For fifty-three years our vows were true
You still love me and I still love you
Do you take this man?
A pledge renewed
To have God's gift; To hold God's view
In sickness; in health
The older we grew
Blessed to still hold our love as new
As twilight comes nearer
Sooner then we knew

Josephine Theresa Eicher
*Landing, NJ*

[Hometown] *Mount Arlington Borough, NJ* [Ed] *BA William Paterson University (education K-8), Med Monclair University and UConn at Storrs (curriculum development), EdD Nova South Eastern University (curriculum development and systemic change—child and youth studies)* [Occ] *teacher* [Hobbies] *reading, poetry writing, biblical researcher* [GA] *having a successful and loving marriage with my husband, raising our two children*

*When my husband was in the early stages of dementia, all thoughts focused upon him and his future care. He deserved the best because he was an exceptional man who put God first. He was an exceptional husband who unconditionally loved me. He was an exceptional father who was "hands-on" from diapers to degrees. He is still all of the above even as his dementia has been identified as advancing Alzheimer's. This poem is dedicated to God's "Perfect Gift" to me however long we have left, for our love will continue.*

## Mis-Capades of the Musketeers Three

A season of testing a matter of heart
With mind on the sleeve wondering, when did it start?
Our yesterdays frolics as we basked in the sun
Let no worries besiege us it just hadn't begun.
Another ball game to watch! Oh we enjoy the TV
And how 'bout a snack? Only you and me.
Running, running to and fro always busy come on let's go.
Feeling the crunch, ignoring the sting
Unaware of what the future would bring.
Well we all had it made or so we thought
But our plans soon changed as they all came apart.
From a hole in the floor and a slide wouldn't work
A family tragedy, it almost drove me berserk!
The yard full of termites, garage door won't close
Where's that vehicle, then this with sister arose.
My mind I left in some unknown spot, my back good one
Couldn't bend or squat and I'm suppose to do what?
A water disaster or just an old cat
The AC had problems, now imagine that.
Musketeers! Where are our swords?
Boxed with our breastplates and the rest of our gear
Stashed in the corner, way back to the rear.
Well, a season of testing and we're not through yet
Like Job I'm afraid we'll get what we get.
The Musketeers will rise as the clouds fade away.
Unpack that box and just ride away, on horses.

Shelley R. Bendele
*Somerset, TX*

[Hometown] *Somerset, TX* [Ed] *Somerset High School* [Occ] *secretary* [Hobbies] *writing, cooking, crocheting* [GA] *serving our Lord Jesus*
*Just a country girl, but a deep thinker. I really enjoy writing and once it starts it just flows. This poem was about true events the summer of 2018 as I'd jotted notes down. It was hectic; we all survived and as it turned out I rode a camel.*

## Spring

Trees bud and blossom
bringing forth
their beautiful leaves.
A thickened canopy overhead
shades the ground below
with a reawakening.
Grass below turns
from a drab yellow
to a vivid green,
turning back into a blush carpet
fit for sports enthusiasts, picnickers,
campers, and stargazers like me.
Flowers bloom and plants
grace garden pots,
where in the winter
they surely did not.
Oh, spring
my favorite time of the year,
a time of repeated promises
and renewal is here.

Julie K. Brincks
*Johnson, KS*

[Hometown] *Johnson, KS* [Ed] *master's degree in early childhood education birth to third grade* [Occ] *preschool teacher* [Hobbies] *spending time in God's word, spending time with family, writing poetry, painting, drawing, walking, and traveling* [GA] *my four children*

*I started writing poems about twelve years ago. My inspiration was the gift that Jesus gave us on the cross.*

## Friendship

Everyone needs a friend in their life
Being a friend can mean so much to
another
Having a friend shows another
They are loved and cared for
Having a friend one can turn to
Having a friend who takes the time to listen
Means so much knowing they have a friend
Who is there when they need a friend
And one's friendship becomes special
When they take the time to be there for each other
And one's friendship grows through the years
When they become more than friends
For thy Father teaches His children many
Different things, the child needs in life
For thy Father teaches His children
How to reach out to another
With love, hope, faith, and friendship
For those are the special gifts thy Father
Gives to his children
For thy heavenly Father reaches down from
Heaven above
And teaches His children to reach out to others
For ones friendship can lead to others
And their friendship is shared with another
And to always be there when one needs
A friend

Bertha A. Garban
*North Brunswick, NJ*

## Seeds

Think of life
As being compared
To the seeds of flowers
All seeds need nurturing and love
To have a chance
To grow and thrive
Resulting is beautiful color
Representing pure perfection and success
Of the completion of life's cycle
Just as individuals marking a milestone,
With the chance to conquer hopes, fears, and dreams
Without all the love and nurturing
Life turns different directions
Resulting in failure and no record of existence
We are all capable of succeeding in life,
When given the opportunity
Yet along the way,
Everything can crumble and fall
With no opportunity, no future
No representation of existence
But, existence in itself, challenging or not
Marks a turning point, a fork in the road
To choose success or not, all challenges faced
in the cycle of life can be conquered.

Candace L. Fresch
*Denver, CO*

[Hometown] *Denver, CO* [Ed] *Oklahoma State University* [Hobbies] *horseback riding, gardening*
[GA] *having my poem submitted for publication*

## New Beginnings—Freedom Regained

Just before the early morning light,
When the Sun peeks into the night,
You can hear the doves begin to coo,
And the owls finish their last hoot.
It is time to arise and meet the day,
Follow the paths that come your way.
God's blessings He will bestow,
As we listen to Him while the sun grows.
The sounds of children all around,
As to school they are bound.
You feel excitement in the air,
As they return for the first day of the year.
Quarantine and virtual learning,
To be with friends, they are yearning.
Isolation, masks, and social distance
Children have suffered the consequence.
Life has been difficult for many,
As the last year has brought change,
Our world is returning to some normalcy,
Since our freedoms have been regained.

Denise E. Bowlin
*Shreveport, LA*

[Hometown] *Shreveport, LA* [Ed] *BA music, MA English, teaching certification—social studies, general science, special education K-12* [Occ] *CEO Fike Family Farm, independent contractor bookkeeping/ tax consultant, retired teacher* [Hobbies] *fishing, gardening, carpentry/woodworking, hunting* [GA] *Teaching over 500 high school students to successfully pass their GED receiving diplomas. One of the most difficult sections to pass is the writing section. All my students passed it on their first try following a set of guidelines I wrote for them.*

*As a retired English teacher of forty-three years, I have been concerned about how the pandemic has affected our children's well-being and education. Since retiring I have pursued my interest in carpentry and building furniture, successfully adding an addition and remodeling my kitchen.*

## Greetings for Someone Special

Another year has rolled around
So herein good wishes do abound
You have been, and are, so special to me
As I am so grateful and hope you see
The love, care and concern I have for you
As my feelings are reliant and so very true
The good times we've spent together
Seems we have bonded as "birds of a feather"
Thankful am I to our Heavenly Father above
For His outpourings of blessings and love
To have sent you back into my life when He did
And experience many fond memories even amid
Complications and craziness of present day life
As we rise above all the noise and even the strife
So, it is with pleasure and without any further adieu
Dear one—I wish you a very *happy birthday*, too!

Martha Bond Branson
*Macon, GA*

[Hometown] *Macon, GA* [Ed] *A. L. Miller High School, Mercer University, Macon State University, Nancy Taylor Finishing School, Crandall Business College* [Occ] *self—property management (semi-retired)* [Hobbies] *collecting antiques, riding and showing horses all over the southeast, writing* [GA] *becoming a mother, grandmother, and great-grandmother*

*I have dabbled in writing poetry for quite some time, but I must confess that I have help—everything is by Divine Inspiration. I sometimes go back to read what I have written, and I am amazed and in awe and express my gratitude to God in humble fashion.*

## Your Memory Lives within My Heart

It seems I hear your footsteps
and you call my name
and I know nothing is ever going
to be the same
It's hard for me to realize you are
really gone
but your memory will live on and
on
When you left you didn't go far
for you are still in my thoughts
and you are still in my heart
I know soon we will be together
again in a world that knows no
death or pain
So until we meet again
sleep for awhile and rest
some too
No one will ever know how I
miss you

Virginia Sanders
*Chapmanville, WV*

[Hometown] *Chapmanville, WV* [Occ] *farmer* [Hobbies] *gardening, writing poetry* [GA] *learning the truth in the Bible*

*I was inspired to write this poem after my husband of fifty-three and a half years passed away. I do miss him but I don't grieve like some who have no hope. My hope is in the Bible and when I read Acts 24:15 where it shows there's going to be a resurrection of the just and unjust I know my husband will live again and that comforts me and just knowing this makes me happy.*

### Live Your Life

If you get stuck in the past, you'll lose the future.
I always let myself go.
A simple way to start a new life:
Get out more, connect with the right people.
Don't limit yourself on what you can do.
If you have a dream, follow it, live it.
If we take it one day at a time, anything is possible.
You are strong. You are brave.
Never let yourself go.
It may help others follow their dreams
And inspire others.

Virginia May Gerew
*Rochester, NY*

[Hometown] *Rochester, NY* [Ed] *CNA training* [Occ] *retired* [Hobbies] *art, writing, and playing guitar* [GA] *I'm still here despite what I've been through.*

*If I can help inspire other people, it will get me going in the right way for myself. A lot of people deserve better.*

## Mysterious Time

Who started time?
Is it when the rooster first crowed?
Could it be a ticking master?
Is it controlled forever after?
Hands developed the clock
Minds assimilated each part
The earth goes round and round
And the sun goes up and down
Does time change speed?
In a hurry? Time wants to drag
Life is good. Time zips by
Waiting, waiting, it almost stops
With human age, time is funny
Early on, it passes quite slow
All want to hurry and grow
Then, boom! Time rushes on
No one can plan when time will end
So welcome each second as a true friend!

Barbara Kay Demaree
*North Fort Myers, FL*

[Hometown] *Muncie, IN* [Ed] *master's in elementary education with science and math specialties* [Occ] *teacher of elementary and adult education* [Hobbies] *exploring life; flying a hot air balloon; being with friends; traveling; volunteering; theater* [GA] *living each day the best I can and having a great family*

*I have always found poetry to be a wonderful explanation of the world around us. It is the magic of words expressed in unlimited ways. All cultures have their own methods to say what is most important in their hearts and souls.*

## Soon

Wine, women and song.
What went wrong?
'Twas a never-ending song.
Now it's all gone.
'Twill hope for a new day soon.
All gloom gone with a new moon.
The newness will be a boon.
Joyous days ahead with no more gloom.
'Twill be a new day to sing.
Bringing on a new fling.
Let freedom ring
Yes! Let freedom ring!
Soon

Guy Brewster Young
*Murphy, OR*

[Hometown] *Grants Pass, OR* [Ed] *master's degree, ministerial degree* [Occ] *probation officer in Alameda County in Oakland, CA; minister in Peoples Temple, San Fransisco, CA* [Hobbies] *paint on rocks* [GA] *being alive at 86*

## Be Ready

Open your eyes
What do you see?
Can you hear
the calling?
Heaven gates are opening
The trumpets are ringing
Are you ready?
Yesterday is too late
Tomorrow may not come
Appointed until the day
Is the time to draw near
Don't turn away
Hear the call
Make yourself
For today He calls

Cynthia D. Wyatt
*Jacksons Gap, AL*

[Hometown] *Millbrook, AL* [Ed] *graduated in 1975* [Occ] *house cleaning* [Hobbies] *reading, writing, and sewing* [GA] *accepting Christ as my savior and the birth of my children*

*My life has been simple, a wife and mother. Then working in cleaning a church so I could be home when my kids got out of school. I feel very blessed. I have been writing since I was twelve. My goal was always to be a great writer. My greatest accomplishment is being a good mother, a good grandmother, and the wife to a man who loves me as much as I love him. I'm very blessed. God has been good to me.*

## The Truest Love of All

Your big brown eyes looked up at me
And I could see the pain.
I knew without a doubt, I couldn't ask you to stay again.
You were going to leave me, this time for sure.
We'd been through this before, but now I knew
No amount of tears or begging could keep you.
I looked in your eyes and saw the love shine.
Or was it just a reflection of mine.
If tears could heal a broken heart.
You'd stay forever and we'd never part.
But God saw you slowing down and your eyesight growing dim.
He made a decision that day
And knew he wanted you with him.
He brushed my tears aside and made me
See that you were only on loan.
Soon I'd have to say goodbye and let Him take you home.
And so sweet Sassy, I'll say to you
Run and play with your departed friends but always look for me.
I'll be along someday, I just don't know when.
But you'll be so happy and you can see again.
Even though my tears are hard to stop.
I know you'll be better there
God let me love you for more than twenty years
When He put you in my care.
You were more than just a little dog to me.
More faithful and loyal than any human could be.
So until I see you sweet Sassy up above,
Go in peace with all my love.

Patricia Nienke
*Ellsworth, KS*
[Hometown] *Ellsworth, KS* [Ed] *some college* [Occ] *retired farmer and stockman* [Hobbies] *flowers, gardening and my Aussie dogs* [GA] *raising two wonderful children*
*Sassy, my little house dog, was the inspiration for this poem. She was so cute and faithful. I bought her for my husband who had ALS. She would stay close to him when I was working in the field or feeding cattle after he couldn't do that anymore. After he was gone, she transferred her love to me.*

## As the River Flows

Cascading down like waterfalls
Gently flows our raging love
Like the powerful current of a mighty river
Cutting through ancient Mother Earth
Warmed by the nurturing sun
Our love is enriched and grows
As the river flows
Or like pulsating stars, bursting
Around Endless suns, our love is eternal and expansive
As the river flows
Our love flows forever and forevermore
As mighty waters ebb and flow
Rushing forward, to a vast ocean of our love
We drink of the rivers waters and are satisfied
For our hearts are full with loving warmth
And intimacy of our companionship
Joy, happiness and lover's delight
Together, we are complete in our eternal love
Our lover's kisses seal our fate
Overflowing in our tender embrace
Rushing, raging, ever progressing, like a mighty river
Within our lover's affairs of state
A tender kiss, a solemn yet passionate embrace
A fiery sky silhouetted upon the river's face
Contented lovers, hand in hand
And our love moves us as the river flows.

Jeffrey Eugene Elliott-Cruz
*San Jose, CA*

[Hometown] *San Jose* [Ed] *adjunct professor, investment advisor* [Occ] *attorney* [Hobbies] *writing, outdoor activities, enjoying grandchildren* [GA] *father of six children and having numerous grandchildren This poem was inspired and dedicated to the writer's mistress, lover and companion, Betty Sharon, aka, Adilene Idalie. She is an inspiring friend, lover and companion.*

## And Life Goes On

You are born, there is a celebration for that—yearly
and early on... throughout, you're treated dearly.

Life goes on, you grow older and older
siblings joined the family and you grow bolder
because if you don't then the world's on your shoulder.

Now you are a teen... thinking life is ever so keen
but the flipside—your parents keep being mean.

Life goes on... the day finals came
you graduated high school, college is your game
a degree to earn and you'll go look for fame.

OPS! Marriage caught you—
children arise—but not on cue.

Life goes on... the goal was slowed down some more,
kids made it out the door, admittedly raising them was a chore,
now grandchildren come and go as we watch them grow and soar.

Life did go on... would I have changed a thing—
others tend to improve my golf swing?

Mary Whelpley
*Laverne, OK*

[Hometown] *Laverne, OK* [Ed] *high school, electronic assembler* [Occ] *retired home maker* [Hobbies]
*writing poetry and stories* [GA] *married for 51 years to the same man*

## Sandcastle

He was the keeper of the castle
In the early morning light.
A truth every thought followed
To show them what was right.
The children in the meadows
Were all dancing for your love
And the songs I once knew were for you.
I heard you were in a tower now
Thinking by the sea.
So I thought I'd come and join you
(The other part of me).
You're brighter and sweeter than anything
'The Wind' could comprehend.
The keeper of the castle
And the keeper of all men.
The sun is a shadow
Hidden deep beneath my soul.
And you keep in the fire burning
Just to let me know.
Now I'm a child in the sky
Crying to be free.
The poets are all waiting
And You're waiting there for me.

Gilbert Reynosa
*La Verne, CA*

*When I was very young, I got very sick and had to spend several months in the hospital. I emerged with such a sensitivity within me, a newness, if you will. Shortly thereafter, I lived in Yosemite National Park for a long period of time and developed my writing technique and began to create musical compositions. I had some heavy influences in my life. My beautiful mother was a main factor, always with her warm love and encouragement. The deep words and music by Cat Stevens and Leonard Cohen were a major influence on my development process. I blossomed into a poet and a singer/songwriter, playing acoustic guitar. I continue to be creative with my masterpieces. Love and peace to all.*

## Summer

Sitting in a lime green
    folding chair,
Hypnotized by the sparkling ocean,
Sly seagulls dance across
    the wet sand…
Season of warm sun returns,
Under a cloudless blue sky,
Massaged to sleep by a sea breeze,
Memorable escape…
Endless innocence of
Rejoicing school children.

Stay forever!

Lynette B
*Philadelphia, PA*

[Hometown] *Philadelphia, PA* [Ed] *AAS in accounting* [Occ] *retired municipal worker* [Hobbies] *collecting 1960s music memorabilia, attending festivals and cat shows, reading, vacations at the shore, people-watching* [GA] *being invited to read my poetry at a literary event for the first time in 1999*

*I love summer! It represents innocence and inspires memories of childhood. I was a shy child who enjoyed reading poetry and, at age fourteen, began writing and haven't stopped. I joined the editorial staff at high school literary magazine and, while in college, I contributed to their literary publication. I had a poem published in the* College Poetry Review *in 1982. In the summer of 1985, I've discovered the vibrant poetry scene in Philadelphia. In 1988 I found my niche with a group of poets known as the* Poetry Forum. *Currently, I am assembling a chapbook of my work.*

## Pillow Chatter

Whether you lay your head on down goosefeathers foam
Rubber, silk, cotton, or the most expensive of materials
The resulting slumber may be hazardous to your life
And limb
Some say talk is cheap. On a pillow talk may be
Quite deep
Secrets, lies, video tape, betrayal, cheating, clandestine
Meetings, stock tips given away markets downward spiral
If humans weren't swayed by romance
To spill all not take the chance
Can pillow chatter turn chaotic?
Sealed lips can make the difference
Between disaster and victory

Sandra Glassman
*Oceanside, NY*

[Hometown] *Oceanside, NY* [Ed] *high school and music training* [Occ] *piano teacher* [Hobbies]
*reading books, learning guitar* [GA] *My poetry and music for a novel about the holocaust are residing in
the Holocaust Museum in Washington DC.*

*I have written many poems about life's different challenges. One of my poetry books has been made into
a screenplay. I have a husband and two adult children. During this year, the pandemic provided lots of
thoughts and subjects. Life, nature, children, the world keeps turning and poets keep on learning.*

## A Second Chance

He was hers
And she was his
From their very first meeting

They grew close through the years
Always together

Then war took him away
She was lost without him

Many years passed
No answer

45 years later—a miracle
God gave them a second chance

They had five years together
And were very happy

They put a lifetime of living
In that short time

Then God called him home!

Irene McFadden
*Conway, AR*

[Hometown] *Conway, AR*  [Occ] *retired*  [Hobbies] *sewing, refinishing furniture, gardening, ham radio*
[GA] *being a mom*

*Daniel went to Vietnam as an army green beret. He served two tours, wounded three times in combat. I lost him in December 2020 to agent orange. I miss you, my sweet soulmate, my first and last love.*

## The Beauty of it All

As I gaze out my window into
A new day created by God
I see the beautiful sunshine
I can hear the birds chirping and the dogs barking
And I see the beauty of it all because a new day
Has come and the winter days and snow are gone
There is peace and joy in the change of the seasons
The flowers bloom in the spring with the leaves so green
Filling the trees and I see the beauty of it all
Summer comes and the warmth of the weather streaming
Over me as I walk along the beach and I see the beauty of it all
Fall comes and we see the leaves change in color and
Fall to the ground in all shapes and sizes
I can see the beauty of it all and I can say
God created it all

Renita Love White
*Robbins, IL*

[Hometown] *Robbins, IL* [Ed] *graduate with a n associate degree in liberal arts* [Hobbies] *cooking, writing poetry and plays* [GA] *having my poetry book published*

## The Glass Rose

An odd thing to see is a "glass rose."
As it lies there so still in its quiet repose.
Its petals etched in place by the artists hand.
Not moving like a live flower on a stand.
Just motionless, not moving a petal.
No life, only made by man.
Her beauty yes, is there, to see.
The *Flower of Flowers*, but no life has she.
Yes, there she lies. Just gathering dust
In her quiet demise.

Vernon Bogle
*Manchester, TN*

[Hometown] *Woodbury, TN* [Ed] *high school/radio course* [Occ] *former radio announcer, now on disability* [Hobbies] *playing the guitar, writing, working, various puzzles* [GA] *writing*

*I seem to live in the abstract, like the "Twilight Zone." If Rod Serling was still alive, I bet he could use some of my dreams, stories and poems on his TV show. I think this poem "The Glass Rose," reflects this. To look at an object, with an abstract view is not to look at it as a thing of beauty but a thing of pity or bizarre amazement. Like my glass rose.*

# Man Is Mind: Maintaining Integrity (by) Nurturing Divinity

As a child, he grabs for a toy.
As a teen, he learns to be coy.
As a young man, his lessons will teach:
Fatherhood and family are goals he can reach.
But as a man grows and expands his mind,
He attracts associates of the same kind.
He sustains growth through industry
And expands his knowledge of divinity.
Physically, a man fights opposition
While strongly defending his own position.
But later he learns to catch more flies with honey,
Not wasting time "earning" dirty money.
As men mature and limit poor choices,
They grow stronger with positive attitudes.
They become examples of good behavior,
Increasing their moral aptitude.
A real man is MIND—
Imam Mohammed taught humanity.
Showing integrity by nurturing divinity—
Standing firm as an ethical entity.

Saisa Bilal Neel
*Annapolis, MD*

*This poem was sent as a Father's Day gift in a tumultuous, pandemic year (2020). It was presented to the strong, courageous, mindful men I know. As an American Muslimah and student of the late Imam WD Mohammed, I learned from him that "Man Is Mind."*

# A Young Black Man Murdered in Hartford, CT

My Shepherd leads me through the valley of thorns.
Wisps of gospel praises soulfully summon me.
Rhyme, rap, beat soothe my soul, set my feet to dance
Yet, through the vale I see myself lie peacefully
arrayed in a stranger's garb.
Gardenia, lilies comfort me basking in my casket.
Family and friends tarry. Weep, wail in haunting grief
Or hold silent in anger, shock, disbelief.
From my place of honor before rows of sanctified seats
I hear whispered snipes, see glazed eyes stare.
What about me? Isn't this my day? My time to smooth
away the rough edges of my life?
Pastor, tell them to celebrate joy at my homecoming!
I am free of the trappings of this earth, free of pain,
free of sirens and lights. My waiting, worry done.
Stealthily they search for my backpack, a vain attempt
to grab some foolish trinket, a key to understand,
desperate to preserve images of already faded memory.
Do they not know my family, my friends are my treasure?
Did I not teach them to love one another?
To be merciful to one another? To cherish one another?
Surrender my children. Give in to the solace.
And remember to tell me of your love and dreams.
 I am but a thought away.

Patricia E. Christie-Brooks
*Manchester, CT*

[Hometown] *Manchester, CT* [Ed] *bachelor's degree in psychology* [Occ] *retired civil rights investigator* [Hobbies] *writing* [GA] *supreme court case on exclusionary zoning, several state cases expanding protected classes*

*I am a seventy-four-year-old white woman, matriarch of a multi-racial family living within the black American culture. My grandson Tyreke Brooks is the third family member to be killed in Hartford, CT.*

# For Those We Have Never Met

We offer prayers for those we know
And for those we have never met
For all of us are shepherds now
Trying not to fret
Our faith is tested every day
In ways we have not known
Yet through these times
We pray to Thee
And give thanks for all blessings shown
Please grant us peace and still out hearts
For we know we are not there yet
As we offer prayers for those we know
And for those we have never met

Karen M. LoCicero
*Mount Pleasant, SC*

[Hometown] *Mount Pleasant, SC* [Ed] *AS degree, early childhood education* [Occ] *retired teacher* [Hobbies] *writing, reading, and gardening* [GA] *marriage of 48 years*

*I have an AS degree in early childhood education and worked for over twenty-five years in public and private educational programs. These included kindergarten, Title I reading, and ESL programs. They all took me on a great adventure that I will never forget. I enjoy writing, reading and working with plants. My greatest achievement has been my marriage of forty-eight years. Thanks, Paulie! This year my father-in-law turned ninety-six. He continues to share with us the lessons of perseverance, endurance, and courage. We are all forever grateful.*

## I Am Happy Among the Trees ... and Others

The park
Look at the branches
of those old trees
twisted ant tortured
by the weather disease.
They stood there and took it...
in rain and in hail
and murmured
mayhem without avail...
There is no mercy in time and in age—
I hear this remark in the whispering wind: "We must go
and turn the page."
Nature
Nature is at war with us;
its furor batters to let us know
to our dismay that tornado,
earthquake erupt and flood
and move to prove we're in the way.
We are supposed to co-exist,
each to benefit both.
If we can't share and we don't care
then the ice will melt…
the sun will burn
then:
it'll be our turn.

Hannie Jacoba Voyles
*Chico, CA*

[Hometown] *Chico, CA*  [Ed] *BA/MA linguistics/English*  [Occ] *faculty and faculty administrator*
[Hobbies] *golf, walks, talks, biking tours*  [GA] *my daughters and my work*
*From the streets of Amsterdam during the Nazi occupation (1949-45), we emigrated to San Francisco in 1950. I had just turned seventeen. My mother, sister, and I settled in SFO where I attended college. Further education took place at University of Colorado and Chico State University. Thirty years later as a faculty member and a faculty administrator at the University and Butte College, I retired and started to write poetry on my early morning walks. Three books resulted: Storming the Tulips—a translation of children's accounts of the war years in Amsterdam. Moments in the Mirror—a book of poetry.*

## 215 and More Remember Them All

Their smiles faded into tears.
Hearts became filled with fears.
Hands tucked hard at their sides,
afraid to show any pride.
Told to be who they are not, their minds begin to rot.
Emotionally injured, physically beaten.
All of them haven't eaten.
Hair cut. Clothes changed.
Any signs of their heritage and they'd be rearranged.
Taught they were lower than low,
scummier than scum.
Some strong ones tried to journey to where they are from—
home they thought.
The ones at the schools all raised and felt a fool.
Lost in confusion as to who or what they are.
Many generations still wear this scar.
215 they found and their remains carry a song.
We are all one warrior in this web of life.
Resilient descendants of those who lived in strife.
We are this new web of life.
We will now make it right.

Janice Yvonne-Daughness Migwans
*Cape Girardeau, MO*

[Hometown] *Chicago* [Ed] *BBA* [Occ] *energy shifter* [Hobbies] *hiking* [GA] *Sigma Alpha Pi*

*A word creator. A joke maker. A smile bringer. A memory that lingers. Manitoulin made. Energy shifter. Two Spirited. Entertainer. Story teller and picture painter. Creator of word illusions.*

## Mother

Mother I wish you were there for me
So many times when I was away
Had no one I can turn to
Was in fear every day

When I got the chance
I would call you on the phone
You would comfort me by saying
Son you never were alone

I've been with you since that day
You left to go to war
I always knew you were safe
Need I say anymore

Those encouraging words you told me
I carry them with me every day
I am now a disabled veteran
Nothing more I need to say.

Kenneth L. Combs
*Pahrump, NV*

[Hometown] *Pahrump, NV* [Ed] *high school diploma* [Occ] *disabled veteran* [Hobbies] *building guns*
[GA] *my daughter*

## Alice Marie

He watches over me,
Little old Alice Marie,
My Heavenly Father sets me free
When I'm down to any degree.

He watches over me,
Don't you see?
I love and write poetry.
I study history.

To be the best that I can be.
I love and care for my family.
They mean the world to me.
And will till the end of eternity.

He watches over me,
As He does the sparrows and chickadees.
He lets me know how to be happy,
Little old Alice Marie.

So if your heart is full of misery,
And life has no meaning or reality.
Remember that He and only He,
Can fill your life with beauty.

Alice Marie Young-Lionshows
*Lodge Grass, MT*

[Ed] *teacher* [Hobbies] *reading, writing, singing and speaking* [GA] *becoming a grandmother*
*Greetings to all from Alice Marie Young-Lion Shows, an enrolled member of the Apsaalooke Indian Nation in southeastern Montana. I am proud of my heritage and my culture and enjoy sharing my heritage with others. I taught elementary school age children for many years. Upon retiring I passed the Crow Tribal Court Bar Exam and now represent defendants in tribal court. In my opinion my greatest accomplishment was when I became a grandmother.*

## God of Nature

Thank you Holy One; God of nature's infinite universe,
for Your sacred breath of transmutable life that enfolds us,
in its generation of imaginations in bodily designs
that enlivens our human nature as our choices define.
Keep us constantly attuned with Your transcendent nature
of spirit around, within, and through our mortal being
manifesting it's omnipresence in all we are seeing,
on the paths we tread through temporal life's inconstancy
to express our innate spiritual qualities
through our predominant human faculties.
And keep us receptive to Your word of guidance,
with its commands for harmony and balance
securing earthly life's amenities through our competency,
with the blessings of Your grace, as we fulfill our destiny.
And strengthen our faith in peace on Earth with liberty,
integrity, and accountability with unity and brotherly love
that pave the highways to Your mansions in the heavens above.

Carol A. Sustarsic
*Willowick, OH*

[Hometown] *Willowick, OH* [Ed] *some college/26 years in legal publishing* [Occ] *retired* [Hobbies] *learning to play a variety of musical instruments but master of none* [GA] *winning first prize for writing the best essay speaking for democracy when I was 18 years old competing in a contest among schools sponsored by the American Legion*

*Composing this poem choosing explicit words from the myriad of thoughts overwhelming my mind, like the virulence pervading the air we're breathing, convinces me of the supernal power in "the Word was God"; Creator of all things made, and the life within our being, as glorified in scripture. But whatever humanity thinks, or believes about the origin and purpose for mortal life, we can be certain that everyone stands to lose the endowed rights to its experience in a defiant rebellion against the commands for its perpetuation by God of nature's infinite universe.*

## Memories of My Valentine Jim

You were my Valentine for 35 years
Today is Valentine's Day
The first time I'm celebrating it
Without you here
Because you are spending
Your 80th birthday
In Heaven this year
We were blessed with a
Special love, it's true
I have you in my heart
But it is broken without you
I didn't want a party
Or a heart-shaped cake this year
I just wanted to be alone
To shed my tears
I lit a candle at church
And said the Rosary, too
This is the way I always
Feel close to you
Tonight I will kiss your picture
Talk to you and hold your
Pillow close to me
Then I will fall asleep
And see you in my dreams

Claire Ruffino Shoaf
*Santa Clara, CA*

[Hometown] *Portland, CT* [Ed] *HSD, attended college* [Occ] *administrative secretary, Union SF Theater Wardrobe* [Hobbies] *knitting, crochet, candy-making for gifts and hospital* [GA] *having a wonderful life and marriage with my husband Jim*

*I am eighty-four years old. I worked as a secretary for twenty-six years and when I retired I started work full time in SF, San Jose Broadway Union wardrobe. We take care of costumes and dress the actors when the shows come to our area. I make blankets and hats for the hospital, and candy-making for friends. I have been writing poetry for friends and family for years. I have a sister Rosalie and brother John, in Connecticut and a family of friends in California.*

## Happy Birthday

I'm writing you this poem
To bring you birthday wishes.
I would have liked to had a party
As long as I don't do the dishes.

I wish I knew how to play a piano
So we could have sung you a song,
Although I don't know the outcome
Of the tunes and our singing along.

This comes with warmest greetings
Which is being sent your way,
Because you are a unique person
In the things you do and say.

Gloria M. Bouley
*Plainfield, CT*

[Hometown] *Plainfield, CT* [Ed] *high school/business college* [Occ] *retired confidential secretary and bookkeeper* [Hobbies] *poetry, photography, knitting, word puzzles* [GA] *won "Golden Poet" award*

*I began writing in the mid-sixties. In 1996, I created my own personal greeting cards. My poems are stories in my life. When I can, I still write poetry. I enjoy wildlife, photography, knitting, and at present work on different puzzle books. I say my prayers every night and thank the Lord for each day. I take it one day at a time and live it to the fullest. I am blessed.*

# Rain Drops

Rain drops
Rain drops
Cool and clean
You are…the most beautiful thing
The dew that you have left upon the ground
Is the most beautiful sight around
The trees and flowers
They love you too
You help spring to begin anew
You help create a beautiful tapestry
For the wandering eye to see

Cecilia Hattendorf
*Apple Valley, CA*

[Hometown] *Apple Valley, CA* [Occ] *retired RN* [Hobbies] *gardening, writing, music* [GA] *Haven't written my greatest poem yet.*

*I have lived in Southern California all my life. I like springtime here. There are many beautiful trees, bushes and flowering plants in this state. Making gardens is a favorite pastime for me, as well as writing poetry. I like writing rhyming poetry. As an amateur poet I am looking forward to studying different types of poetry to enhance my writing abilities in hopes of appealing to a broader audience.*

## A Storm Story

As we huddle with foreboding, we're trapped
In our own anticipation, grim and terrifying.
The storm is coming our way, unleashing fury
That recalls the poet's "woman scorned."
Beyond mollification, now past the point of no-return,
The storm rages on, as if intent on wreaking havoc
In vengeance.
Gripped with terror but defiant, I load my flashlight
With new batteries as the settlers of old loaded
Their rifles when they headed west in their
Covered wagons, never knowing when they might,
Along the way, have to circle their wagons.
But you don't circle your wagons to greet
An approaching storm! You bide your time,
With your flashlight at the ready,
Then, at a time of its own choosing, the mighty sun
Comes out of hiding behind the clouds. It flashes
Its irresistible smile upon those shaken and anxious.
We're suddenly made aware of what it is we've just
Been through: one noisy storm but not the "pitiless" sort
There was no havoc wreaked in vengeance.

Sugwon Kang
*Oneonta, NY*

[Hometown] *Oneonta, NY* [Ed] *Columbia University, PhD political science* [Occ] *professor of political science emeritus, Hartwick College, Oneonta, NY* [Hobbies] *playing the piano (classical music) and painting* [GA] *Fulbright Senior Scholar (2008-09, South Korea)*

*English is my second language, and I find it an impossible language really to master even as I take much satisfaction in noticing my own small improvements from year to year, now speaking as an octogenarian. The language amazes me, especially its capacity for growth, which I can't say I always rejoice in. It was one of the principal reasons why I made the decision many years ago to stay in this country for good. "I came, I saw, I stayed."*

## She

She hides her pain and says she's fine
She'll get through it all and at the end she'll shine
She would cry in private so no one would see
She was scared and depressed to a certain degree
She was overwhelmed and scared to be alone
She had to start over all on her own
She put a smile on her face and tried her best
She dealt with her feelings that made her so stressed
She knew what to do to get past all the hurt
She learned to recognize her own self-worth
She'll rise to the occasion and come out strong
She realized who she was all along
She had her family and she had her friends
She knew they'd support her all the way to the end
She knew that with time her pain would fade
She's proud of the progress that she has made
She is strong and proved to be a survivor
She realized she is one hell of a fighter

Tisha Rodriguez
*Riverside, CA*

## Nature Made

A white bridal veil blows with the south breeze,
Designed and completed on top of a juniper bush.
Completed by a patient spider, it's beautiful as you please.
Transferred to bride's shining hair and held with a pin.
A glowing bride of small stature, she will take her vows,
At the side of her groom in front of their preacher.
The vows made together to love, and care for each other,
So strong to have lasted fifty-six years.
Memories linger,
Tough decisions made together with her work as a teacher,
His work as a factory supervisor and farm owner.
They had a family and stayed true to each other, no fears.
Now that he left for heaven, she holds his memory close.
Each day she looks at the family picture. She says a prayer.
Before turning off the light at night, she turns in the bed where
They slept so many years, shuts her eyes to sleep.
She is proud, staying true to the vows
Made so very long ago, memories recalled by viewing a
Spider nature made white bridal veil.

Bonnie Neuman
*Evart, MI*

[Hometown] *Evart, MI* [Ed] *education* [Occ] *art in public school* [Hobbies] *travel, family, exercise, hugs with great-grandchildren* [GA] *sharing, love, hosting students from foreign countries*

*I have lived for eighty-six years and live in the same home I came to as a bride in 1957. We had four children, eight grandchildren, and are expecting our ninth great-grandchild. I have traveled to visit our Youth for Understanding students homes in Spain, Netherlands, Hungry, Romania, Germany, Norway, Chile, and Japan.*

## Follow the Science

Novel coronavirus on the horizon,
Not to worry per the WHO.
Sickness and death tide,
Disease spread worldwide.
Lockdown guidance,
Follow the science.
Social distancing,
Double masking.
Businesses shut down,
Closed streets in town.
Restricted churches and beaches,
Eliminated school choices.
Listen to the silence,
Follow the science.
Government lied,
Statements unverified.
Listen to the silence,
Follow the science.
Listen to the people clamor,
It's getting louder.

Lance S. Loria
*Montgomery, TX*

[Hometown] *Sleepy Montgomery Texas on Lake Conroe.* [Ed] *BS degree in accounting, Stetson University, DeLand, FL* [Occ] *currently semi-retired/self-employed management consultant/CPA* [Hobbies] *writing (of course), toy trains, financial markets, reading, and cooking.* [GA] *by use of a Heimlich maneuver; I saved the life of a neighbor's young child who was turning blue and choking.*

*I've lived a life filled with professional accomplishments of which I'm proud however, I'm most proud of my two children. One is a school teacher with two sons who are young gentlemen. My other child is a talented musician, song writer, and more who works within the creative music industry. I'm now in my seventies living life comfortably in my lake home where writing is a pleasure and not a pressing deliverable of my profession.*

## Endless Love

When I was a little girl all I ever wanted was to be a mother. How lucky I am to be blessed to be a mom, a grandmother, and a great-grandmother. There is nothing more special than a soft kiss on your cheek or a big hug around your legs when they run across the room to greet you. Every time is like the first, like it's been forever since they saw you. Little ones are so easy to read; they love you unconditionally and completely. They are not just connected to your heart but also to your soul. I could never imagine how a mother could love more than one child the same. Now I know with each new little life that comes into your life your heart grows. There is always room for one more and more and more. They all have their own personalities and little attitudes, which makes them all special in their own way. Loving a child is so easy; sit with them on the floor and play or dance and spin around to any music at all. Read to them, rock them to sleep; it takes so little to make them happy. Listen to them—really listen—you might just learn something. Love them, enjoy them, and bask in their happiness every second. They don't stay young for long. The love for a child and the love of a child is endless.

Margaret Beach
*Mechanicsville, MD*

[Hometown] *Mechanicsville, MD* [Ed] *high school* [Occ] *business owner*
*I am a wife of fifty years and a mom, grandmother and great-grandmother. I became a poet after I lost my son tragically. I found a poem he had written that touched my heart. I sent it in and it was published. I have been writing poems ever since. I believe he left me this gift so I could bring beauty into the world without him and because of him. I also have my own business now.*

## My Gift

A special gift, from me to you.
This empty box, yes, it's true
Please don't be blue.
Because you'll fill it
With all the cards I'm sending you.
So when you're grown
And I am gone,
We'll still be together far, but near.
If you're feeling down and sad,
Just touch your heart,
I'll cheer you up, my dear.
Just remember your grandma's
Love is all for you.

Dyan R. Ramos
*Milwaukee, WI*

[Hometown] *Milwaukee, WI* [Occ] *retired* [Hobbies] *swim* [GA] *being a grandmother*

## Then All People Will Have the Power to Go On!

People live, people love, people die.
People have the power to go on!
Isn't it great, so much to do, so much to say.
Somewhere to go, somewhere to stay.
People play, people laugh, people flirt.
People work, people hurt, people get left behind.
People live, people love, people die.
People have the power to go on!
People are bruised, people are pained.
People are abused, people are killed!
People can change, people can improve.
People can live well and help others excel!
People are happy, people are at ease.
People can uphold the laws, people can enjoy.
People live, people love, people die.
People have the power to go on!
We say justice for people, we say all people are equal.
Yet we leave people who are weak, sick, poor, elderly,
Of mixed race and of unusual gender
To stand alone without enough people to help them!
As death will surely take us all, can we engage those in need
To live a better life and by our deeds enable
Under-served people with the power to go on?
If yes, then all people will have the power to go on!

Brenda Kay Miller
*Hoboken, NJ*

[Hometown] *Hoboken, NJ* [Ed] *Bachelor of Music from Heidelberg University, Tiffin, OH & Master of Music in vocal performance from Cleveland Institute of Music, Cleveland, OH, opera studies at American Institute of Musical Studies, Graz, Austria* [Occ] *retired music teacher, singer, and pianist* [Hobbies] *drawing, painting, reading mysteries, action novels, and romance stories* [GA] *to greet each day with determination and grace Brenda Kay Miller is a forty-year member of the Soka Gakkai International, which is a Nichiren Buddhist organization. She chants Nam Myoho Renge Kyo to raise her life condition to be in rhythm with the universe and helps others do the same. Brenda has been a singer, conductor, and voice and piano music teacher for over fifty years. She has written several music compositions, poems, and is now trying her hand at pencil and water color artwork. Ms. Miller, originally from Ohio, moved to New York City after a brief opera career. She now resides in Hoboken, NJ.*

## Sharing Foxholes

We of the World share tantamount foxholes,
Ducking terror's blitz of malignant hate.
Silence malediction from nescient gholes.

Colors of humankind coalesce proud souls,
Veracity, democracy connate.
We of the World share tantamount foxholes.

Equable climates gyre to mob control,
Contracted thugs traduce the free speech state.
Silence malediction from nescient gholes.

Dire issues we face!  Take the ozone hole!
Toil as One to halt thawed ice mass spates.
We of the World share tantamount foxholes.

Trash and plastics gorge the world's toilet bowl.
Raping Earth's rain forests just must abate!
Silence malediction from nescient gholes.

In so many languages alarms toll.
Pinpoint Earth's dilemmas to ruminate.
For We the World share tantamount foxholes.
Silence malediction from nescient gholes.

Jan L. Hetherly
*Scroggins, TX*

[Hometown] *Mount Pleasant, TX*  [Ed] *BA in fashion design, fashion merchandising from Texas Christian University*  [Occ] *WombBooks.com, creator, owner, writer, illustrator, voice-overs*  [Hobbies] *floral design, gardening, silk painting, cooking and entertaining*  [GA] *awarded a Poet Fellow by Noble House, London, England, 2006*
*I have enjoyed many forms of creativity through the years, painting with pastels, and silk ink paintings, making jewelry by the lost wax method and precious metal clay, pottery, and crocheting.  But when grandchildren began to arrive, I created The WombBooks, in audio format for babies in the womb, video format for infants to age 4, and hardcover books.  I spend hours a day in my studio with my Woombees, the little characters I created for the books.  I wrote the stories in poetic form with rhyme, rhythm, and music enlightening babies womb experience.  How blessed am I!*

## Springtime, a Rebirth

From coldest winter, springtime brings new birth
The farm gone the new we all behold
And joy again does come to Mother Earth
More precious than all silver and all gold
The grass again it shows an early green
The Lord do sing so sweet in the trees
And love is once again found on the scene.
And lovers woo, you know the Lord our God.
And Old Man Winter has to go away.
The snow melts where once white upon green
And children camp outside to run and play
And youth and all things good as this are found
Yes springtime is a time on man's Earth.
And tis also renewing of the earth.

Lewis Walling Findley
*Port Wentworth, GA*

[Hometown] *Port Wentworth, GA* [Ed] *high school* [Occ] *retired janitor* [Hobbies] *web surfing*

# Down into the Darkenss

The ground is frozen under your feet
It is cracking under your weight
It threatens to giveaway under you
Through the cracks of frozen earth
Ice cold water escapes the broken shards
It was only yesterday that a smile was upon you
In a blink of an eye everything changed
Deep down into the darkness you fell
Now the ground is threatening to consume
Threatening to drown you
The ground is breaking around you
You cannot breathe
The darkness consumes your will
Deep in the darkness there is a light
A soft sweet ray of hope
A hand in the freezing darkness comes for you
It grips you tightly pulling you out
Back into the light, the warmth, back to life
To hope and happiness

Brittany Sarkozi
*New Boston, MI*

[Hometown] *South Lyon, MI* [Ed] *graphic design degree* [Occ] *Nissan parts specialist* [Hobbies] *candle making, music, writing* [GA] *being a published poet*

*Music is my passion, I can play six instrument. I wish I had more time to play every instrument ever made but my writing has always been my first love. I enjoy writing and expressing myself through words.*

## From Earth to Eternity

It is true. No, it's really true.
I am not the best Christian.
But, I try hard.
I seek to love God;
To serve other people;
And, to reach the world
As I travel along life's highway.
It is by the power of God
Working in my heart
I can make God happy,
Become a man after his own heart.
So, as I move from earth to eternity,
Taking one step closer
Each day to Jesus,
I can make God happy!

Bill M. Watt
*Junction City, KS*

[Hometown] *Ottawa, KS* [Ed] *PhD communication* [Occ] *university professor (rt)* [Hobbies]
*racquetball, chess, Go, NASCAR* [GA] *forty-four years teaching college/university*

*Friend and colleague Ron Brown once gave me the high compliment saying, "You aren't the best Christian
I know, but you try the hardest." So, with the power of God working in my life, maybe, just maybe, I can be
what God wants me to be and He will be pleased with me.*

## End of the Plague

Like a breath of this
Rain-freshened air,
This is the end
Of the coronavirus outbreak.
Across the street
A flurry of white
Apple blossoms drift down
On fresh breeze,
The apple tree framed
By now, clear azure sky.
As I tread the sidewalk
To the mailbox,
And maybe an acceptance note
From a poetry publisher.
I need to get the mail
But I pause to breathe the fresh air
And gaze at the apple blossoms.
This fleeting moment is
White apple blossoms on a wet bough
And the end of the plague.

Richard Stepsay
*Aurora, CO*

[Hometown] *Denver, CO*  [Ed] *BS in creative writing*  [Occ] *peer specialist*  [Hobbies] *writing, coin collecting*

## My Dream Kitty

Little bitty, bitty,
Oh, so sweet kitty,
How I wish you were mine.
I'd love you and be so kind,
Little bitty, bitty,
My sweet dream kitty.

Becky Johnson Richardson
*Boaz, AL*

[Hometown] *Boaz, AL* [Ed] *equivalent to a bachelor's degree in English* [Occ] *retired IBM manager, staff technical editor and writer* [Hobbies] *life in general—when you retire, life in general becomes your overall hobby* [GA] *still working on it*

*Grandmothers are the ones who have the patience to teach grandchildren little songs. This poem is meant to be sung to small children so they will go to sleep clutching their stuffed kitten or real kitten. I hope many, many children learn to sing this and that it becomes as meaningful.*

# Sedition

Who's to say, what to say,
Is it wrong, to have a voice,
So strong…
And to wonder why,
So many must cry,
and
So many must die…
Is it the broken promises…
With no reasons why…
Or
Is it the fat cats…
Or
The street rats…
With empty facts and too many hacks…
Who's to say
The right way or the wrong way…
Because on any day
Be it may…
The solution will
Find a way.

Rodney Peterson
*Bedford, OH*

*I live in Bedford, OH. I love writing; I am a hopeful believer. Would love to fly to the moon.*

## Sister Sunshine

Spoke to Dad last week
He said he felt as if it was the end...
End of what, I immediately queried
He said he had bad fatigue, soreness, and a headache that did offend
I asked him if he had been vaccinated and which one he got
He said he had and said the one he had gotten...
I said I had gotten the same vaccine and
I told him that soreness, headache, and fatigue were side effects that soon would be forgotten
Dad thanked me for the information
He said he felt and sounded a whole lot better with the insight...
I was happy to put his mind at ease with the information
To which he called me Sister Sunshine, with my light shining bright!

Saundra T. Russell
*Tucson, AZ*

[Hometown] *Tucson, AZ* [Ed] *RN, MA* [Occ] *retired* [Hobbies] *poetry and crafting* [GA] *50 years a RN, over 30 years a RDN, and a former member of the Academy of Nutrition and Dietetics, and is in the PoetryFest Hall of Fame*

*Dedicated to my dad, LeRoi T. Russel who passed away in Nassau County, NY twenty-six days prior to his 95th birthday (7/22/1926-6/26/2021).*

## Angel Beach

Tucked neatly away
On beautiful winding roads
Through the giant forest
Of Wisconsin's noble pine
Cozy streams lay hidden
Near a cattail grove.

Powder blue skies with
Ruffled clouds from a painting
Flowers in a field surrender
Their charm of magical colors
A priceless Monet in the waiting.

Nearing this lake of wonder
As the sun and shade glisten
Shining through each and every pine
Now we shall walk on the sands of time.

Angel Beach once drenched
With one thousand angels tears
Holding the sand rains of humanity
Until God's serenity calmed their fears.

Rebecca A. Borreson
*Sparta, WI*

[Hometown] *Sparta, WI* [Ed] *high school* [Occ] *unemployed* [Hobbies] *gardening, fishing, hiking and boating* [GA] *being a mother of two children, surviving two types of cancer*

*I live in a small, unincorporated city out in the country. It is small, yet larger than life with nature's beauty,; truly I enjoy all the giant pine trees, bluffs, valleys, Sopher Creek, and the Mill Pond. Fishing, hiking, and camping are a great joy to me as is my family—the best joy of all! This poem was inspired by the beautiful drive to a state forest on a rustic road, that eventually brings you to an amazing campground, no electricity. Just all natural. The lake is the first thing you see as you pull in.*

## Creation, It Is All to You

Creation, your eyes are open, yet you refuse to see,
Your ears are open, but you don't hear Me.
In your darkness, suddenly I will come like a thief.
Open your eyes and ears; there is little time left.

Do you believe that I lived and died for you?
My heart is still pierced for what you do.
There are tears in My eyes, I constantly shed,
When my creation refused to hear and believe.

The grass is still green, embraced by the sun,
Enjoy the flowers that bloom at their own time.
Treasure the moments with friends and loved ones,
For in a blink of an eye, everything will be gone.

Don't ignore My messages and warnings.
Don't ignore My wishes and commandments.
Look around you, what do you see on your path?
Storms, plagues, and calamities are My wrath.

So, Creation be strong, you have been warned.
Be on your knees; repent while there is still time.
Rest assured I promise, I am always with you.
Follow and stay with Me, Creation, it is all up to you.

Virgilia Aberilla Smith
*Marshall, MI*

[Hometown] *Marshall, MI   USA*  [Ed] *Bachelor of Science in elementary education and registered nurse*  [Occ] *retired registered nurse*  [Hobbies] *traveling, writing, painting, gardening, dancing, and reading*  [GA] *mother of two, retired nurse after 44 years, acrylic painter, lyricist of twelve songs, published poet, and writing a memoir.*
*This poem was inspired by a vision of Jesus on February 23, 2021. I have been on the computer writing my memoir, which is inspired by my spiritual dreams. My eyes were tired. I closed my eyes to rest them. I was fully awake. Suddenly I saw His face. He had a crown of thorns. He looked very sad. He had tears in His eyes. His face was bruised and bloody. It was brief. I painted His picture. I placed the painting on my bedroom altar. God is good all the time. Praise the Lord.*

## Christmas Blessings

To my friends and family on Christmas Day
May the angels in Heaven for you play
May you receive your heart's desire
And may new dreams our Lord inspire.

May all your hopes and wishes come true
May you walk in all that God has for you
And may God's peace and love enthrall
And into satan's snares may you never fall.

May you walk with a light and bouncy step
Towards the people you haven't ministered to yet
And may the power of God through you flow
To help the little people whom no one knows.

May you constantly hear His voice
May your heart be tender and in Him rejoice
May your tongue bring blessings to all who hear
And may you feel God's presence always near.

Shalom Christina Zoë
*Roswell, NM*

[Hometown] *Roswell, NM* [Ed] *bible college* [Occ] *homemaker* [Hobbies] *I'm writing a book of Christian science-fiction, tetherball* [GA] *When I was in grade school, I saved three little children lost in a snowstorm.*

*I think the most important thing a person can do is lead someone to accept Jesus as their savior because that is eternal. As a small child I went to Heaven and saw Jesus and angels so I know Heaven is real. As for me I'm seventy-two. The world considers me handicapped. I use simple words because I want everyone to understand my poetry. I'm writing my first book called Purple Eyes. It's a Christian science-fiction book. I love to decorate and want my home to be beautiful and full of peace.*

## Love's Power

Love can have the power to bring
Happiness
and joy to everyone
That lets the power inside.
Real
Love can heal a broken heart and
Bring peace to the one who's heart
Has been broken.
Letting their light
Shine again knowing that you have
Nothing to fear but fear itself and love can
Heal scares that were there since the
Beginning of time.
Making you a whole
New person that can walk around with
There head held high.
Showing the
World what love can do.

Angel Heady
*Cumberland, MD*

[Hometown] *Cumberland*

## The Third Bathroom

So much confusion with people today.
Remember when you were either straight, bi or gay?
Being in front of a restroom never caused such gloom.
Choose the door the left or right could take all night.
Do you flip a nickel to choose?
No just take the one in the middle.
Mothers dress their sons in pink dresses,
while girls cut their hair in sinks making big messes.
Guys with man purses,
and women saying they are male nurses.
"Do you feel like being a man or woman today?"
"Say I find that statement insulting."
"Against nature we should be revolting."
"I feel like a transgender."
It's like a man and woman put in a blender.
So many terms to identify what you think you are;
but others will tell when you walk in that bar.
To find what you are grab a beer and look in the mirror
A rail between your legs? You are then a male.
Bumps on your chest? You can figure the rest.
You think you need special terms to identify you?
Civil rights and courtroom fights; laws that are new
it's not what you think you will be.
It's just that you in need of some therapy.

Robert John Vogt
*Schenectady, NY*

[Hometown] *Schenectady* [Ed] *BS in graphic design* [Occ] *supervisor airport parking* [Hobbies] *drawing, writing poems, making art craft masks and photography* [GA] *poems published*
*Went to school for drawing but found I was actually better at writing according to my teachers; although not with spelling and grammar (thank God for spell check). To me a poem should rhyme even though many tell me mine really don't (thank God they needn't). I use poems to express my opinions on different events and current topics, such as birth or gun control which gets a rise out of many people. I'm not heavy into poetry so my influences are of the mainstream although fitting for myself—Dr Seuss and Edger Allen Poe.*

## Dear Heart

Another winter morning, bright with crisp air
my lungs can only welcome,
each in-breath infusing the tender membranes
and instilling the coursing flow
to my pulsing center,
by now, a trusted, reliable friend, a dear heart
that keeps me going,
pumping away,
minute after minute, hour after hour,
day after day, month after month,
for 94 short years, stuttering once or twice
to let me know,
nothing lasts forever.

Except change, maybe, when, just like that,
I will become what I have never been before,
a consciousness
freed from its mooring, alive now,
in a new state, with others, beyond belief,
where my heart's pulse has given way
to timeless contentment
and love is all there is.

Robert Skeele
*Anacortes, WA*

[Hometown] *Columbus, OH* [Ed] *BA, humanities, BD Christian studies* [Occ] *retired college dean* [Hobbies] *walking, writing, reading* [GA] *self-published 10 books, mostly poetry*

*The second stanza came to me weeks after the first and is based on my understanding of near-death experiences. One medical doctor who has made a study of near-death experiences has said that there have been enough validated experiences to conclude that consciousness can exist, does exist, independent of the brain. Such a phenomenon has been described in the book* Proof of Heaven *by Dr. Eban Alexander, a neurosurgeon who himself underwent surgery, and in the process—after all monitored body functions had shut down—experienced what he called "Heaven."*

# Aslan's Freedom

Old Eden is Eve's damnation
New Jerusalem is eternal creation
No freedom in Eve's destruction
New Jerusalem is eternal destination
Salvations is freedom from Hell's dominion
Aslan is freedom!
Creation is kingdom of Adam's dominion
Aslan is freedom!
Aslan's kingdom is eternal freedom.
Holy, holy, holy
Adam's kingdom is earthly dominion
Horror, horror, horror
Death is Adam's Eden prophecy.
Woe, woe, woe
Breath is Aslan's Eden mystery
Freedom, freedom, freedom
Eve? When is your sting?
Now! Coronavirus!
Eve, who is our king!
Aslan: forever with us!
Now I speak Aramaic
Mene mene, tekel, parsin is Eden
Numbered, weighed, and divided is Eden's fate.
Dominion, dominion, dominion
Old Eden is Adam's kingdom
Now Jerusalem is Aslan's freedom

Timothy A. Wik
*Elkins Park, PA*

## Rhubarbie

Looking good as a Rhubarb should
And standing long and lean
Magenta hue looks good on you
Man, you're the Rhubarb queen

Your veggie style is versatile
You sure are cute as pie
You're groovy as a smoothie
That anyone would try

Rhubarbie stalk you are the talk
You've really set the bar
Nutritious and delicious
A veggie superstar

You're no will o' the wisp—but in strawberry crisp
You're such a tasty treat
You're a crimson sensation and in my summation
You simply can't be "beet"!

Tracey Travis Lee
*Landenberg, PA*

## Breathe

in the magic of the morning
beside her sit
with yours, trace her lips
as her eyes smile
forehead and nose you kiss
in between coffee sips…

Erin Antonino
*Methuen, MA*


## The Pig in the Spotlight

Yes, she was a happy pig in the spotlight
everyone made over her.
Plus she was Mom's girl it seem
the pig grew up and all was okay.
In time she married and had little pigs
but the day came when pig lost her mom
and a heating stove exposed
that changed the pig; she was going downhill
not taking care of herself.
Plus other people and family seem to fail her.
It took her life, for she was left
a dirty little pig in the spotlight.
After her death the Lord made her
a little white pig in the spotlight
with her mom where she is happy again.

Betty J. Bible
*New Oxford, PA*

*This is in memory of my sister, Joann.*

## Pretty, Quick Draw, and Watch Turkey

In Jamaica, the old days, in jovial times between
Fern Gully and Dunns River Falls, we laughed when we were
kids, our animals spoke. Pretty, our one legged green
parrot bellowed, "Junior, put on the kettle!" He
whistled. The dogs came running, looking for us. He
oinked for Quick Draw, our pink pig, who lived with
them, sat on the front stoop in the pack, accepted by
us all as a dog. He would follow us to the Bush, never
wrong, resolute until slaughter day and put on the
table. (I was in Miami then.) I could never eat a beast
I knew, one with a name. I was there in spirit, in
spirit in Colgate. Times familiar, happier, we were
closer. Animals were friends. Watch Turkey, a lover, never
gobbled aggressively. He was King of the Hill. Watch
Turkey, better than the dogs, my friends afraid to pass
him. He never pecked. (Uncle wanted geese who would do
the job.) They would have been out of place, unkind
as were geese I knew in Florida. (Roosters pecked, too.)
Our chickens sang every morning, better than an alarm
clock. Toby, a little burro, sauntered about with all and
sundry, laughed with us. Things were jovial there in
Jamaica in our little farmhouse between Fern Gully
and Dunns River falls in the old days, back in me
childhood, in our memories, gatherings, we reminisce.

Romy du Jong
*Cocoa, FL*

## Find Your Happy Place

Find your happy place... it's soon time to rejoin the human race!
Find your happy place... Is it in the USA? For 245 years, the
home of the brave where thirty-three million eagles soar.
Listen, you can hear us roar?
Find your happy place...is it in the countryside
by a warm and toasty fireside?
Find your happy place...is it up on the roof or
hanging with your dog who is half wolf?
Find your happy place...is it on a dock by a bay
where it's a quiet place and you can feel the cool spray?
Find your happy place...is it hanging out on a ship
where the music is bliss?
Or on a deserted isle
where you might want to stay a while?
Find your happy place...just pray and go there and live
with grace...

Roberta Elizabeth Hartley
*Pittsburgh, PA*

[Hometown] *Glenshaw, PA* [Ed] *Holy Ghost High and The Art Institute of Pittsburgh* [Occ] *Verizon Communications retiree* [Hobbies] *writing, photography, art, gardening, cooking* [GA] *not realized yet*

*This poem is dedicated to my sister, Sandie. I am the youngest daughter of four and I have a younger brother. In school I excelled in art and was chosen to go to sat. classes at the Carnegie Music Hall in Pittsburgh, PA for four years until we moved. I was in spelling bees, won races, and sang in the school and church choirs. When I was older I won photography contests including a Kinsa award from The Pittsburgh Post Gazette for Kodak's fiftieth year. I helped build my first home at thirty-three and was semi-retired at age forty-eight to care for my mother. I used to make up stories on a rainy day.*

## Together We Can Make It Right

I guess I'll never understand,
The hatred that engulfs this land.
A place once filled with hopes and dreams,
Now will self-destruct it seems.
If our time is running out,
Isn't it time we think about...
How we want to leave this Earth,
And live our life for all it's worth.
If everyone would start to care,
With open hearts our love we share.
Then perhaps the world would unite,
And together we can make it right.

Mary A. Lindsay
*Kingman, AZ*

[Hometown] *Kingman* [Ed] *some college* [Occ] *retired* [Hobbies] *writing* [GA] *my daughters, grandkids, and great-grands*

*I picked this poem because of the turmoil that is running rampant through this country. Hopefully it will open hearts and eyes.*

## The Essence of His Soul

A bliss from above he sent to me
with his heart-shaped dreams
made up of mystery and devotion
to thee. A quest to thy unknown
he goes on to find thy one and only
missing piece of this shattered
heart of mine.
Night after night he so willingly
oh so hopefully journeys through
thy unknown in search of whatever
it may be that my heart would
need to be whole again.
Unknowing of his own strength
that he possesses within to heal this
heart of mine. For 'tis he and he
only who holds within thy power
to complete me.
A dreamy night's vision he has brought
upon me with thy warmth and safety
only his arms can bring to thee
each and every time he raps them
around me.

Gohar Minassian
*Los Angeles, CA*

[Hometown] *Los Angeles* [Ed] *The Art Institute of Santa Monica, animation* [Occ] *visual development artist specializing in Rococo* [Hobbies] *singing, painting and writing romance/fantasy genre stories* [GA] *gold medal from United States Congress*

*My poem is inspired by my favorite fairy tale from childhood to adulthood,* The Neverending Story. *As a child I was deeply inspired by the courage of the character Atrayu in* The Neverending Story. *I am a 2008 Congressional Award gold medalist, a 1st degree black belt in Tae Kwon Do and a poet. I hope to have more poems published in the years to come.*

## The Girl on Your Arm

In all of our years together
I was the girl on your arm
When we would run into an old flame
I was always so proud because
I was the girl on your arm
That was years ago and now
When I happen to run into you
There is a new girl on your arm
I just never thought that I would be
That other girl
The girl watching you
With another girl on your arm

Elinore J. Krause
*Renton, WA*

[Ed] *high school, some college courses and training* [Occ] *loan review, now retired* [Hobbies] *art and poetry* [GA] *my two sons*

*My poems are usually very personal, something good or bad that has happened to me. I find them very healing.*

## The Toilet Paper Pandemic

During this COVID-19 stuff,
People can still smile!
   I know the times are rough,
But just listen to me for a short while.
   With people making a run on toilet paper
When COVID-19 doesn't give you the runs,
   I think it is a silly capper,
And a huge waste of funds!
   Please don't just guess what the symptoms are?
Get the facts!
   'Cause guessing won't get you far,
Nor will panic fix a fart!
   So why not enjoy life?
Worry not what toilet paper will do for you.
   Love our Lord Jesus Christ
And forget about the COVID-19 loo!

James M. Wilson
*Roseburg, OR*

[Hometown] *Roseburg, OR* [Ed] *GED and some college* [Occ] *watchman for a logging company*
[Hobbies] *poetry, wood working* [GA] *being ordained as a minister*

## Attacking the Human Spirit

Upon the core of the human spirit, COVID-19 declared war.
It has attacked our need for physical contact, so to the outside world, we are told to close the door.
As human beings, we must come together in this crisis that plagues us.
Letting the dividing line of hate and judgments, between us go, will shield our faith in humanity from rust.
Gender is really the only difference in our bodies, so, most differences are created in our minds.
There is but one race, the human race.
Once we see that, to one another we can be so kind.
COVID is putting the human spirit and faith to the ultimate test
My heart weeps because humanity has not been giving its best.
But that does not mean that we cannot change it
Dig down deep within the human spirit, the fire is there, it just needs to be lit.
Humanity has been through worse and done far worse to one another than COVID-19 has done.
But this virus and social crisis has failed to recognize the fire within the human spirit.
We will keep burning!
We will not run!

Joylene Marie Rios
*Sacramento, CA*

[Hometown] *Sacramento, CA* [Ed] *Bachelor of Science in human services and current Master of Science in clinical mental health counseling student* [Occ] *student, fashion designer, and author* [Hobbies] *anything creative* [GA] *the day that I stopped letting my epilepsy control my life*

*Although I wrote this poem in 2020, it still holds true to just how much COVID-19 has impacted humanity. I hope that people will read this and it will make them take a look at themselves and try to change any negative behaviors and/or thoughts that they may have/exhibit towards another fellow human being.*

## Ode to Gordon

He was a great person,
a family man, a friend
to all who had ever met him.
He was someone you could
rely on and look up to. He had
a terrific attitude, always
looked on the good side of
things, always smiling or
laughing. You couldn't help
but love him; I know I did!
I'll never forget what he did
for me. He was uncle, mentor,
and a friend to me! I'll miss him!
Here's to you, Gordie!

Deena L. Carlson
*Longmont, CO*

[Hometown] *Longmont, CO* [Ed] *high school graduate* [Occ] *sales clerk at a thrift store* [Hobbies] *writing poetry, playing the piano, bingo, needlework* [GA] *staying sober for eighteen years*

*My inspiration comes from life's lessons and events. This time it was because of my uncle's death. We were very close. He was the father figure in my life. Because of him I'm a better person.*

## The Butterfly

I sleep, safe and protected in my cocoon
A keeper of dreams
One day I awaken
Wings wet, and trembling with joy
I soar, the sky my canvas
The wind my navigator
I light on a flower before you
You stare
The light reflects my radiance
I am life
On my wings I carry your dreams
Come follow me, I whisper
The journey waits
You smile and shake your head
I fly away
You stare
Your eyes blaze with dreams to be

Lynn G. Armstrong
*Hammond, LA*

[Hometown] *Seattle, WA* [Ed] *Institute of Children's Literature, Long Ridge Writers Group* [Occ] *retired senior housing property manager* [Hobbies] *reading, crocheting, and painting* [GA] *publishing my first mystery novel 2020*

*The Butterfly is dedicated to my late husband who loved butterflies and saw them as a symbol of life and teaches us the importance of living life to the fullest as we are here for such a short time like the butterfly.*

## Friends

There are many ways to define the word, *friend*.
It may be someone who listens to
You when things are not going
Your way.
And you can count on them to say
Something to brighten your day.
It may be someone who lends a
Helping hand.
Because at some time, they have
Been in your shoes and understand.
It may be someone who makes you
Laugh because of the silly things they
Purposely say or do.
Even when you feel sad and don't
Feel like smiling, they will keep being
Silly until they make you.
However you define the word *friend*, it will always be
The same. It's a person who makes
You feel warm inside just by the sound of their name.

Sherry Denise Doyal
*Centre, AL*

[Hometown] *Centre, AL* [Ed] *certifications in various medical and writing fields* [Occ] *administration assistant* [Hobbies] *making jewelry* [GA] *my poetry being published*

*I am currently living in Centre, AL with my mother Dovie and my four-legged son Dusty who is a dachshund/ Chihuahua mix. I have been working at MDS Gadsden, AL for twenty years. I've been writing poetry and stories since I was a young girl. I have been published in America and England.*

## Teaching a Child How to Accept Death

When a person or animal is hurt, sick, or so old they cannot do anything but lay there and no doctor or medicine can heal or help them, God sends His angels down to gently put them to sleep and take them to Heaven. In Heaven, God makes them well and they never need medicine or feel pain again. Sometimes, unhappy people pray for God to take them to Heaven. When we know someone who is sick and in pain or unhappy, we grieve for them. That person or animal may want to live, but not being able to feel joy or do things by themselves may say, "It would be better if I were to die." Many times, when God hears this, He sends His angels down to bring the souls of our loved ones to Heaven. Their bodies stay here but that special part of our loved ones goes to Heaven to be with God, and we gently let their bodies go.
In times of the coronavirus, sickness and death, it's comforting to know our family members, friends, and pets who die are with God. He always takes care of us and them. Although death is always hard to understand, it is a relief knowing our loved ones who die are happy, healthy, and safe with God.

Linda Beth Thomas
*Aurora, CO*

*I chose this subject because I believe there is truly a need for children to understand death and dying. With the coronavirus, accidental and natural death and the increase of deadly violence, children need to be comforted with an image or explanation of what happens to a person, or animal who dies, or is near death. This is not written as scripture but it addresses the issue of death in a comforting way. I must add that this explanation is softer and far more comforting when parents also teach their children how to pray.*

### Dear Francesca

Eyes shimmer sky-kissed blue.
Cheeks whisper a rosy hue.
Smiles and laughter breakthrough,
When we play fun peekaboo.
Lips create Cupid's bow.
Hair sun-kissed strawberry flow.
Sense of calm rests below,
As I watch you bloom and grow.
Painting radiant beams,
With irresistible gleam.
Dancing through rich daydreams,
Developing self-esteem.
Little sister that's true.
Learning skills each day anew.
Following what you do,
Little angel, all day through.
Frankie's July fifth debut,
Smiles and laughter breakthrough.
Open ever watching you,
Eyes shimmer sky-kissed blue.

Barbara McGuire Fiore
*Melbourne, FL*

[Hometown] *Melbourne, FL*  [Ed] *registered nurse*  [Occ] *retired*  [Hobbies] *golf, biking, writing*

## Before Amanda

I was writing before she was born
Took to the details at 9 and by 13 I was sworn
It was my fuel; my forum, my soul, my heart
Every judgment exposed, by piece, by part
Then I closed my eyes and dropped my pen
I lost my words until she entered in
Some will say everything counts, everyone matters
Words written by tyrants rising corporate ladders
We shine if they let us; our souls they batter
I didn't count and I certainly didn't matter
Judgments made, I dropped my pen again
Watched as folks shattered lives, with a grin
She represents the voices of the souls of our times
People now hear the rapture through her rhymes
Either we overcome or we remain the same
All voices are needed; it's how we gain, remain
She gave us a seat at the table, thoughts now sustain
She brought us opportunity to rewrite the books
A small pebble makes an enormous splash, a new look
We change from hopeless to hope at last
I'm now 61, with pen in hand and a new task
No more guises, no judgments, bullies step aside
This is our wealth, our guide
Brought together on a tailwind, strong, new stride

Julie Mandell
*Poway, CA*

## Our Freedom

"Our Freedom" comes at a high cost
The meaning it now imparts
Just to know it's almost lost
Americans, vow in your hearts

To show your American pride
Stand up, it's time to be counted
Our heroes didn't let it slide
A task they did undaunted

Many dying on a battlefield
In blood shed around the world
From wounds that never healed
To flags waving above unfurled

If our heroes could see us now
They'de be crying in their graves
Our foes want our backs to bow
Only in hope, God now us He saves

We're fighting a foe from within
America is shaken to its core
Let's pray they do not win
Or a free America will be no more

Harriet Kriner
*Taneytown, MD*

[Hometown] *Taneytown, MD* [Ed] *business school* [Occ] *former caregiver to disabled veteran*
[Hobbies] *reading, stamp collecting, poetry writing* [GA] *being published in poetry*
*No matter your race, color or religion, freedom should become dear to your heart and to know that we have been overtaken from within saddens me for all the soldiers who had given their all in sacrificing their lives even upon returning home to die for the freedom they were duty bound in giving. Now to have our history removed is a dishonor to those soldiers in what they died for like: freedom of the press, freedom of speech and freedom of religion or just plain freedom. May God bless America again.*

## The Carousal

The carousal is silent, the tents are coming down
I watch the saddened weeping of the lonely misfit clown

But why is it all over? Why did it go so fast? With great
Anticipation we thought that it would last.

The lights, the sounds, the laughter, the smells of food
So strong, why would it not continue, go on and on and on.

Still everything seems empty, a slowly gathering gloom, no
More anticipation instead a sense of doom.

The people have departed, a staleness in the air a child's
Lost toy, a broken cup, an old stray dog that can't get up. If
Only I could interrupt this darkened cloak of sadness.

I do so want to be a part, to have some gladness in my heart.
To find some goodness in each day, to try and find a different
Way to muddle through the madness.

I want someone to really care, someone who says "I am aware"
Of all the endless torment. I want to know I'm not alone one
Special person all my own. I need to know what is my worth?
Why I am living on this earth?

Just like a star up in the sky I'd like to know before I die—
Did my life really matter?

Or was I like the weeping clown, who stood and watched the tents
Go down and wondered if I'd be around to watch the horse go up
And down upon the carousal.

Jo Ann Blunkall
*Paonia, CO*
[Hometown] *Girard, KS* [Ed] *high school* [Occ] *mother and homemaker* [Hobbies] *reading, drawing*
[GA] *surviving*
*I am an eighty-year-old grandmother living in a small town in Colorado. The ideas for my poems just seem to enter my head from no particular place. Thank you for inviting me.*

## Guilt

Guilt is not something you are born with. It is like a seed planted deep inside your gut during a specific time in your life. And this seed grows and limbs spread and branches intertwine. Before you know it, it takes over every inch of you. Sometimes branches snap off and you feel a little peace. But those branches grow back and the tree stands tall for many, many years to come. And it consumes the air around it and makes it hard for other smaller trees to survive. No matter if you feel like you can free yourself from the grasps of the broken twigs, you will always feel the guilt inside.

Stephanie Day
*Long Beach, WA*

[Occ] *retail* [Hobbies] *writing, photography, art, poetry* [GA] *two sons, living on the beach*

## Free to Be Me!

It's a long hard struggle to finally find oneself.
Daily wondering where one goes from here.
After diapers to teens,
Your children all grown to now where you used to be.
I pondered the situation,
Planning a not-so-busy yet tedious day;
Thinking what now, 'I'm free.'
'Free to do and be what?'
The harried days are over, balancing career and family,
Playing the roles of super mom and social politics;
But "Life is meant to be made, not just lived," right?
So it was once said..., or is it?
Alas! A ray of light dawns—a new mission statement!
Based not on who I was,
Definitely not a 'whom' I hope to be;
But only just simple me!
Free to be me as I am, wiser with experience,
Though novice to this new vocation.
Where all I have to give today is me,
Living one day at a time, as I choose....
Accountable only to me and my Maker,
Where in the end, all that I can be *is* just me!

Joanne Marshall
*Greenland, NH*

[Hometown] *Greenland, NH*

*Initially upon retirement, I found myself still trying to fit my old life and rituals into my new-planning schedules, making to do-lists, etc. Without the challenges of work and family, all became very tedious and unfulfilling. It was such a freeing experience when I finally realized that there were no needed obligations outside of those I set for myself. I was free to be me to choose the things I really enjoy like writing and painting, sharing more quality time with family, friends in community, and most importantly me and getting to know me better*

## Universe

Why does the universe keep spinning?
Spinning out of control
Why does it keep winning?
Not allowing it to grow
Putting us back together
Just to let us go.
Oh damn you universe
You gave us every test you had
The test of time
Love, you gave Love, you tore apart
Even death, we survived
Time to want
Time to heal.
Universe that led us back to be
Now let the time be ours
A life time of pain
Now almost gone
Is he strong enough to stay?
Will we let it grow?
Love like no other
Safe within each other
A lifetime we will go…

Corinne A. Soutra
*Easthampton, MA*

[Hometown] *Hatfield, MA* [Occ] *Radon Tech* [Hobbies] *swimming, quilting, boating* [GA] *getting back into competitive swimming at 50, swimming in many senior nationals*

## My Wish List

Wishing for more than I had in the past
Was a dream alas
I knew never to be fulfilled
Why not ask for everything though
A wish is just a wish after all
A list was made of wants and needs
The perfect person God created for me
All the things I needed and wanted
Someone who would love the real me
I didn't really believe it true
That someone like that could exist
Except hidden deep in my dreams
A wish is just a wish after all
One special ingredient was added
A special prayer said to Heaven
To someone with power greater than me
After ten tiring years the wish was fulfilled
Amazingly someone was sent from above
The perfect person God created for me
Matched together by our pastor no less
A wish isn't just a wish after all

Diane Carson
*Goodyear, AZ*

[Hometown] *Goodyear* [Ed] *BA in psychology* [Occ] *self-employed* [Hobbies] *writing, gardening, recreation,* [GA] *raising strong successful children while single, working, and going to college*

*Writing is my passion. My friend always said if you want to know how she feels wait until you leave and she sends you a text and that's so true. I am pleased to say I changed the end of this poem from still waiting to love, to fulfilled love since I got married two years ago. Wishes do come true. I also moved from Illinois to Arizona and am working on a novel.*

## The Mind's Journey

Oft in the dim, dark night
memories of one life
meander through the mind.
Thoughts of bygone times float
in, out, in, around and around,
recalling the good, recalling the bad.
In musing, reliving, remembering
with the mind seeing the past.
Some thoughts were only mundane,
some perchance were uniquely wonderful.
And all were neatly wrapped
and tied with shining ribbon
of one's own mortality.

Helen-Anne Keith
*Chelsea, MA*

[Hometown] *Chelsea, MA* [Ed] *college BA degree* [Occ] *retired* [Hobbies] *painting, beading, organ playing, knitting, genealogy, writing* [GA] *my children's success in life*

*At age 101, I'm still on my feet with the help of a cane or walker so I can enjoy a restaurant meal or visit with family members or friends. I love my condo with its harbor view, but most of all I am proud of my five children—their achievements and successes. My six grandchildren carry on in each unique way, and, oh yes, the two great-grandsons.*

## Sad World

Such is this world we live in today
A deranged and hurtful place to stay
Killings have happened since beginning of time
Most people see no rhyme

But there is an answer to why all this violence
It started back millenniums and was not in silence
Should not come as a great surprise
For an angel in Heaven against God did arise

He made himself, so came to be called Satan and Devil
He called God a liar and became the great rebel
This angel was a liar to the first human pair
Bringing all of their offspring into great despair

Our sad world today is a result of this rebellion
Then a blessing from above made us to be boughten
One day soon we'll be from this sad state rescued
Look for the reasons of our sad world, I request you

Genevieve M. Votra
*Potsdam, NY*

[Hometown] *Potsdam, NY* [Ed] *house wife* [Occ] *corrections* [Hobbies] *braiding rugs, writing* [GA] *publishing a third book*

*I have loved writing from a young age. Being a housewife with five children and husband to care for did not afford me much time for writing. Since I've retired I have more time to write down thoughts, feelings, and experiences. I also take note of other people's thoughts and experiences I love the opportunity to publish poems because many are in way of expression!*

# Time

I know time
I saw it crawl on my grandmother's hand
It slipped to her neck, to her wrinkled face
Then I saw her last look
Stretching her arthritic fingers to make a hook
With my child's hand
The last fruit of her life
As if she said
This is the length of time
I had in life

Mitra Pourmehr
*San Rafael, CA*

[Hometown] *Tehran* [Ed] *geologist* [Occ] *teacher* [Hobbies] *reading and writing* [GA] *most of all being a mom and a wife*

*The place I grew is always yesterday. It is the land of Shahrzad, the story teller. The land of poets: Hafez, Sadi, Rumi, Sohrab, Forogh, Nima, Shamloo, and many others. The land of children who talk poetry before they learn their alphabet. When I was fourteen my father gave me a notebook to write my journals. Now when I turn the pages of this old notebook, I feel the passage of time. My name, Mitra, comes from Zoroasterism. In old Persian mythology it is the deity of sun. I am a retired geologist, living in California. I am honored to have poems published by Eber & Wein in many anthologies.*

## Sugar Ridge

Sugar Ridge not sweet but named from sour sarcastic pun
Filled with adversity, heartache, and pain
Growing up there was full of hard work, love, and fun
Especially days smelling plum blossoms after a spring rain
Smells of honeysuckles, clover, daffodils filled the air
Where the outhouse, pigpen, and chicken coop are no more
Where children ran hills and hollers with their feet bare
Gone the sweet aromas that made it wonderful to be poor
Smells of burning fields and fresh plowed ground
Burning hickory, boiling water, killing hogs and stewing lard
Now only the odor of cut grass, wild onions and garlic abound
Mixed with the smell of primrose and sweet shrub permeate the yard
Sugar Ridge, home sweet home of the Hoppers
JM, Leecie, Bobby, Diane, David, and Glenn
The home burned, reduced to a pile of bricks, ashes, and copper
No one lives there since death, marriage, and life caused the end
"Welcome Home to Sugar Ridge" a saying by dad told to mom one day
Her constant plea to leave Godforsaken Perry County and go home
No satire for Sugar Ridge in its grandeur and magnificence today
A reminder of family, peace, and serenity despite where you roam
Thank you, God for giving the Hoppers Sugar Ridge and love
As we enjoy the beauty of the good Earth, we call Sugar Ridge today
It is nothing compared to the joy, comfort, and hope from above
Sugar Ridge is a reminder where there is God's will there is a way

Bobby E. Hopper
*Jemison, AL*

[Hometown] *Jemison, AL* [Ed] *doctor of ministry, BA, history (major), English (minor)* [Hobbies] *woodworking, antique cars* [GA] *Andy, Angela, Aaron*

*Lisa and I live on small farm called Sugar Ridge Farm and Ministry in Jemison, AL. Dad's comments to Mom when returning back home from Sunday afternoons trips to where he grew up was the inspiration. Dad would always say, "Welcome home to Sugar Ridge."*

## Dusty Roses

Today I threw away some dusty dried roses.
I had kept them like they were prose,
given to me by the man I adore,
To whom I gave my life through good and strife,
only to become his wife.
Those dusty roses were once live and bright,
as a sign of his love without a fight.
Through the darkness and the light, we have survived.
As a couple, one would never contrive.
Here we are in our golden years,
still calling each other honey and dear.
I hated throwing away those dusty dried roses
that spoke to me as much as prose.
As we near the end of our walk,
we find we have less about to talk.
Though we are together as one,
the time has crept by, not just as fun.
For it takes work to make it endure,
as true love has no cure.

Elaine R. Fleming
*Little River, SC*

## The Enchanted Forest

As I start up the trail where the land meets the sky,
I wonder, will animals join me or are they too shy?
A bobcat to my left, moving with anxious stealth,
Eye on a rabbit, unaware of what will be dealt.
A rippling stream ahead, movement at the side,
A beautiful fawn deer, thirst not to be denied.
Near that oak tree, walking bold and unafraid,
Long ears of a coyote with tail in bushy braid.
A cackling cry from that small clearing in the trees,
A pair of wild turkeys, singing in different keys.
Along the trail, ahead, a red fox running with zest,
Determined to catch a rodent that just left its nest.
A squirrel busily jumping from tree to tree,
Proud of his skill and chirping with glee.
A stump on a knoll suggested a short rest,
Hawks circling above in hunger quest.
Finally the end of the trail came into sight,
The sun emerging more radiant and bright.
The lesson of this walk, what could it be?
Be tolerant of difference, enjoy the right to be free.

Garry O. Hanson
*Florence, KY*

*I am a semi-retired consulting engineer who enjoys the challenge of writing poetry as a pastime. I own a mostly-wooded acreage in an area that is quite remote and fifty miles from where I live. There is a log cabin situated on this property, which I refer to as "My Castle in the Wilderness." I greatly enjoy walking the trails on my land and observing nature at its best. Added personal benefit is gained from pictures taken on my trail camera. "The Enchanted Forest" is based on this experience.*

## A Star in the Night

A star in the night
Is shining in the Western sky;
It glows so bright
To say it is no lie.
A spirit guides its way.
She comes from a planet far.
She wishes for a new day
To hear a message say
That her green world is alive.
It blooms in the spring,
A promise of a busy hive,
A bounty of sweetness will bring.
She was a dancer in her world;
She spun on tiny toes.
Now she spins where she was hurled
Against the winds that blow.
A little voice calls her to return
To toss her head and whirl.
There is a greater truth to learn
In a wider world for a small girl.
She watches from her starry realm
And wishes for a bend
In time to make all things return
Her story to an end.

Judith Parrish Broadbent
*Chapel Hill, TN*

[Hometown] *Chapel Hill, TN* [Ed] *master's plus* [Occ] *professor and writer* [Hobbies] *writing, gardening* [GA] *my children, grandchildren and students*

*Judith Parrish Broadbent is a poet and author who is also a teacher. Her poetry reflects her love of her children and grandchildren and the earth.*

## All Alone

A single one…only one
standing all alone,
the saddest somber face
in her garden home.

Where have all the others gone?
It was best for them to leave.
But, oh, she misses them so much…
she's lonely as can be.

Slowly going to rest awhile,
she safely follows her crowd.
When springtime comes around again
they'll show their brightest shrouds.

Many brilliant characters
stand quite tall and proud—
fragrances they give to you
so eagerly and loud.

Joining many others
in multi colors bright,
they will show much happiness
as they drink the warm sunlight.

Anna M. Barnes
*Sioux City, IA*

[Hometown] *Sioux City, IA* [Ed] *high school* [Occ] *retired* [Hobbies] *gardening, writing poetry* [GA] *my family*
*I am an eighty-one-year-old great-grandmother and enjoy writing poetry very much, even though I'm not a pro. I also like flowers and love to garden. My yard is filled with tulips, iris, daffodils, coreopsis, honey suckle, and many more. I have six great-grandchildren and they are my pride and joy! I like to share my joys with them.*

## Hurt

I thought you love me. I am small
I depend on you that's all
But you hurt me, you should let me go
Give me to someone you know
Now it's too late, you've taken my life
My mother was so stressed she will never be
At her best. I am sorry, Mom, if it's my
Fault, now I am with angels who love me more
I will never be hurt no more. You and I
Came along ways together. Now we part
And that's forever.
Goodbye, Mom. Get it together

Peggy Thomas
*Cincinnati, OH*

[Hometown] *Cincinnati, OH* [Ed] *high school graduate* [Occ] *retired* [Hobbies] *sewing, making comforters by hand* [GA] *giving whatever I have to people less fortunate*

# Who Am I?

Who am I? Who am I?
My mama gave me a name…Who am I? Who am I?
Whose blood runs through my veins?
My color has been somewhat altered
No, Mama! It's not your fault!
Someone violated your beauty…Someone rearranged my birth
Someone invaded our land…Someone cursed the earth
I would be who I am…If they had kept me where I was
I was there years ago…I was black beautiful
And truly pure…This is so I know for sure
Black my story, Not His-story
Whose lesson did they teach?
What message did they preach?
To know myself and love me too
To know what they did…And did not do
They did not see what God had created
They saw black! And that they hated!
Who am I? I often wonder…Who am I? They put us under
Beneath their feet—damn those chains
Their history is written, it still remains
To learn my history, to embrace my culture
To love my people and myself is something I must find
Who am I? Who am I?
Is always on my mind…

Chanda M. Boone
*Louisville, KY*

*My poetry is written from real life experiences of not only myself but others as well. My hope is that each reader knows and feels my message in form of poetry. Poetry with a purpose best describes my style. This gift is to be shared given to inspire, heal and to comfort. The issues of today are relevant and prevalent. I write my poems to give the reader insight to words of wisdom and truth. Speaking the truth and opening my inner spirit in poetry is a blessing. My prayer is that…it is, and it does.*

## America

America, the land of the free and home of the brave.
People flee to her from all over the world, their lives to save.
She has stood a beacon for all the world to see.
Within her land there is freedom and liberty.
When they come to America from their very dark place
They will find people from each and every race.
Lady Liberty invites you with light in hand.
You may come in if you love this land.
We do have laws you must obey.
They are set in stone if you desire our way.
Assimilation to our constitution is what we require.
Violence and hate we will never desire.
America has done a lot for the freedom fight,
Fighting many wars when it is for right.
We do not conquer and hold their land.
Our aim is to free people who on their own cannot stand.
We have always placed God in front of the battle.
We knew the enemy He would surely rattle.
May we never forget that wonderful rule.
Without God we become the obvious fool.

Sonja Lee Goldsmith
*Vero Beach, FL*

[Hometown] *Mora, MN* [Ed] *high school and technical college for banking* [Occ] *bank teller and data processing* [Hobbies] *writing, amateur photographer of God's creation* [GA] *20 years of being a good US Navy wife*

*My poems are inspired by the happenings around me. Sometimes I cannot write at all and other times it flows like a river. I wait for the inspiration.*

## All As One

Straight or gay,
No one can say.

Transgender change,
No one can gauge.

Black, brown, or white,
A comfortable sight.

Young or old,
Embrace and hold.

Rich or poor,
Matters only one's core.

Quick or slow,
Created so.

Disabled or able,
No need to label.

Mentally broken or sane,
Dealing with this we gain.

Those foreign or near,
We need not fear.

All the world is in our heart,
For all eternity we are part.

Joan Ball
*Floral Park, NY*

## The Real Pandemic

The real pandemic is not COVID-19 but our youth killing each other
He sings "Pop, Lock, & Drop – it"*
but I know my hip will pop its socket
Tells me to meet him at the "Curbside"**
I am wondering if I should abide
He says he "Know Who I Am"***
I wonder if he is my friend
She says she wants to have "The Conversation"****
I am curious what she has to mention
They play their music and sing their songs
rap, hip hop, techno, rock all about life's wrongs
So very young, just beginning life
all of it full of strife
I listen but don't understand
why they have to play with guns and think it is grand
shot, killed, dead as can be
yet they continue so they can be free
Where does it end?

Darlene Thomson
*Newport, RI*

[Hometown] *Rhode Island* [Occ] *retired* [Hobbies] *pottery* [GA] *being mom and grandma*

*As they kill each other even if their friends *Huey- "Pop, Lock & Drop It," he was shot, **Lil Marlo - "Curbside" he was shot, ***Tray Savage - "Know Who I Am" he was shot, ****Chynna Rogers - "The Conversation" she committed suicide. All of these people are under age 35. I have been published by Noble House, The Who's Who of International Poetry, Today's American Poet (all three anthologies), Eber & Wein Best Poets of 2015, and my Facebook poetry group will be publishing a book in September of this year called A Woman's Perspective.*

## The Rose

Back in the woods
where nobody goes,
by an empty old house
grows a red, red, rose.
The rose tells the story
of the love that was there,
in this deserted old house
now empty and bare.
Out in the yard
where the lady stayed,
she planted the rose
while her young children played.
Now the children are grown
and have all moved away,
but the rose lives on
this very day.
What happened to the woman?
Nobody knows.
Perhaps she is buried
beneath the red, red rose.

Patricia Joy Brumfield
*Tylertown, MS*

[Hometown] *Tylertown, MS* [Ed] *high school graduate* [Occ] *retired GMAC, Jacksonville, FL*
[Hobbies] *poetry, flower arranging, fine art* [GA] *long life, good health, and a great husband and family*
*I am age eighty, married, and have two grandchildren. Poetry has been a hobby for fifty years.*

## Written Witness

I struggle to witness aloud you see,
So as a written witness, this is my plea—
Don't be crass or hard-hearted.
Death will come and you and God will be parted.
Eternal life, I wish for all to receive,
Just ask Him into your heart and life and believe.
He said, "Take up your cross and follow me."
I said, "I will," and a written witness I will be.
Until Jesus calls for me, and I am with Him
For all eternity.

Shannon Louise Young
*Jacksonville, AR*

[Hometown] *Jacksonville, AR* [Ed] *communications degree* [Occ] *kitchen person at Little Caesar's*
[Hobbies] *writing, singing, reading.* [GA] *being published in Eber & Wein books.*

*I wrote this after a Sunday school lesson one Sunday talked about being a witness for Jesus. I've always wanted to be a witness for Jesus, but I was never sure of how to do it. I tried to tell a family member about Him, and he wasn't receptive to it. From that point on, I struggled to figure out how to witness for Jesus properly, and then I realized through my poetry journal, with my poems that are God-centered, I am witnessing for Jesus through them.*

## My Scotty

You couldn't miss them
His beautiful eyes of brown
Or that ever smiling face
That rarely turned to a frown.

His smile suddenly ceased one beautiful March day
Someone took his life you see
In this world he would no longer stay.

So many hearts broken a vast hole did he create
They took my young man away not even 23 yet.
March 8, 2005 is a day I can't forget

Like a glass my heart was shattered
My soul was pierced and forlorn
My mind was torn and scattered.

How do I find that smile again?
How do I find the laughter he gave?
How do I find the unending joy?
Deep in my heart and mind there I must save.

He has been gone now for such a long time
No more sparkle no more shine
Taking him from us was just such a crime.

Donna M. Smith
*Lawrenceville, GA*

[Hometown] *Detroit, MI* [Hobbies] *writing, drawing, painting, designing interior spaces* [GA] *five children and nine grandchildren*

*My beloved son was murdered on March 8, 2005. I miss him so dearly*

## Desire 1977

The old yelled,
*Evil!*
The young sang,
*Revolution!*
Faces painted white, seven-inch heels, tights
Going to rock all night.
*Rock* and *roll* grooves the body.
*Rock* and *roll* moves the mind.
*Rock* and *roll* drowns the hate.
Eyes fixated,
As his hands move across her body
His fingers squeeze the strings on her neck,
The chords scream,
*"Light me on fire!"*
Sticks pound on their heads,
'77 Was the year to rock
To chase *desire*
To follow the man and his band.
A summer of fast cars and painted, souped-up vans
And a man with fast-moving hands.
Watch the stars while moving to the groove.
Sleep under the moon.
Hoping freedom never ends,
The love that lights the *desire* on *fire*!

Tammy Mustapha Johnson
*Sergeant Bluff, IA*

[Hometown] *Sergeant Bluff, IA* [Ed] *BA in English and secondary education, MA in bilingual education and English language learning* [Occ] *high school English teacher* [Hobbies] *writing, music, reading, knitting* [GA] *obtaining my master's degree*

*I am a seventies rocker who loves to listen to the music of the seventies. I write about music, musicians, and cars. I am currently working on a novel about a vampire who loves to sing.*

## Off to School

Leaves kiss the ground on a brisk November morning.
Our winged friends scurry south,
In brace of the white wall to come.
A chilly wind sweeps in,
The hairs on their necks rise in attendance,
Saluting the guests as it fades into oblivion.
Steam from fresh coffee is pulled from its vessel,
Wafted away by the break of dawn.
The Daily Gazette is a pace away.
Crystallization of water vapors seal the paper
To the tar beneath a pair of loafers.
A few drops of warm brew sizzle
As they deconstruct surrounding ice particles.
A singular wave is targeted at the yellow tanker
While the printed words of the day are
Cradled on the trek to safety.

Michael Fiore
*Schenectady, NY*

## Darkness of a Soul

Darkness lurks in the depths of the soul, where light,
love, and happiness once dwelled.
With forgotten promises and cruel words,
love was lost in silence.
Because of you, now, darkness lurks,
in the depths of my soul.

Margaret Rene Mendez
*Decatur, IN*

[Hometown] *Decatur* [Occ] *retired nurse* [Hobbies] *writing* [GA] *my sons*

## Tears in Rain

As the night sky shines above my head
the world's pain in my stead.
I reach out with heart and hand,
with love and peace I make my stand
to end the pain
and end the fear,
On this poor earth, that I hold dear.
She quakes in fear
and cries in rain
and burns the trees
and floods the plain.
The answer here, is bring her peace.
Make the hate and violence cease!

Robin Alix Menzies
*Lake Havasu City, AZ*

## The Tree

When I was fourteen,
The world was in raging color.
Electric blue skies spread
Over seas and sands.
Dull gray trees erupted in
Orange and yellow and red,
Only colorful in death.
I felt like a tree
Decaying on the inside,
Choked by the ivy of an identity
That wasn't mine.
My chlorophyll stopped
And my leaves blossomed.
For a few short days,
I ruled the world
In robes of fiery leaves
Dappled in auburn and ochre.
I wore a crown of branches and berries
Woven together like the perfect lie.
When I was fourteen,
The world was in raging color
And I was a tree in autumn.

Erin Joy Maas
*Atlanta, GA*

[Hometown] *Atlanta* [Ed] *high school* [Occ] *student* [Hobbies] *ukulele, singing, writing* [GA] *winning my high school talent show*

*I've been writing for as long as I can remember and writing (decent) poetry since fifth grade. I love to draw inspiration from the world around me and how I fit into that world. I hope to continue writing poetry through college and for the rest of my life.*

## New Life

A friend of mine
Who's true and kind
Has found a true love
That said "Will you be mine?"
A love that is not selfish,
Ungiving, untrue
But one that is ever giving
And says "I want only you."
This love has no boundary;
It's to the ends of the earth.
All the silver and gold
Cannot add up to this love's worth.
Their new life together
Is fresh and brand new;
No one can come between them
And make them untrue.
Your hopes and your dreams
Are now in your hearts
Sharing them together, never depart.
You have waited so long
For your love so true;
Keep him in your heart.
Now let your life start new.

Barbara Reimer
*Cave Junction, OR*

*Retired twenty years law enforcement, working in the jail, 911 operator, trainer, and hostage negotiator. Now enjoy my writing, gardening, and traveling with my husband.*

## The Cycle

As the earth rotates, orbiting the sun,
our summer, fall, winter, and spring
seasons are born.
Whether it is gorgeous, comfortable,
or miserable for some,
One thing is certain, seasons begin,
and seasons will end.
And so, the cycle begins.
Mishaps are predictable,
blessings are comprehensible
and, all things encountered, somehow
will find amend.
Like the seasons, it rotates around and
back to us again.
For each season, whether summer, fall,
winter, or spring,
the test is endurance,
while maintaining assurance
that the end is near.
So, there is no need to fear
because seasons begin, and seasons will end
as the cycle rotates itself once again.

Annette Whitaker-Moss
*Grand Prairie, TX*

[Hometown] *Dallas* [Ed] *bachelor's degree—business management* [Occ] *payroll and HR benefits administrator* [Hobbies] *photography and writing* [GA] *writer/author/publisher and photographer*

*Annette's ability to express herself led to her first book of poetry,* One Heart to Another, *and later her second book of poetry,* Another Heart to Another. *Her work appeals to the heart and soul of all readers and is featured in many collections of poetry published worldwide. After writing her first and second book of poetry, Annette wrote her first novel,* Good Kid in Trouble *then her second novel* Shundra Henderson, Thorns and Roses. *She tells stories through pictures and books as a professional photographer and a published author while representing the promise of new beginnings!*

## Ode to Mom

So many thanks yet to say,
but all of tomorrows
are now yesterday.

It mattered little the strength
of your son
when God said, "Come, your
reign is done."

I'll remember always the cards
I gave you,
they turned my siblings a
crimson hue.

So as the song goes and I quote,
"Sail on, Silver Girl,"
sail into paradise's joys
to the open arms of you boys.

Sister Mary, bless her heart,
is now our family's matriarch.

As we take you to your final rest,
we know in our hears, Mom,
you loved us all the best.

Your son,
Bill


William E. Muehlmann
*Midland, MI*

[Hometown] *Midland, MI* [Ed] *two years tech school NIH* [Occ] *x-ray tech* [Hobbies] *fly fishing,
hunting, golf, carving decoys* [GA] *marrying Nadine*
*Mom had nine children. No two sexes together boy then girl for the nine. Each of my sisters had an older and
younger brother. We lost the youngest brother, then six months later we lost our oldest one. We always kidded
each other saying, "Oh ya Mom loves you best."*

## God Guide Me

God you've guided me through the storm
God you made a way when I couldn't see a way
God oh God you've guided me through all my trials and tribulations
God guide me please without you I'll be lost
God guide me keep guiding me when I can't go anymore
Oh God I couldn't do anything without you
Keep guiding please keep guiding me
God guide me

Lakisha Deaon Todd
*Brandon, MS*

[Hometown] *Jackson* [Occ] *Walmart, Dollar General* [Hobbies] *reading, writing* [GA] *having kids*
*I am an author as well. I published a book of the same name.*

## Awakening

Speak your mind, even if your voice shakes. Yes, your heart will break. However, at least you will feel more awake. Because you will no longer have to act fake. And just remember, that at the end of the day, you gotta do what you gotta do. So, always stay true to you.

Chelsea A. Hoffner
*Dover, DE*

*Hello! So, I have been writing poetry for over twenty years now. Poetry has definitely become a passion for me. I think this because it helps me to express emotions that I would of otherwise kept inside. Poetry is my escape and I absolutely love it!*

## Christmas Spree

I was shopping one day
But my funds were low.
What can I do, Santa,
I just have no dough?
With laughter on his face
And a fur cap on his head…
No need to worry, my dear,
"Charge it," he said.

Well, my list is complete
My shopping is done.
I never spent a dime
But had lots of fun.
So, when you go shopping
Spend your days at the mall
Keep in good spirits
And may God bless you all.

Kathleen Brown
*New Port Richey, FL*

*I was born in Dublin, NH. Early years settled in Rensselaer, NY. Worked sixteen years in banking in Albany, NY. Married, had two wonderful sons, traveled to Colorado Springs, CO. Attended college and made "Phi Theta Kappa." Worked ten years in probation and six years drug and alcohol clinic. Worked seventeen years in retail then retired to NPR, FL. My greatest achievement was raising two great sons and sharing my love with two grandkids. Now a widow I wanted this little poem to add a bit of humor to a shopping day. I have been thankful to God for each and every blessing.*

## Perception

I am but a figment of one's imagination
Floating through the vast emptiness
Of what we call home
Yet each of us is somehow still all alone
No creature who walks
On the face of this planetary body
Can define the confines of another
Yet we all say we're sister and brother
My appearance is as you wish it to be
Because that is how you have decided to see
Therefore I am to you as you wish me
Rather than as my true identity
And when another gazes upon my form
Then once again I will magically conform
To their own definition of "the norm"
And so are we constantly swimming in the perfect storm
And one day shall I meet my great maker?
The ultimate creator?
Will they understand the complex creation
That together encompasses my very being?
Or must they mold me
Into a figment of their imagination too
Following their own desires
Just as we all do

Reva Kalene Holmes
*Helena, MT*

[Hometown] *Helena, MT* [Ed] *high school* [Occ] *student* [Hobbies] *swimming, baking, reading, writing poetry, and animals* [GA] *becoming a published poet*
*Stereotypes cloud our perceptions of others. They mask the true identity of our fellow human beings through preconceived notions, which often are untrue. Yet, it seems that without stereotypes our society would be unable to function because we are unable to interpret others outside of our own desires. This begs the question of a higher being, whoever that is, and their perception of us as individuals. Who are we, really, if nobody can truly see us?*

## Half-Baked History: Peach Cobbler

History gets baked
leavened, over-salted;
too many hands try to knead
honeyed honesty gets assaulted.
Two ovens overheat
as the eggs start to hatch;
rollers are revolting
tender chicks peck the latch.
No master chef is summoned;
as neighbors watch, they're floored.
The chaos wins, brown blood does, too;
caramel lies stick to the board.
No bake sale for this saga—
too few trays of truth appear.
Fast-food pre-wrapped egos,
hark these lessons, future years.
No eraser, no censor,
no gallant call to arms—
the recipe clearly stating, on all others, render harm.
A leader rules from top to under—
bad smells, untruths prevail.
No spine, no core beyond the term—
justice bites your tail.

Rozann Kraus
*West Stockbridge, MA*

[Ed] *in process* [Occ] *arts activist* [Hobbies] *life* [GA] *being sane*

*Rozann Kraus dances, runs, writes, and agitates daily, with time to frolic with her beloveds.*

## His Infinite Majesty

Great open door, grace.
Life's open view eternity.
The grace of God that brings salvation has appeared to all men.
One plants the seed and another waters but God gives the increase.
The word was with God and the word was God.
All things were made by him. In Him was life;
and that life was the light of men.
The light, that all through Him might believe.
The true light, which lights every man that comes into the world. As many as received Him, gave them power to become the sons of God, to believe on His name born by the will of God. Truth the Father's word, not in letter but in power; living enlightenment His spirit. Where the spirit of the Lord is there is liberty. God's word, His omnipotent love yours. Believers in beloveds love endowment. Beautiful for situation, the joy of the whole earth. Master, redeemer, savior, friend, king, brother. Remain in it…the word: Him.

Tina M. Clymer
*Joplin, MO*

[Hometown] *Tampa, FL* [Hobbies] *cooking, poetry*

*America is still beautiful, just exercise your faith. He has crowned the good with brotherhood but you must turn back to grace. Gratitude receiving a cleansed existence is still free. Remember to do mercy, kindness, and righteous judgment and you will be again liberty. Eagles' eyes watch, their strength sure, protect, rest and nourish well. Encourage all grow leading endowed spirits. The beautiful US. Wherever the body is thither will the eagles be gathered together.*

## Bonded

The fragrant wind caresses a wan mist
And iridescent shafts of chrysoprase and gold
Illumine a sallow earth.
Amidst the splendor of nature, I denuded stand,
No longer plaintive, as I basked in a volatile delight.
The blatant mind surges,
As the billows in a tempestuous sea,
While I shuffle in the hysterics of love.
Anon, beyond the silvery linings of dawn,
On the gossamer wings of Astarte.
Love's diorama fills the balmy air.
In silence we meet, in silence we greet.
A winsome smile bewitches the soul with rapture,
In extricabley bound we saunter on.
Now she denuded too, heads to the aqueous spray.
Where waters warm and aphrodisiacs cleanse the soul.
We dwell in a world sublime,
Our lips in juxta meet, the cheeks grow flush,
With rosy brilliance.
And a thousand angry passions stroke the mind,
As prostrate we shroud Mother Earth.

John Alfonso
*Tamarac, FL*

[Hometown] *Tamarac, FL* [Ed] *business administration* [Occ] *retired* [Hobbies] *fishing and writing*
[GA] *having my family*

*With no formal training in poetry writing, I consider this talent a gift. Begins with an idea or a line that follows another. On a dream, I have the ability to put on paper or to express that which I feel. Never knowing the title, upon completion it presents itself. Born in Trinidad West Indies, lived in New York, Texas, Belize, and Florida, my present home. This poem is dedicated to my brother Parieso G. Alfonso.*

## The Virus of 2020

A year of pandemic has almost come to an end.
The year twenty twenty was more like an
enemy not a friend.
Many were crushed, yet some up to the challenge
At times it seemed quite hard, for life to find a balance.
Here we are in twenty twenty are still facing
trials of the past, and some have just began.
With a new president in office, new laws will be made,
The past four years under, even good foundations
are starting to fade.
Surging gas prices are seen all over the land,
This all started with one stroke and a land.
Internet gets hacked causing slow down through
out the land.
As well as our borders have gotten way out of hand.
Who can blame people for wanting to live in the USA,
But as with everything there is a right and wrong way.
Riots and crime worsening in cities everywhere.
I guess more of Jesus gospels need to be shared.
The virus has still hurt the world, in twenty twenty-one,
yet It's grip seems to be loosening with less stress and
more fun.
So help us Lord as we finish up this year.
Let us push forward with courage and a lot less fear!

Rick Lee
*Liberty, KS*

## 'Neath Fluttering Sails and Whispering Winds

For fun and sun and something new,
I recommend dear one that you
do fast escape with boat and friends...
'neath fluttering sails and whispering winds.

Aboard a boat on waters blue,
you'll find your worries soon are few,
and stress of life will fast be trimmed...
'neath fluttering sails and whispering winds.

The drift of time midst breeze that sings,
while to your skin the soft spray clings,
will quick and sure all pain rescind...
'neath fluttering sails and whispering winds.

It matters not to where you go,
important is just that you'll know
the feeling as real life begins...
'neath fluttering sails and whispering winds.

Robert G. Rohland
*Savannah, GA*

Bob Rohland was born and raised in Bethlehem, PA. He played football and basketball in high school and at Penn State University, with the highlight of his basketball career coming 1954, his junior year in college, when Penn State took third place in the NCAA playoffs. Immediately upon graduation from PSU in 1955, he entered the army, and then served in various locations around the USA...plus two years in Korea, three years on Okinawa, two years and eight months in Vietnam, three years in Thailand, and four years and six months in Italy. The preponderance of Bob's service, at troop level with special forces and conventional parachute organizations, was eventually interrupted by volunteered-for attaché duty in Rome, where he remained on parachute status for the complete tour. He retired as a lieutenant colonel in 1984. Bob and his college sweetheart, Grace, were married in 1955 and remain the proud parents of four daughters. He completed his college days in 1982 when he graduated with a master's degree in public administration.

## Time Capsule

What is my body but a time capsule
Of deferred hopes and dreams?
I'm layers of sewn skin, bone, and muscle, of fat that bursts at the seams.
My stretch marks are an allegory, a sketch of an intimate story.
Twisting, turning, splitting into deltas, winding into deep swollen streams.
What is my body but a time capsule, preserving ghosts of memories?
I'm tainted by shadows of his shackles, still clutching my wrists with voracity.
Lemon-faced ogres kept me, prisoner, in a smeared web of conspirators.
Their mouths contorted into semblances of smiles, misshapen by split, sour, sore, crusted lips.
Their chests were hollow cavities, revealing pulpy, decaying hearts, bruised like rotten fruit.
Festering with insatiable, rancid hunger, their thirsty mouths watered with longing for prodigal power.
Greedy fingers reached inside my chest, searching for my soul.
Wanting to rip it, fragment it to the point where it
was identical to their deformed, vile black hole.
What is my body, if not a warrior? Trained to protect my passion.
So I tore open the delicate, netted prison. Only then realizing it was a fragile barrier.
The ogre's grin distorted, and I seized its decomposed core.
Leeches slithered up my arms, but they, I ignored.
Aortas splintered in branches, dripping frosty, pungent sludge.
The ogre's grip released, increasingly weak.
My body had conquered the beast, and to it, I held no grudge.
What is my body but a time capsule? A eulogy for the demons I defeat.
What is my body but an altering work of art, built to preserve my warm, ripe heart.

Jordie G. Cornfield
*Essex, MA*

[Hometown] *Essex, MA* [Ed] *sophomore in high school* [Occ] *high school student* [Hobbies]
*screenwriting, poetry, baking, playing Scrabble with my mom, making outfits, songwriting, playing with my
dog Cooper* [GA] *being published 2 (now 3) times before 18! Also, I have a 4.4 GPA, Woohoo!*
*This poem is about an abusive friendship that I was in. I like to see this person as nothing but an ogre. They are
not a demon, because demons hold power and strength. This person was not powerful, as they were fueled by
their own insecurities and inner emptiness. I wrote this poem as a reflection of my own personal journey, and
to assure those who are struggling that they have the power to free themselves of the fragile prison.*

## You and I

Through trials you and I
you are with me
even though I have never known you.
I know your fret, same as mine.
Your hurts are my compassion; my soul aches.
Yet, I never knew your name, your smile, your laugh.
Your presence is with me; I feel you,
yet, my eyes have not seen your face.
You are every part of me;
the air you once breathe, I now breathe.
A faint difference now—thank you!
I breathe with ease, more than before.
Still looking over my shoulder, but with ease.
You carried it away from me, again; I thank you.
Trusting it will not return; if so, you are with me.

Catherine J. Broussard
*New Orleans, LA*

[Hometown] *New Orleans, LA* [Ed] *master's in social work* [Hobbies] *writing poetry, short stories, designer* [GA] *mother to 3 of the most amazing adults, grandmother to 7 of the most astonishing souls to grace this earth*

*My Name is Catherine Johnson Broussard. I am an African-American poet and a lifelong resident of New Orleans, LA. I have a master's degree in social work from Southern University at New Orleans and am the owner of The Wedding Broom Company of New Orleans. I am the mother of three amazing souls and the grandmother to seven of the most precious gifts one can ask for. I am also the author of* His Words, *volume II, a collection of inspirational poems. Spanning over years the thoughts of Him has been my solace; words written on scattered paper, now in His time, my words have come to be.*

## As Seen on TV

This product cleans better, that product slices and cuts better and this one does this and the other that. These products come with a satisfaction guarantee or your money back.

These "As Seen on TV" products can also be found and purchased at major retail stores without bemoaning wait of the four to six weeks for delivery of the order.

To my observation, I began to notice that these products are short-lived and don't bother to exist anymore.

Hans Jurgen Hauser
*Queen Creek, AZ*

[Hometown] *New York* [Occ] *cleaning crew member* [Hobbies] *reading, going to movies, attending church* [GA] *graduated from high school as valedictorian*

*I have been doing freelance writing for many years expecting to achieve success. My poem, "As Seen on TV," expresses my feelings of how I get excited when a new product captures my attention and fails to maintain its longevity.*

## I've Stayed Much Too Late at the Faire

I've stayed too late, so very, very late,
Oh! I've stayed much too late at the faire!
I remember a time when the lights were ablaze,
And we played and we played, in the penny arcade.
And with friends and lovers always at my side,
We observed the exhibitions, and rode all the rides.
And with laughter and frivolity our ever reactions,
We took in all the fair midway exhibits and attractions.
Always enjoying the days bountiful carefree play,
We feasted on cotton candy and drank pink lemonade.
But those days were another place, another time,
And I was young, I was innocent, and in my prime.
And lasting relationships were not my pace.
And so not to take place.
And now I set on a bench alone at the end of the pier,
Watching the setting sun slowly disappear,
Into a still water grave of the horizon's gray-colored veneer.
Chiding myself for not being in my youth, more honest, with
Others, and careless with truth, and being immature with
Regards to my relationship longevities, I always
Cast my lot in personal relations curt brevity.
But those, then were my mistakes, my foolish
Decisions and one's fate, (especially at this late date) does not allow
One to make, in realizing one's mistakes, new revisions.

John Knowles Probst
*Quincy, CA*

## No Longer

The tears in my eyes are because of you—

When your fingers wrap around mine
whenever they have the chance.
When you lay your head on my shoulder
and hold me close.

When you kiss in the morning
and always at night.
When you leave in the morning
and your scent lingers on the pillow.

When I catch you smiling at me
whenever I look at you.
When you come looking for me
when you can't find me.

The tears in my eyes are because of you.

I no longer have to be afraid;
I no longer have to feel alone;
I no longer fear the unknown;
I no longer wonder where I am supposed to be.
I no longer wonder what it's like to have
found the love of my life.

The tears in my eyes are because
every time we say I love you
it means my dreams have finally come true,
because of you.

Deanna Marie Soost
*Watertown, MN*

[Hometown] *Arlington, MN* [Hobbies] *nature photography, farm life, fishing* [GA] *being selected to be published 6 years in a row*
*I write what I call poetry, always open to interpretation. Some are made of the darkness inside me, some are glimpses of my past, some are the happiest moments in my life. Writing saved my life, and being able to share it with others has been a lifelong dream. Enjoy!*

## Ethereality

Welcome! Bienvenue
Omnium - gatherum "Poets" meritocracy extrapolation
Abreast flexibility one's own Chronicle accentuation
Moment by moment, laddered pari passu access way
Vis-a-vis prima facie "om" magnum opus desideratum
Magler momentum destination Zodiacal quantum
Fortoken childhood, unmourned multilevel rebuff
Inspired hardships! Reality optimistic scale enlinker
Tra-la-la econium petaled words "qua" free thinker
Fieches d'amour, Cosmos meandering, ah mosaic
Bonny! Lavander-aloe summer pond aural love todas
Altruistic victorious journeyed warrior crossroads
Avens perfumerie blowy, bird-of-paradise landscapes
Mesolithic omivorous link, prehistory mesmorism
Superlative solar system, topiary plantae empiricism
"Tic-toc" mirror - like hapatic seed! Tic toc
Time and chance prodosy, temporal crenelated loconic
Sky dawning, populistic longivety lucious tonic
Chacun 'a son gout
Peter Abelard, theology rooted creation Keystone they
Alpha human and nonhuman, anaphoric anorning lluaby
Justified seal, scriptual transmigration memorandum
Supernal aurorae, rediscovery or Time purism bloomful
Abaeterno reaffirmation life-form gyration doomful
Illation root, ode consummation, moony postlude

Mary R. Martinez De Arellano
*Chamisal, NM*

[Hometown] *Chamisal, NM* [Ed] *Associate of Arts degree* [Occ] *100% disabled - hereditary blindness* [Hobbies] *devotional prayer, wildlife and domestic care, cooking, viewing the world through movies, sharing poetry when asked* [GA] *world acceptance, determination, survival tactics, educational field, self - explanatory knowledge*

## Rise Like the Phoenix: A Poem for St. Vincent & the Grenadines

He was a young boy from an island town
Had big dreams until his world came crashing down
The volcano erupted
And the lava and ash came down
Destroyed everything in its path
He said I guess nothing last forever
I just want better
But everything keeps getting worse
Went from Covid to now this
How will we ever recover
It's one thing after another
Everyone is hurt
We all feel pain
But as long as we got each other
We can get through anything
'Cause I'm your brother and you're my sister
I got your back
I hope you know that
We're in this together
In the good and the bad with God by our side
We know He'll provide as we rise and shine
Like the Phoenix from the ash.

A. E. Charles
*Stone Mountain, GA*

[Hometown] *Stone Mountain, GA* [Ed] *Master of Science* [Occ] *data analyst* [Hobbies] *writing poetry, creating music, and podcasting* [GA] *publishing my two poetry books* The Experience *and* The UnderGrad Collection

*I would like to dedicate this poem to the people of St. Vincent & The Grenadines, which is an island located in Caribbean and is where my family is from. The volcano on St. Vincent, La Soufriere erupted on April 9th at 8:41 am after forty-two years. As a result of the volcano erupting it has forced people to evacuate their homes. It has also caused heavy ash to fall across the island killing crops and animals, as well as lava flow which killed lots of fish in the ocean. On top of all of this St. Vincent had to deal with heavy rain fall which caused flooding and mudslides. The island is also still dealing with COVID-19 as well and is still recovering from that. So I just wanted to write a poem to encourage and uplift my people in St. Vincent & The Grenadines spirits and bring more awareness to what's going on there. If you can help please send donations, big or small every little bit helps and is appreciated. I hope you all enjoy the poem!*

## My Forever Love

There's a love that burns deep within my soul,
The ignition of a passion that I don't want to control.
I want to be able to tell the world I love you;
I am confident the universe has opened its gates for just us two.
The path that lies ahead will be one of true measure;
We will find along the way that we are each others most precious treasure.
My day doesn't start when from my bed I arise;
It starts even if through a photo when I look into your eyes.
We are prone to days of joy and laughter;
Here's hoping they last throughout the hereafter.
You are the one for whom my feelings are sent from above;
I am elated to call you my friend, my heart, my baby, my forever love.

Diann C. Lloyd
*New York, NY*

[Hometown] *New York, NY* [Ed] *Walton High School* [Occ] *special officer* [Hobbies] *watching movies, basketball, and poetry writing* [GA] *having a published book of poetry Dee Dee's Innermost thoughts*

*I've been a lover of words forever. Poetry has always allowed me to express on paper what I've wanted to verbally. This poem was inspired by the love of my heart Rachelle. Also a lover of poetry, she is my muse, may she continue to inspire the creativity that lies within me.*

## Bubbles

Sometimes I feel outside the bubble.
Looking in able to hear
But floating in and out,
Not really there as I'm about to pop
Sometimes I feel left out of this bubble.
The conversations aren't always my favorite
But I stand and listen,
So I guess that's my fault,
Sometimes I am a bubble.
Floating only long enough
To get the best then leave
Feeling let down as I do so…
I guess that's on me,
Sometimes I am removed from this bubble.
I fall away in my mind
I feel I don't belong so I drift away
I do it to myself, I know.
I am the bubble.
So beautiful, shining with many colors
But I live a short life
Flying but falling, lost until I pop,
Like a bubbles lost in the wind.

Elena N. Rodriguez
*Longmont, CO*

[Hometown] *Longmont, CO* [Ed] *high school* [Hobbies] *drawing, D&D, video games, chemistry, guitar/ukulele, and singing* [GA] *being able to go to Odyssey of the Mind world championship and being a finalist of Colorado in 2018*

*The first time I shared my poetry was in fifth grade during a class poetry slam. I won and that further sparked my interest in poetry. From that point on, I found that expressing myself through poetry was calming and it allowed me to center myself. I am so happy to be able to share my pride and joy with you. Poetry is an expression of how we see the world and that is enthralling.*

## Trails

The beaten path bent backward upon itself
As we followed
The gilded orb beat with a fury of its own
As with parched lips we sought moisture
It was so clear that day
The trails led all way and to each
Its own story to tell

Eric Bonholtzer
*Huntington Beach, CA*

[Hometown] *Arcadia, CA*

*Eric Bonholtzer's work has appeared in numerous publications. He is a USC graduate with a master's degree in English from the California State Polytechnic University, Pomona. Eric has received numerous awards for his writing including taking first place in the fiction and poetry categories of the College Language Association Creative Writing Contest as well as receiving the Ted Pugh Poetry Award. He has written two short story collections, Enter the Abyss and The Skeleton's Closet, as well as a collection of poetry entitled Remnants & Shadows. Eric's work has appeared in many anthologies and he is a regular contributor to several national magazines. He is the author of the interactive text-based action/suspense game, It's Killing Time, where players are put in the shoes of a high-priced, world-traveling assassin. In addition to writing, Eric is also a civil litigation trial attorney.*

## Unsung Harmony

We all have our own melody,
A song to sing, to hum,
To our own beat.
Some scream it as a slogan,
Asserting themselves to the world.
Some recite it as a poem
Delicately treading through life
As an ode to beauty, to joy!
Rarely, some chant it,
Surrendering to the sacred truth, illuminating lives.
Some synchronize it to
The symphonies of the worldly orchestra.
Some choose to play their solo flute.
I hum my tune under my breath
With the occasional stray notes
Escaping into a lilting melody.
But, in your quiet silence,
I can hear...
Your hymn, radiating from your soul,
Its rhythm, pulsating from your heart.
I can see...
The unsung harmony of your secret song,
Gleaming in your expressive eyes.

Shraddha Jaideep Bhat
*Lisle, IL*

*I have studied architecture and since architecture is called the mother of all arts, I appreciate art in all forms. I love to read literature and poetry and like to express myself through poetry, articles, and short stories. My poems, articles, and stories have been published in several periodicals. I write in my native language Marathi as well as in English. My grandfather was a well-published author and my mother is an accomplished poet. I can say that I got this gift of writing from them. A collection of my poems called Kaleidoscope was published in 2020.*

## Missing

Home alone again
No one filling in
Gaps in this story of mine
Whenever rainstorms fly
Whatever tumbles by
Nothing to dry my eye. Fine!
Seems like night all day
Thoughts full like buckets
May be leakin' on the wooden floor
But you aren't walking
You're not talking
You sure can't come stumblin'
Through this open door anymore
'Cause your missing
and I am wishing you weren't in my head
Instead I think of how you bled me dry.
No longer cryin', grieving, dying
To call you "Darlin'" anymore
Just wanting day to shine
Nights to be mine
and someone to pine for me like I'm missin'. Fine!
Got nothing more to dread
Once you aren't here to leave me anymore.
Grateful to move on now you've gone missing. Fine!
Rainbows all the time.

Betty Bonds Hatfield
*Louisville, KY*

[Hometown] *Atlanta, GA* [Ed] *BS in nursing, Vanderbilt University* [Occ] *retired* [Hobbies] *reading, writing, getting out in nature, and traveling* [GA] *children, grandchildren, being married to the same wonderful man nearly 45 years!*

*I love writing poetry and lyrics.*

## In the Manner of Poe

Once upon a midnight dreary,
as I pondered sad and leery,
thoughts about my sweet Lenore.
Only thoughts, and nothing more.
For Lenore had left me early,
leaving me all sad and teary,
with the memories of yore.
Memories only, nothing more.
Suddenly there was a knocking,
as of someone softly tapping,
tapping outside my front door.
Tapping only, nothing more.
Never had I been so fearing,
as I asked, steadily trembling,
"Who's that knocking at my door?"
Silence answered, nothing more.
Bravely gathering my senses,
and without further pretenses,
I quickly opened the door!
'Twas Lenore at my front door...
to be mine forevermore.

Felipe Chacon Jr.
*El Paso, TX*

[Hometown] *El Paso* [Ed] *two years of college education.* [Occ] *retired* [Hobbies] *writing, music, singing* [GA] *I have received praise for my work from as far away as England.*

## When We Were Young

When we were young and didn't have a care
We'd run and play and hide everywhere
We didn't pay attention to night or day
All we wanted to do was laugh and play

When we were young we had show and tell
We wished upon a star and threw coins in the well
We didn't think about how clothes are made
All we knew was they got worn and would fade

When we were young and turned on a light
We didn't have a clue what made it so bright
We knew what to do when the street light glows
All of us drank cold water from a garden hose

When we were young and we wanted a new toy
We were told that Santa might bring it with joy
We filled a glass with milk and cookies so he's fed
All we had to do is be sound asleep in our bed

When we were young and we were sent off to school
We looked towards the teachers to teach us the rule
We think it's sometimes boring but we had to attend
All we really wanted to do was just make a friend

Robert Lee Stephenson
*New Egypt, NJ*

[Hometown] *Elizabethtown, KY* [Ed] *AAS in computer science* [Occ] *retired* [Hobbies] *fishing, writing poems, classic cars, camping* [GA] *graduating from college*
*My wife Sue and I live in New Egypt, NJ. I have been interested in writing poetry since I was a kid. My father was in the military so we moved around a lot and I went to several different schools; the places we travelled to and the friends I made over the years give me many stories and adventures to tell. After my wife retires next year, I plan to sit on a dock by a lake and write poetry about life, people, and the world we live in.*

## Do I Belong?

Do I belong?
I am part of a family,
at least I think I am.
I have two parents and siblings
with whom I live,
but, do I belong?
As kids we notice that Mom and Dad
might favor one sibling more.
We have all seen this.
Now we are all grown with families of our own,
but yet I feel like I'm on the outside looking in.
We all go through the motions
but somehow I am lost.
Do I belong?
I feel a distance between us
but that closeness we shared is no longer there.
Things have changed more it seems.
Do I just go on like all is fine?
Maybe I should hold my silence
and just keep wondering—
do I belong?

Deb Alpaugh
*Turbotville, PA*

[Hometown] *Turbotville, PA* [Occ] *paraprofessional for special education* [Hobbies] *writing, cooking and baking, canning, and pulling mini horses* [GA] *having my three kids*

*I enjoy writing poetry and magazine articles. I am working on a manuscript, but it's in the early stages. I enjoy spending time with my family and enjoying the outdoors.*

## The Play of Life

Close the curtain, the show is finished.
The story for the play was unique.
A new beginning during the first act,
Hear the actress, she begins to speak.
This is joy, not easy to explain,
Deep in the veins, so near the heart,
Talking to all with a small quiet voice.
Just notice the scene and surroundings.
Sounds familiar, the actress speaks clearly,
Breathing slowly, struggling for breath,
Humming softly to herself.
First act is finished, curtain comes down.
The second act begins with a burst of joy,
Waiting to hear the outcome, announcing with pride,
Actress proudly exclaims, "It is a healthy baby boy!"
The curtain closes a second time.
Clearing the stage, showing the progress of years,
Curtain goes up, young man now on stage,
Learning, working, slowly his mate and family appear.
The stage is now crowded with family and friends,
Moving along, going separate ways.
The stage grows quiet as easy time ends.
Now this man on the stage is growing more quiet,
While his family appear and watches nearby.
The audience knows the play will end,
The curtain will fall, hanging their heads to cry.

Patricia Montag
*Colo, IA*

[Hometown] *Whiting, IA* [Ed] *University Of Northern Iowa Teacher's College* [Occ] *homemaker*
[Hobbies] *writing poetry, reading, gardening* [GA] *raising six children*
*During the ninety-two years of my life, first was being born the second daughter to Ruth and Eddie Langren. Loving school, it was easy to manage perfect attendance for many years. After graduating from Whiting High School, my next challenges were two years of teacher's college and teaching. My life has been devoted to my family, marrying and raising six wonderful kids, first on the farm and later in Ames, IA. Since losing my husband to death, I am living in our home with the help of our children. I enjoy writing poetry, reading, flowers, and the great outdoors.*

## Hound Dog

My dog used to listen to Bach
While running around on the dock.
Till a gal pug he spied
With a collar tie-dyed,
So now he just listens to rock.

Richard Eugene Breese
*Youngstown, OH*

[Hometown] *Youngstown, Ohio* [Ed] *BA American History* [Occ] *Retired* [Hobbies] *student of the lute* [GA] *68th Birthday*

*I write poetry to make people laugh. Whenever this occurs life is great. For as someone once said somewhere that a giggle a day keeps the doctor away.*

## Lost Emotionally

I wanted to make a difference
To help! you in some way
You don't need to say it
Nor ask me to stay
I realize I did wrong
I meddled in your life
Not easy to forgive, nor to forget
I tried to be a friend
I got sucked into your personal problems
I'm sorry if I hurt you in any way
But now who, listens to an old man
One that you might not understand
I needed to delete and take
Myself out of line
And proceed with my life
But something you did and said
Motivated me to be
And feel as a better person
I'm only human, and not always right
Our emotions of love and life, its an endless fight

Jose Guadalupe Valdez
*Othello, WA*

[Hometown] *Othello, WA* [Ed] *11 1/2 grade Othello high school* [Occ] *retired from work of 28 years* [Hobbies] *camping and hiking on weekends* [GA] *to pay my home and become a US citizen*

*Going to high school I wanted to be a poet someday. My lit teacher said if I became a poet I will help many people understand it. So I wrote a note to her, how she motivated me to create my own poems: "Poetry: A Work of Art," "Ideas of our Mind," "Feelings from Our Heart."*

## Love of Ocean

Being by the ocean brings back memories of young,
salt air always tingles your tongue.
Waves so great, land crabs scary,
so walkers be wary.
Starfish beauty, shells in a sand dune,
will become part of the collection soon.
Finding shark teeth sprinkled in the sand,
provides a challenge different from the land.
At sunrise the sparkling sun rays spray the
water like a jewel while waves rush in every which way like a duel.
The salt air and breezes open your mind,
there's no better way of relaxation to find.
To sit and watch waves on the ocean—
what a great creation, and it becomes a great form of meditation.
Vacationing at the ocean is an exhilarating find,
but leaving makes me feel empty like leaving part
of me behind.

Carolyn J. Hopp
*Olmsted Twp, OH*

[Hometown] *Olmsted Township, OH* [Ed] *high school, some college* [Occ] *retired administrative secretary* [Hobbies] *poetry, reading, crafts, hiking, walking, zoo, watching waves* [GA] *marriage, children, grandchildren, family, friends, and poetry*

*My husband Don and I reside in Olmsted Township, OH. We have two children and two grandchildren (Ryan, a lacrosse player and Emily a nursing student). We have many bird feeders and an abundance of flowers and plants in our yard. Hobbies include looking for artifacts such as arrowheads and gemstones spending days at the Cleveland Zoo, and hiking in the metroparks various sites. I am an avid reader and enjoy poetry. My love of the ocean and waves started at age four on vacations with my family. We are blessed to have family and friends.*

## Alpha-Omega

Beyond the mind exists a desert universe,
That mocks the intellect of homo sapiens,
The personification of infinity transcends space and time,
The cause of causes manifests ultimate reality,
An eternity of knowledge freely granted unconditionally,
To all who genuinely choose to accept the divine gift,
Imperfection vanishes as ultimate potential is realized,
Love is triumphant and peace is forever.

Richard A. Sano
*Sammamish, WA*

[Hometown] *Albany, NY* [Ed] *BS education State University College, Oneonta, NY; MA liberal studies Wesleyan University* [Occ] *retired federal* [Hobbies] *playing jazz piano, reading non-fiction, Italian cooking* [GA] *improvising on the piano, college education*

## The Heart with No Name

The heart with no name creative
its story using kindness and understanding
when you're lost, be yourself and follow
your heart call to the wild seeking
the unknown be brave push away
the fear relace it with the wonder
and a curious and step forward go
straight not knowing the strength
the heart meets new challenges
that makes the heart ask questions
Some answered in time some never
get ask some forgot and lost in this moment
of choices leading the heart to
meet the call of the wild leading with
the understanding of the kindness
it has to have to make its own story
But the heart has no name but
shared and filled with goodness
by those who have met or passed by
thus heart creating a feeling that teaches
the heart how to love showing
the lost that the heart with no name but
has a story of being true to itself

Jeana Lynna Tilley
*Danville, AR*

[Hometown] *Bakersfield, CA*  [Ed] *high school*  [Occ] *elder care*  [Hobbies] *reading, writing*  [GA] *being a wife and mother*

*My name is Jean Lynna Tilley, a wife and mother. I live in Arkansas and was born in California. I love to write poems and love animals. My family is my world and without them I wouldn't be who I am.*

# Grand Frondescence Lure Unfold

There's rejoicing in life's splendor
and lush green foliage cajoled,
where once there were sparse boughs austere,
now grand frondescence lure unfold.

Pink magnolia claim grandeur,
while white dogwood display impose
magnificence in spring's splendor,
and grand frondescence lure unfold.

O, buttercups dot the lush ground,
verdant fragrant grass has bestowed
a silent expression around,
with grand frondescence lure unfold.

Olivia Serena Snead
*Harleysville, PA*

[Hometown] *Harleysville, PA* [Ed] *bachelor's degree in business administration, a diploma in creative writing* [Occ] *unemployed* [Hobbies] *writing letters, continued education, exercise, reading* [GA] *bachelor's degree in business administration*

*My poem was written from the sheer joy of spring. Currently, I'm studying various forms of writing—essays, short stories, and different types of poetry. I've joined a mystery book club. My long-term goals are to complete a book of poetry, revise a collection of first draft private investigator short stories, and a biography of my late youngest son.*

## Destiny

Start out by trying to be a little kinder
with the passing of each day.
To leave only happy memories
as we go along our way.
To use possessions that are ours
in service full and free.
To sacrifice the trivial things
for larger good to be.
To give of love in lavish ways
that friendship true may live.
To be less quick to criticize
more ready to forgive.
To use such talents as we have
that happiness may grow.
To take the bitter with the sweet
assured it is better so.
To be quite free from self intent
whatever the task we do.
To help the world's faith in God and right
no matter how things run.
To work and play and pray and trust
until the journey's done.
God grant to us the strength of heart
of motive and of will.
To do our part and falter not
God's purpose to fulfill.

Rena Winters
*Las Vegas, NV*

[Hometown] *Las Vegas* [Ed] *master's degree* [Occ] *adjunct instructor at college* [Hobbies] *writing* [GA] *employed for years as Hollywood film and television writer*

*Anyone can change the world. We just have to try. If we follow our destiny, all will go well.*

## Let the Inside Out

I live here, inside this mind of mine.
A safe place to hide.
I leave the misunderstanding world outside.

Inside, I'm not lonely nor defeated.
Energy grows inside and amongst my thoughts,
Energy worth consuming.

There's no place in this world for all that I hold inside.

Passion grows deep within me.
A voice inside me that hopes to sing out loud,
Not to be seen nor acknowledged but to be freeing.

The world pushes on me.
Reminds me that to be free in this world
I must be free within me.

For I am the only one who can see me.

Lisa Marie Roth
*Petersburg, WV*

*For those who know me, know that I am a quiet, deep kind of soul. This poem brings light of that. I love to be creative in many ways. My motto is "Inspire to be original." I am blessed with many inspirations that allow this all to happen. I want to thank my husband, Alex, and our two beautiful, amazing girls, Zenna and Hayley. Without them life would be dull and left without sparks. To all those who truly support all that I am and do, it means the world to me.*

## That Train

I stepped into that train
like so many before
When that last hit was gone?
I had to get me some more
It was all that I wanted
It became my best friend
Everything I was doing
Would soon come to an end?
Hurting not only myself
But also those I loved
I was on that train of addiction
With whistles blaring above
My life was falling apart
Slipping away really fast
I had to get off of that train
Knowing the ride wouldn't last?
Making my way to the caboose
All the way at the end
I closed my eyes and I jumped
Into the hands of a Friend
My Friends name is Jesus
And He can be your Friend, too
If you find yourself on that train?
He's on the caboose waiting for you!

Eric Steven Voehringer
*Eustis, FL*

[Hometown] *Eustis, FL* [Ed] *addiction counseling* [Occ] *lawn care* [Hobbies] *volunteer for One Heart for Women and Children* [GA] *being grateful*

*I spent twenty years in addiction. I have been clean for almost twenty-three years now. I am a husband, father, and grateful recovering addict.*

## A Special Mom

My mom is a special lady,
for she gave birth to me.
And when you count the other two,
we all add up to three.
Two red-haired boys and one blonde girl
into this world she brought.
Teamwork, friendship, and honesty
were the philosophies she taught.
We'd sit on the arm of the living room chair
while she would read to us.
She'd share some of life's experiences
and she told us not to cuss.
We've pushed her to the limit
and I'm sure when she'd lost all hope,
her little darlings found redemption
after washing out their mouths with soap.
Some moms are gone forever
and no longer can we see.
But in our minds they've never left
for they live on in our memory.
And some day when we're talking
I'd find out that it's true;
that your mom is a lot like mine,
for she is special, too.

Gary G. McDonald
*Heltonville, IN*

*It is four days before mother's day. I was born on Mother's 21st birthday. She passed away at age ninety-three eight years ago. She had Alzheimer's. She sacrificed much raising us three kids without any child support from Dad. She loved us kids, God, and America. You probably couldn't count all of the people who called her a friend. I am presently eighty years old and have been married to my sweetheart Brenda for fifty-five years. We have three kids, six grandkids, and four great-grandkids. I am a navy veteran.*

## In Front of the Moon

We stepped outside.
He hoped to snap a photo,
One to catch the biggest moon
That we would see this year.
A harvest moon is what we used to call it
When on a night as clear
It beamed as bright and low and near.
We held hands for just a moment.
Then my ego stopped the magic
When I mused my head of graying hair
Could measure up to such a light.
And I felt it loosely lifting
In the playful night time air.
Then, glancing down from moonlight
It seemed our luck was always going to last.
It's held out favorably in the past
And still seemed solid as this newly-poured and
Polished City Cement Pathway Square!
I reasoned this in momentary silence
While standing there.
Then,
I watched him as he turned and set the camera.
And the smile I held was timed to hold,
According to instruction, just long enough
For him to click another lifetime moment,
With such care.

Lavonne G. Rytting
*Houston, TX*

[Hometown] *Salt Lake City, UT* [Ed] *BA University of Utah where I graduated in English the year of 1961* [Occ] *taught English for 3 years in public high school, worked as an interior designer for twenty years* [Hobbies] *poetry, gardening* [GA] *seeing 4 children reach their educational goals, all the rest is good news from that I am now eighty-three and two of my poems are in two of your volumes of amateur poetry works. I have been writing poetry now for six years and it has been rewarding personally, and interesting to my family. I am presently working on a collection of thirty. It was exciting to see your notification and send you another of my poems. I have four children, eight grandchildren, and a cherished sixty-three years of marriage.*

## Karen

K stands for kindness
that only a heart can give
Key for solidarity
Symbol of loftiest deed.
A is for achievements
That gives honor to our life
A towering labor of love
Because of Jesus Christ.
R is righteousness
Embedded in the heart
Greatest joy in life and living
A heart's desire for being.
E is excellence
In all life's endeavor
Elevated from the clay
Distinction forever.
N is newness in spirit
Since Jesus shed His blood
Salvation at the Calvary
Life's journey to carry

Adelfa Gonzales Lorilla
*Seagoville, TX*

[Hometown] *Lambunao, Iloilo, Philippines* [Ed] *PhD in education/major in English* [Occ] *retired* [Hobbies] *reading and writing* [GA] *raising eight good children for the Lord*

*This poem is an expression of love and appreciation for our daughter, Karen. She is the first blessing, out of the eight children, with whom God has gifted us. To God be the glory!*

## Memories

Denise was born with a gift of the very best kind,
Beauty and intelligence as she stood in line.
Sparkling blue eyes and dark curly hair,
Her sweetness was really beyond compare.
Friends were amazed as her talents came soon,
While still just a baby she could carry a tune.
About beautiful songs that she could sing,
By being so tiny it was a wonderful thing.
Her God-given graces were ever so good,
But health was not given as well as it should.
Don't worry, little Denise, God has His hand on you,
The hard times came, but you always pulled through.
School was a problem; making friends made you shy.
You learned how to talk to other kids and you really did try.
A new Dad, a new school, a new house and more changes,
You had fun in band with the clarinet's musical ranges.
Norton High was the place to be—Larry and Susan were there.
Graduation and then to Akron U., where no one could compare.
You worked at Summa about the time you found love,
A love that was made in Heaven above.
His name was Larry Ferrell so tall, trim, and handsome,
From then on he held your heart for ransom.
A beautiful November wedding and life planned so well,
Then adopted a baby we named Jon Ryan made life swell.

Frances L. Kalapodis
*New Franklin, OH*

*This poem is to honor the life of my daughter, Denise L. Ferrell, who was a mother, sister, NaNa, and dear friend to many. She has returned to the arms of her loving husband and they have reached "Infinity Together." She lived a gentle, honorable life, and will be always an example of Christian love.*

## Time Never Stops

In a world where time never stops, days are long
Nights too short, memories of the past cannot
compare with love of the present we much share
Birds fly high to sit among the trees, flowers in
rainbow colors as far as the eye can see
Blue skies, winds gentle breeze, with fresh air
after a spring rain
Oh! such beauty to see as animals roam free in meadows
of green cared by the hand of God Almighty
Love is the light of tomorrow, beauty in a child's
smiling face, where war is no more, children have
plenty, countries do not judge by power and race
As elders of this Earth, let's not repeat the past
much sorrow, year's of pain
Our future is beyond me, what will it be no one can see
We leave this land to the new generation who will bring
healing and peace to our nation, may we be forever free
Our land is beautiful, take care of her forever to be

Alice France Ellison-Crampton
*Logan, UT*

[Hometown] *Boston, MA* [Ed] *2 college degrees one in funeral services, travel and business management* [Occ] *retired* [Hobbies] *poetry, hook rugs, reading and helping animals in need* [GA] *getting awards in poetry for my poems*

*This is a poem for the hopes of the next generation of children to live in peace and beauty. I have been writing poems since 1980s and live alone with my five boy cats. I hope to put all my work into a poetry book someday and share them with the world.*

## F.I.R.E.—Forgiving in Rough Environment

October 2, 2018 was a sad day,
When a fire took all my worldly possessions away!
This journey to healing has taken over two years,
Filled with moments of sadness and tears!
With the help of faith, family, and friends,
That sadness has come to an end!
After moving four times in a year and a half,
God has taken me on a new path!
I am now divorced and alone,
But at peace in my new home!
Pandemic or not, God has given me a reason to smile
And continue to do His will mile after mile!

Sandra Defaye Banks
*Atlanta, GA*

[Hometown] *Atlanta, GA* [Ed] *BA mass communications* [Hobbies] *dancing, reading, and walking* [GA] *meeting Oprah Winfrey and taking a picture*

*I have had some serious tests over the last few years that I have turned into testimonies. I love to write poetry to help me through these situations.*

## Moving Forward with Faith

The wind travels rightward
through the space
between the verdant terrain
and the white stratus face.
In its direction,
a fog sheets a mountain
to the point the wind's path
becomes a closed intersection.
The wind, however, continues
to follow its natural instincts
by flowing around and above
the mountain but never sinks.

Ian Alexander Sloan
*Upper Marlboro, MD*

*The wind is analogous to a person following natural instincts to push through mental and physical obstacles.*

## Believe in Yourself

We attract into life that which we dream of most...
Imagine most vividly!
Follow your spirit voice,
hold close your dreams,
They are achievable!
Listen to the wisdom of your soul.
Dance to the music in your heart.
Rise to conquer every challenge before you.
Treat yourself to time...for that is all life offers.
Remember life does not grant us....
Days without pain, laughter without sorrow,
Success without struggle nor sunshine without clouds.
Realize the power is within you,
Summons the strength inside for every day.
Comfort for the joys or fears.
Remember, there is always a light from within
To find your way.

Lois Ann Goldstein
*Lewes, DE*

[Hometown] *Lewes, DE*  [Occ] *retired*  [Hobbies] *writing*  [GA] *author of "Dust from the Attic"*

## Feed

I'm starting to remember...

I was aboard the USS Georgie when we hit tuff terrain, torrential down pour
The wind continuously sucker punched us in the face
As I lose track of the scenery and steered directly into the deadlights

Awake, unconscious, my surroundings become uncanny
With the smell of circus food accompanied with the appropriate music
A yellow slicker and mixed serology, inhuman bite marks and floating...
Then I see your glowing eyes through the darkness

I'm sorry, I don't currently feel like floating
Wait...you stupid bitch those words were never spoken
You need to check your third-party sources
Because your game of telephone tag is clearly twisting the facts...

I know this trick
I have been studying the lure behind it for years now
I understand the inner and outer workings of a clown
So, let's just exchange smiles...

So, I implore you tempt me with a balloon
No, you stupid bitch that is not the right color
I want the mischievous red one that holds all the secrets
And with a sleight of hand, guess what I am going to do...

I am going to pop it
The blood will plunge your face
As my fist connects with your face
A direct hit to vocal chords
You will never understand, you dug your own grave
And I no longer have a problem pushing you in

Shaunna M. Ingrassia
*Holbrook, NY*

## Birthright

Reflection of a long cracked mirror
bears a cameo pink soul
capturing her childlike youth.
Her tear-stained eyes
were like chilling rain
running its course down the windowpane.
Movement in unknown dark waters,
always a reminder,
tangled with sin.
An error of misconduct,
or so they say.

Myraka Jones
*The Villages, FL*

[Hometown] *Lady Lake* [Ed] *certified death doula* [Occ] *artist* [Hobbies] *kayaking* [GA] *giving birth to my son*

## American

American,
stand as one voice, amongst a multitude
of people woven in the same stars and stripes
fabric as I and recognize you for who you are, a human.
American, see that our humanity is being challenged
and attacked by acts, concepts, and euphemism that is
dividing us into them, they, she, and he.
Only so that a small percentage of profiteers could
stay relevant.
American, persevere in light of the hate and envy
that's been unleashed upon our humanity in order
for us to be effective against those two components.
I'm going to need the help of my fellow humanity
because that's exactly what's at stake, humanity...
American, can appeal to our humanity and ask that we
stop desecrating the sacrifice it took for us to be
free, independent, and united, with indifferences,
towards each other because we're all benefactors of
our nation founding principles.
As one humanity and one American...

Emmanuel Lopez
*Salinas, CA*

[Hometown] *Salinas, CA*  [GA] *sharing my passion with all of you*

## Grandparents

There are not many things
I wouldn't give
to see you smile
or hear your laugh
just once more,
because even the moon
slumps its shoulders
in a deep despair
from your absence;
but also like the moon,
I know you are there
even in our darkest skies,
and I will feel
your love
for a lifetime
without needing
to see it.

Alyssa Rose Packard
*Plainfield, NH*

[Hometown] *Meriden, NH* [Occ] *medical insurance biller* [Hobbies] *writing, reading, making art*

## That Blooming Onion

How often I have ordered
A blooming onion,
Delighting in a gentle ritual
Of peeling each delicate petal,
Then dipping it slowly,
Rhythmically, into a pungent sauce,
Knowing how sad I would be
To touch the last petal.
This strange, inviting ritual
Is a subtle imitation of life.
Some petals are brown,
Withering and uninviting
No matter how tasty the sauce;
Yet, as the layers fall away,
They become healthier, stronger
And sweeter to the tongue.
Each petal beckons me
To participate in this ritual,
To celebrate the power it holds,
To dance once more.

Mary Marlene Daley
*Roseburg, OR*

[Hometown] *Roseburg, OR* [Ed] *junior college, online college courses, business and life experience* [Occ] *retired* [Hobbies] *writing, bowling* [GA] *raising my beautiful children and spoiling my grandchildren and giving them a love of reading and writing*

*For a half century Southern California was my home. I loved her vitality, her uniqueness, her versatility and the beauty of her people. But all good things come to an end and I found myself longing for a place of my youth, where time didn't seem to be in such a hurry and where people wanted to know your name. I moved to Roseburg, OR, a delightful little town, in 2014 with no regrets, other than being a distance in all directions from my family. The American Northwest is breathtaking and brings one's soul to life. Its flavor has blended well with my taste for beauty and serenity and provides a treasure chest of poetry and prose. I am where life has chosen I should be.*

209

## Truth

In silence of word and frozen in place,
I searched the world for truth's sad face.
For truth had discovered
that there was no other
to follow in suit
to speak the truth.
Why? I feared, but dared to ask
was this such a daunting task?
Why did the people flee
from what was made to be free?
What was intended
became descended
from lies,
hidden in a deep disguise.
No one knew
the masked shrew
that taunted, tempted,
and never relented.
Illusions of a haunted past
created a narrative that would last.
Confusion had led to this illusion,
that finally exploded into delusion.
The lie that was believed
is what the world received.
The bed we choose to make
will forsake the truth we fake.

Christine M. Bowen
*Douglasville, GA*

[Hometown] *Douglasville, GA* [Ed] *college* [Occ] *life coach/brain health coach* [Hobbies] *art* [GA] *published lyrics and books*
*My name is Christine Bowen. I am an author, a life coach, and a brain health coach. I am a lyricist. I wrote the lyrics for the three albums of the band True Witness. I live in the Atlanta area. I am married with five children and five grandsons.*

## The Inquisitive Traveler

Traveling to a new town or city is exciting
While taking walks down a path or on a boardwalk
Where local artists eagerly create
And display their best masterpieces yet
Gentle to subtle detail as the sounds and melodies
Move in your soul to embrace their cultures refined.

Because your whole world is a playground
To discover what washes up in the universal tide
And the best of times you might recall
Is talking to the people of each vidid place
Learning their stories and chasing ideas
Of local cuisines yet to be tried.

This curious traveler was a celebrity chef
And a great storyteller who connected with many
He traveled parts unknown around the globe
Where a passport gets you into each diverse location
Within this vast world we hold dear.

He just may return one day
And walk with all of us once more
People are unique, and self-expression is key
As a dearly remembered nomad travels
To find his next meal and a smile.

Mariah Ann Delorenzo
*Homeland, CA*

*I was inspired to write my poem, "The Inquisitive Traveler," in 2018 and dedicated it in honor and memory of Anthony Michael Bourdain. He was an American chef, book author, journalist, and travel documentarian who starred in programs focusing on exploring international culture, cuisine, and the human condition. Sadly, on June 8, 2018, Bourdain died by suicide in France while filming his CNN hit series, "Parts Unknown." Bourdain captivated my interest in his travels, fine cuisine food, and cookbook recipes.*

## The Seductress

The wind—feel me—I'm warm or cool
The tree—touch me—I bend but don't break
I'm no one's fool

The rain, fluid or solid, feel with the face or hand
The ocean—many moves with waves—ups and downs
for woman or man

The flowers with beautiful blooms; enjoy the sweet scents
The bees, making honey; lick and taste it, it's their intent

The sun, upon rising produces such heat
The moon, in control of such mysteries, in its shadow, a retreat

The fruit of the earth, nourishment within
The love of it, the need for it; embrace it, my friend

The spirit of the artist, creating from the soul
The Creator pulling you forward for stories untold

The longing for expression, as in nature, comes comfortably
The inner me, the outer me, it's all of me you see

The chance to get a glimpse of the fiery sparks inside
The assurance that I'm my very best guide

The seductress comes in many forms
as each stage of life you approach

The best friend you'll find is—you!
The seductress—your own coach!

Sherry A. York
*Arab, AL*
[Hometown] *Guntersville, AL* [Occ] *retired RN* [Hobbies] *cleaning, reading, yard sales, writing* [GA] *55 years of marriage (to the same man)*
*I am a seventy-four year old great-grandmother. My life has mostly been lived in the "care" arena of life, therefore feelings mean so much to me. Nature plays a great part for all of us as we age. The feel of wind, sun, moon; the beauty of trees and flowers and fruit for life are so important. A "connection," I suppose, is what inspired this poem many years ago.*

## Nature

Its purity and innocence, its life and breath
Apparent by growth and destruction
Nature is seen, heard, tasted, smelled,
felt by all, healing and science, death and decay.
Nature reflects God's divine wisdom and intent
to create, multiply, and replenish the earth.
All viable in the Darwinism of the life cycle.
Hail, lightning, and thunder
Hurricanes, tornadoes, storms, and tsunamis
Cardinal of nature with purpose.
Medicines, diamonds, and pearls are
nature's resources.
Chemical composition are integral elements
in the earth's crust.
The ocean minerals, pivotal to man's survival
critical resources deep within the seabed's
untapped resources to the average man.
The mountains, valleys, lakes, rivers, forest,
volcanoes and wastelands are God's creation.
One cannot separate God from nature
they are intertwined and interwoven together
to the mystery of humanity and the human race.

Bobbie Norris Chambliss
*Fayette, MS*

*I attended Alcorn State University, received a bachelor's and master's degrees in elementary education and guidance education with a certification in mental health. I am a retired mental health professional who is writing poems and poetry. I enjoy reading and doing self-reflection. I wrote and self-published my first book. My greatest achievement was becoming an ordained ministry/Evangelist.*

## Dawn

a columbine, lustrous
   on the beach,
flushing shell-pink light-
   tipped
and radiant...
   curling over sun.

Joh Cambilargiu
*Tooele, UT*

## Deep Sea Duality

I'm fighting.
Yes, fighting these demons, with love.
These demons that don't know love.
How love.
What love.
Love.
So, this war I wage.
This war I hold, held deep within,
subsides.
This cage, once locked.
Only when I wanted change, and I ached
and ached
did those demons, demons I once held, unlocked.
Loved.

Austin Leander Phillips
*Lawrenceville, GA*

## Thanks for Your Light

Thank you, Stranger
For giving me a part of you
For being so selfless
And knowing exactly what to do.
Throughout my life
I made many mistakes
Thinking I was happy
Until came confusion
And body aches
I made unwise choices.
Lived life high through a blur
My brain in a cloud
I did not deter.
A part of my body
Gave up in loud protest
I survived on medication.
I was unhappy and stressed
Now, through your donation of life
I get a chance to make it right
And know that when we meet up in Heaven
You will be proud that you
Gave me your light!

Dora Elia Gonzalez
*Harlingen, TX*

[Hometown] *San Benito, TX* [Ed] *associate degree in childcare and development, bachelor of arts in English, minor in sociology* [Occ] *elementary school teacher* [Hobbies] *writing, reading, arts and crafts, gardening* [GA] *publishing my poetry*

*I like to write about certain emotions that I feel during important events in my life.*

## Never a Waste

Every single day I try to go outside
By the end of the day, I'm still stuck inside
I dream of going out, I want to explore
I know thru that door there has to be more
I'm desperate to know how to get thru this
The clock is ticking, but something's a-miss
I look out my window and see beauty, it's true
But I don't deserve it, so it must be for you
I'm stuck in here, my life goes no further
Because one day, I know I'll be murdered
I pray that one day when I meet my demise
That the ones I love will think I was wise
Sometimes I wish I would be called home
Someday I'll look back and see how I've grown
It's obvious to me that people don't care
Sad but true, I just wish I was there
My faith is deep, in my blood and veins
I need no pity, I am not insane
Soon I'll be gone, and they'll have nobody to blame
They could have known me, and that's just a shame

Tracy Lorraine Ross
*Port Angeles, WA*

[Hometown] *Port Angeles, WA* [Ed] *high school, beauty school, certified nurse's assistant training* [Occ] *cosmetologist, CNA but now have PTSD and disabled* [Hobbies] *reading non-fiction, writing for an outlet, rock-hounding, fossils, researching, self help, boxing my punching bag* [GA] *my 2 Children Jeffrey Don Price 37, Katie Lee Gilbert Lord 27; they are miracles to me*

*I lived in Port Angeles most of my fifty-seven years. I've been married twice. I have two children thirty-seven and twenty-seven. I was a cosmetologist most of my life, then my second child was born with cerebral palsy, so I became a CNA. My second husband was abusive while our daughter was home on life support. I had a melt down and sent my daughter to live with a nurse for most of her life. Now she has two Moms. I'm happiest I've been in a very long time. I even leave my house now.*

## Everyday Life

Off and running I go,
as time approaches for school.
Chaos and madness reign supreme,
as 1,2,3, boys onward they go.
Like mini tornadoes
scattering Cheerios and whirling papers
bustling in the aftermath.
One shoe is gone, Heaven forbid.
Meltdown town, here we come.
Whew, that shoe is found, disaster averted.
Now my coffee, oh where may you be?
Not in the microwave, that's yesterday's cup.
Then it's "Honey, where are my keys and phone?"
Rushing out the door, no time for a kiss goodbye.
Honk, honk the bus is here.
One child mad because he couldn't take his toy.
When morning madness ends, time to breathe.
Here comes boy #4 with my now empty coffee cup.
Giggly, little grin he asks, "Mommy, more please?"

Brenna Reeter
*Chula, MO*

[Hometown] *Chula, MO* [Occ] *CNA at local hospital* [Hobbies] *reading, trail walking*

*I live with my husband of fourteen years with our four boys on a hobby farm. I am a nurse's aide at a local hospital. I enjoy our local church activities as well as spending time with family and friends.*

## Together Again

Their arms reached out beseeching...
Why have you abandoned us,
did we do something wrong?
We have no one to hold, our laps have been empty for so long.
They huddled together circling, sheltering the heart which was beating slower and slower and slower, clogged with the dust of avoidance.
I could no longer walk past looking the other way.
Their loneliness started to worm into my thoughts and their despair circulated deep into my veins.
I took a soft cloth and rubbed their backs with fragrant oils, they began to shine with a golden hue.
I tenderly massaged the heart until its pulse began to race. I lit a light to chase away the darkness.
I gathered the others and we sat upon their laps, lounging against their backs, as their arms began to warm.
We rested our hands upon the heart, which gathered in our laughter as it basked in the candlelight.
For that one night, all was right,
we were a family dining together again.

Cheryl Holloway
*Jacksonville, FL*

[Hometown] *Savannah, GA* [Ed] *master's in nursing* [Occ] *retired registered nurse and aspiring writer* [Hobbies] *writing, acting, stand up comedy, and reading* [GA] *motherhood and now grandmother of a princess*

*Poetry is my first love in writing. I enjoy searching for words that can paint a picture and bring emotions out to share with others. I started writing poetry seven years ago after the death of my best friend and soulmate in life. Poetry allows one to write out the darkness and make room for the light in life. Poetry reaches across the chasms between people and provides a bridge in which to connect to one another. It is communication at its purest.*

## God Is Real

The day had come when I was told
A tumor they had found
And after hearing all that news
My life became unsound
The treatments started out quite well
Then slowly wore me down
The time had come to seek more help
From the hospital uptown
And as I lay there helplessly in a room
I occupied
Comfort washed all over me
For God was at my side
He came and sat with me each night
And gave me strength to heal
Ten years ago I fought that fight
I know that God is real

Eleonore Charlotte Hinkson
*Goldsboro, NC*

[Hometown] *Goldsboro* [Ed] *high school, some college courses* [Occ] *retired executive officer for board of realtors* [Hobbies] *ceramics and assorted crafts* [GA] *opening my own business*

*I was born in Germany and now live in Goldsboro, NC.*

## November Is Eternal

My child, you must know
you are not forgotten, you were
God's most precious gift given to the world.
So many years ago, somebody came
before you and like you he left in
pieces, too.
My dear child if I could see you through
my tears I should cry forever then.
I wish you come through the wind,
I wish you come through my dreams.
You left one cold November without
Knowing you left a November eternally mine.

*To Gabriel Vargas*

Rebecca Deciga
*Brighton, CO*

*My poem was inspired by my friend's son, who died in a firehouse trying to save his mother. On November 16, 2016 both died. He was an organ donor.*

## The Babbling Brook

The babbling brook recites tales centuries old,
Speaks to me of sourdoughs and panners of its gold.
The trees surround brook, the sky enfolds the green
Little fishes dart about, birds complete the scene.
A tiny branch floating by tells another tale to me.
"I came from the sky above from on the tallest tree.
I saw the panners one and all abuse the little brook,
He fed tiny fishes and his gold they all partook."
Only one ever said "thank you" or even gave a nod,
As brook fed and clothed them with his golden rod.
That one was a poet, well known in the least,
Blessed it with his verse and for the fishy feast.
"The brook did recover, it took a long, long while."
The little branch he told me, told me with a smile.
As I walk through the forest and stop by the brook,
He passes me a drink, near the best I ever took.
He keeps his tales a secret in his book of gold.
With closed eyes I listen and hear them unfold.
The golden leaves are floating from the sky above,
Brook's friends are saying, "Adieu, adieu, with love."

James Arthur Hipsher
*Beaverton, OR*

[Hometown] *Igloo, SD (no longer exists)* [Ed] *college degree engineering* [Occ] *retired US Treasury* [Hobbies] *writing poetry, books, golf, performing, teaching, playing the harmonica and piano.* [GA] *making it to the ninth decade*

*Poetry to me is a blessing that speaks volumes with brevity. As a husband, father, grandfather, college grad, 1968 Vietnam vet, retired thirty-five years. US Treasury employee and reached the four score mark. Poetry remains the heart and soul of my being. I am a poet, musician, author and perform recitations of one to two hours of many poets' works as well as my own, always from memory free as a community service and have for over fifty years. Nature is always a great poetic adventure subject.*

## The Next Life

When I leave this world, I hope that someone will remember me,
Not by my indiscretions of the past, but what I turned out to be.
Will I again be able to see the ones I loved so much when I was here,
Or will I just see that they will never again be near.
I've often wondered what Heaven would turn out to be;
Often I've prayed that one day there would be a place there for me.
In my heart I've always believed that I've done the best I could,
And praying many times that I forever would.
My mistakes of the past, I can only hope will not follow me,
And that in the end I'll be where I've always wanted to be.

Louis M. Graziaplena
*Orlando, FL*

[Hometown] *Baltimore, MD* [Ed] *high school graduate* [Occ] *retired Maryland state employee*
[Hobbies] *reading, writing poetry, fishing* [GA] *4 years and 4 months in the US Navy, National Service Medal*

*Louis is of the Italian heritage. Both of his grandparents were born in Italy. He was born and raised Catholic. He has been living in Orlando, FL since June of 1995. Louis has two children—a daughter he lives with in Orlando and a son who lives in Bear, DE. Lou retired from the MVA in Glen Burnie, MD after thirty years. He also retired from the state of Florida after six years service. Lou has four grandchildren and two great-grandchildren.*

## Broken

Sitting here at the kitchen table looking out into
the darkness of night so broken-hearted won't even
allow myself to cry not one tear can fall from my eyes
cannot show weakness, not for a lie even though my
heart is in so many pieces because I believed the
things that were said I trusted things would change
even when they never did I went along for the ride
knowing it probably was all a lie I will never
understand how you could speak harm on your
own mother, now I'm sitting here broken like
shattered glass mangled inside while smiling
on the outside because I believed all your lies
now I'm simply broken and tore up inside

Karol Earlina Toliver
*Jacksonville, FL*

[Hometown] *My hometown is in Bolingbrook, IL* [Ed] *I am in the process of getting my bachelor's degree in English with a minor in creative writing at UNF.* [Occ] *mail handler with the United States Postal Service with 24 years of service this year* [Hobbies] *watching Marvel and DC movies, and reading* [GA] *I just finished my first screenplay.*

*I am a mother with four beautiful children and a Nana to two. I love being with family when time allows. I look forward to graduation next year so I can travel out of the country. I'm looking forward to living my best life.*

## Following in Your Footsteps

The temple Kinkaku-ji is reflected in the still water
The cherry blossoms create a natural frame.
I turn and pose for a picture.
I am standing where my grandfather stood.
Snow still paints the wooden houses white
In Ishikawa mom tries
Gold covered ice cream.
Did you eat gold covered ice cream Grandpapa?
It is quiet,
Despite the crowd of visitors,
The Hiroshima Memorial
Is simple.
I take our 100 paper cranes
We folded
And hung them with the rest.
We can hang these cranes together Grandpapa.
The deers rub their heads against my leg
Bowing to receive their treat.
Did Grandpapa feed the deer like me?
Tōdai-ji Buddhist temple is grand,
I slid through the "nostril,"
To seek enlightenment in the next life.
 "Oh Kaire, you went too fast,
I didn't get a good picture!"
My fellow travelers protest.
I hope Grandpapa was granted enlightenment in the next life.

Klaire Karina Suzanne Mason
*Brookhaven, GA*

[Hometown] *Atlanta, GA* [Occ] *college student* [Hobbies] *traveling, writing, listening to music* [GA]
*publishing a poem in Emory's* Lullwater Review

## Mia

I reminisce about all of the moments she was there—
the times I looked around the locker room
comparing myself to them,
all the times he chose someone else.
Every time, she stood by my side.
I remember times so dark
I thought I was not worth saving,
but she was always there, holding my hand.
Whenever I needed her,
she cradled and comforted me.
Senior year of high school, everything changed.
Our relationship became wearisome.
She held me close when I needed someone—
So close she was suffocating me.
I felt as though I didn't need anyone else,
so I pushed all others away.
She was controlling me,
but every time I tried to let her go, I couldn't.
I needed her.
I don't think of her often, but when I do,
her presence feels just as compelling
as she did when I met her:
beautiful, exquisite, inviting and warm.
Controlling, dominate, and dangerous.

Amore Norell Berger
*Watertown, CT*

[Hometown] *Torrington* [Ed] *criminal justice major* [Occ] *head teacher* [Hobbies] *crafting, reading, crocheting*
*When I think of all the things I was supposed to succeed at so far, I feel insignificant. However, I have done a lot that many people do not see or know. This is my second publication with Eber & Wein, and I am happy to say that a coping mechanism has turned into a hobby. Without my past experiences, I would not be where I am today, and I am proud to be who I am: shaping little hearts and minds every day. I can show my students that anyone can be an author; you just have to put your mind to it.*

## Job Description

I'm often asked, by inquisitive minds
As a poet, what do you do?
My answer feigns the illusive,
With hope to the rare and few.
I seek to express the human condition
In words that color and texture
The tapestry that I weave. . .
Though at times the product seems
Unfinished, and an area rug
Is the remnant to leave.

Timothy John Mattson
*Los Angeles, CA*

[Hometown] *Los Angeles, CA* [Ed] *BA psychology, MBA management* [Occ] *retired* [Hobbies] *most sports, golf, sudoku, new tool technology, cosmology & physics, chess.* [GA] *publishing my first book of poetry in 2020*

*I've lived with privilege and poverty, as well as, both strength and injury. My interest in poetry began late in my life during three years of homelessness, and has continued to now. For the past eight years, this effort has given me some meaning and direction, to express my thoughts in a great variety of ways. As a self-described, "warrior poet," I'm hopeful to continue these battles for years to come.*

## I Don't Lie

She's sure you know,
when she walks in the room;
If you should miss it,
she'll let you know soon;

She's only got her in mind,
she's taking you for a ride;
Tame you if she can,
if not, eill she tried;

With eyes as blue as the cloudless sky,
hair like the blackest night;
Tongue with the fire of satan's den,
a look that an kill, I don't lie.

Her skin so fair, so soft, so white,
her words so tender in the night;
Then you're awakened by her violent dream,
you look at her and you scream!

Her eyes are as red as the setting sun,
her hair standing right up straight;
Her tongue got a split down the middle,
she wants a meal, and you're the bait your heart's on a plate.

William R. Miller
*Janesville, WI*

[Hometown] *Janesville, WI* [Ed] *high school graduate* [Occ] *retired union construction laborer* [Hobbies] *hunting fishing, drummer singer, poet, writing short stories and songs* [GA] *learning to stay positive even when times are hard*

### Ode to the House Cat

An alley cat's world is trouble and strife,
And a barn cat's a pet until he finds a wife.
The wild cat has claws like the point of a knife,
But a house cat's a kitten all of her life.

Marian Louise Malone
*Lincoln, NE*

[Hometown] *Lincoln, NE* [Ed] *two associate degrees* [Occ] *retired, do a lot of volunteering* [Hobbies] *freelance writing, antiquing, knitting, adult coloring* [GA] *getting my poems published with Eber & Wein*

*I have always enjoyed a close relationship with my grandmother. She loved animals, especially cats, as much as I did. She also read to me from the time I could sit up and taught me to love all forms of literature, including poetry. Today I am enjoying a quiet life with my cats.*

## The Traveler

I am a time traveler wandering through space
and time. Walking down a path unknown a road
to finding a true love that I need to call my own.
I am a traveler searching for the truth like the
gypsy that I am. Traveling through the years in
space and time. Looking for that guy who will
be mine.

I am a traveler, traveling upon the open seas.
My face is not my own and no one sees.
I am that traveler who never has doubts about
the unknown. Thinking back to the places that
I have roamed. I am a traveler I have now
found what I seek. My soulmate who will
love me forever and that feels really great.

Traveling from upon those open seas, together
we have become one walking down that path
unknown. Together we will forever roam.
Knowing we have found our home.
I am that time traveler who now can travel
back in space and time with my soulmate—I can't
wait. We will go into the future where we will
roam, finding new adventures, a place to
settle down with a brand new home.

Cheri Campbell
*Omaha, NE*

[Hometown] *Omaha, NE* [Ed] *high school* [Occ] *service associate* [Hobbies] *writing poetry, storm chasing, reading* [GA] *to publish a novel*
*I was born in Omaha, NE. I have lived here all of my life. Started writing poetry at a very young age. I like to hang out with my family and friends when I'm not working. There are many things that inspire my poems, most come from life and stuff I feel.*

## Man in the Cage

Man life was so simple back then.
Playing football with my brother in the house right before Dad comes home
The fear of getting caught used to be the thrill,
Having fun was my priority,
Nowadays I look to the left nobody, I look to the right nobody
I look at the back know all I see is anxiety mixed with shameless doubt
I look to the front there is a cage
Wait who is the man in it, this man looks like he has been going through it.
He stares at me, then yells at me, *"Let me out."*
There is my anxiety again
Ughhh, I hate this feeling, the chills it gives me.
Who caused this? Did I do this? No,
Where is the self accountability
Why this man stares at me? I do not know.
This man looks like me. Oh crap this man is me,
What have I done
What have I done to me,
When did this start?
When did I start to doubt myself?, When did I start not to feel loved?
Look at it now, how my self doubts wrecked me.
He is waiting to come out, I must let him out.
God please help me escape!

Otito E. Nzesi
*Silver Spring, MD*

[Hometown] *Silver Spring, MD* [Ed] *bachelor's degree* [Occ] *marketing specialist* [Hobbies] *writing poetry, cooking* [GA] *graduating from university*

*A couple weeks I have graduated from Frostburg, MD, but I still do not know what to do with my life. So I wrote this poem inspired how I out my faith in God to get me out of this—clear up this foggy situation.*

## Sitting by the Creek Makes Me Glad

Sitting by the creek makes me glad.
I think of all of the good times I've had.
Catching fish and skipping stones,
Feeling great all through my bones.
Whether by myself or with a friend,
I felt like it was the living end.
Laying on my back and staring all around,
looking at the sky or at the ground.
They truly were peaceful times,
enjoying all of nature's signs.
Seeing a rabbit or a squirrel at play,
I really didn't want to go away.
So find a creek and stay awhile,
I'm certain it will make you smile.
It will take your mind off all the hustle,
and calm you from the entire bustle.

Jim Lee Shanabarger
*Clearwater, FL*

[Hometown] *Clearwater, FL* [Ed] *high school graduate, honorably discharged from USMC* [Occ] *retired* [Hobbies] *writing poetry, watching television, surfing the Internet, going to the movies with my wife* [GA] *performing a Blues Brother's tribute act in front of 72,000 people*

*I really enjoy writing poems. I especially enjoy writing about Jesus Christ. He's my Savior and my dearest friend. I have a website where I publish a lot of the poems I write.*

## Glitter Royal Blue Poinsettia

A large glitter royal blue poinsettia
arrived at our house as a gift.
Though blatantly unnatural, it was attractive
in a seasonal sort of way:
"where the treetops glisten" and
"in the lane, snow is glistening."
The natural white bracts of this plant
had been sprayed with harmless royal blue dye,
and then festively sprinkled with
thousands of minuscule flakes of lustrous plastic,
resembling confetti in a ticker tape parade
down Broadway in New York City.
Some new white bracts peek out
like an old lady who quit dyeing her hair.
I realize these new designer poinsettias
are regarded as the fashionable glitterati
of flowers adorning winter holiday homes.
Regardless, my own money will be spent
on the indigenous cultivars in shades of
crimson, white, scarlet, coral, and pink.

David Mayer Gradwohl
*Ames, IA*

[Hometown] *Lincoln, NE* [Ed] *PhD in anthropology* [Occ] *Professor Emeritus of anthropology, archaeology, and American Indian studies* [Hobbies] *walking, hiking, reading, music* [GA] *co-parenting three wonderful children*

*I've written poetry since I was a child, mentored by my mother, Elaine Mayer Gradwohl, who was a wordsmith and lover of poetry. I treasure the writing and poetry classes I had in high school and college. In my younger days, I liked mountain climbing and backpacking.*

## Eyes

Eyes that see the darkness of the world
Eyes that see the sadness of all
Eyes that see so much despair
Eyes that see and question
Eyes try to focus
Eyes see nothing
Eyes pleading
For change
Now
Before
We have lost
All hopes and dreams
Of a better place
Where light banishes dark
Where solutions are working
Where eyes can see beauty again
Where eyes see compassion for others
Where eyes recognize an answer
Where eyes see the reflection
Where the view becomes clear
Where the arrow is
Pointing backward
Towards home
Towards
Me

Melanie K. Graves
*Zephyrhills, FL*

[Hometown] *Willowick, OH* [Occ] *retired* [Hobbies] *writing poetry, reading, painting, planting flowers, baking* [GA] *I am an author of one poetry book that was published November 2019.*

*I have been writing poetry since early 2018 after retiring and relocating to Florida from Ohio. Inspiration for my poems is found in nature, life experiences, faith, famous quotes, or a specific word.*

## Fighting the Battle

We know that you are tired and battling
Battling for all of us; strangers and loved ones too
We know that you are fighting the hard fight
A fight that you never imagined having to fight
We know that you are on the front lines
That you may not get a break
From clocking in to clocking out you always fight
Not just for us, but also your family
As you help people that you may or may not know
As you give of your time and strength
Your sweat and your everything just like family
You give your life and love for others
No matter how tired you get, you keep going
As you continue to fight, we will walk beside you
We will follow your example
You are our heroes and the greatest and we praise you
Today we thank you and pray for you
Our amazing heroes, family, and friends
Remember that we are grateful and we love you
Remember that we care about you
We honor and love you
You are on our minds and in our hearts
On a daily basis as we pray for your safety
From start to finish and the time in between
We could never be more grateful
To those who are fighting the battle

Laurie Ann Monica Dain
*Akron, OH*

[Hometown] *Akron, OH* [Ed] *associate's degree in business administration* [Occ] *administrative assistant* [Hobbies] *writing, singing, piano* [GA] *being published in two books*
*I dedicate this poem to those who are on the front line of this coronavirus pandemic. Thank you for your time and dedication to help people whom you may or may not know. I am very grateful. We are all very grateful.*

## A Day's Drive

A drive along the coast sees open life along the sea
Feeling the soft wind blow through one's hair
With soft wind whispering *You're a beautiful site*
The suns setting—soft rays bounce off the moon
Revealing life's end to another day and the
Beginning of nighttimes beauty is revealed
Stars so bright they light up the black hastened sky
Yet so full of vigor the sky sparkles with emotions
It fills one's soul with excitement and puts a beat into
Your heart—seagulls not to be seen—only shadows
Flying in the night—the pounding of waves on the
Shore make the sounds of life revealed
Shooting stars fly past looking for a place to go
Not knowing where they came from
The sun coming up in the east signals a night's end
With the sun's rays a new day begins
And another day's drive begins—Anika
"I could conquer the world with one hand
As long as you are holding the other!"
On a day's drive

John E. Contreras
Valencia, CA

[Hometown] *Valencia, CA* [Ed] *Heritage University, London* [Occ] *retired/author* [Hobbies] *fishing, golfing, music, writing* [GA] *surviving the Vietnam War*

## Crème Brûlée

Splattered
The crème brûlée pastry pan
I have paid the price
Second degree burns
My right foot
My left foot, my left arm
Oh, what a pain
A rising temperature to 275 degrees
Rained down hot water, hot cream
Streaming down my cook shoes
Splashed in the air
Yelp for help!
Adrenaline peaking the extremes
Wishing cold water could have been a better splash
Only ice-cold water had saved my blistering skin
Numb
Temporary moments felt like a century
My chef's reaction misty to be a concern
Humor was a response to my accident
Could bear enough to wear shoes
Shoes the very moment were
Brown paper towels wrapped around my feet
Forced to walk a block down to CVS
For a doctor's response
A horrid moment of my life
Following day
Ambitious
Passed my NYC permit test
Oy vey, what a painful way to see the light!

Lissandra Molina
*Bronx, NY*

## America

It was all fun and games until prom was over
no one knew how uncomfortable her heels had become
how her makeup made her eye itch
how her head hurt from the continuous guitar strum
the after-party was all anyone talked about
she took off her shoes and headed to the bathroom
she made her way down the hallway and
peered in through a door
the sight before her was scary, unnatural, and impure
he threw himself off the girl and ran away
he didn't realize that she saw his face
she rushed in to help the girl who was full of fright
and alcohol on her tongue
and called a cab that took them out of sight
the next day she went to the police station
she reported what she had seen
the policeman told her he'd look into it
a weight lifted off her shoulders as she
resumed her daily routine
she went to school on the following Monday
she thought it was something out of a dream
rumors were spread around her that were not true
she didn't know he was the captain of the football team

Sarah J. Lemesh
*Brownsville, PA*

*To all the women who mustered up the courage, and to those who are still in the process.*

## Ink

When I was little,
my stories were all in crayon.
They were bright,
colorful,
and honest;
that was before everything turned to ink,
from an old gel pen,
inconsistent,
dull,
and dark.
And now here I am,
almost sixteen,
changing,
learning,
studying,
about to turn to the next blank page.

Ava Madison Lo Manto
*Rochelle Park, NJ*

[Hometown] *Rochelle Park*  [Ed] *high school*

## Shallow to Deep

Asking for help
Feels too exposed
Showing vulnerability
Treading lightly in the shallow
Perfection, perception
Keeps you at arm's length
The positive persona
Keeps me from showing my scars
Searching for peace, bracing
To ride the wave of emotion
Grieving on my own, alone
Isolated yet safe
Masking the flaws
Minimizing the pain
Hidden is the inner beauty
Drowning beneath the façade
Growing closer is stalled
Until I am brave enough
To reveal my true authenticity
By inviting you into the deep.

Robin Jenest Lezotte
*Davidson, NC*

[Hometown] *Franklin, MA* [Ed] *MBA* [Occ] *higher education* [Hobbies] *writing, traveling, spending quality time with friends* [GA] *being a mom to my precious daughter, Rachel Elizabeth*

*After losing my beloved mother, Marjorie Mae, earlier this year (2021), I reflected upon the journey of grief and loss.*

## Our God

Our God has an awesome imagination.
When he looked out in space,
He spoke the world into existence.
First thing he spoke was the word,
Then he divided it between day and night.
He added the water and plenty of land.
He spoke fish of all kind into the sea
And filled the sky with beautiful birds.
Then he made animals of all kind,
But then he noticed something was missing.
He said: I will make me a man.
So he took the sand from off the land
And formed him what is now called man.
He breathed life into the form he had made.
He noticed that Adam as he called him,
Was all by himself and lonely
So he said: I will make him a mate.
As the story about Eve goes on,
She disobeyed God and wouldn't listen.
So for punishment today,
Old satan is still loose.
He will tempt you and try you
Like he did Eve. This is God's world
So don't let satan deceive you and take it.

Elizabeth Fredricks
*Port Saint Lucie, FL*

[Hometown] *Olcott, WV* [Ed] *high school* [Occ] *retired riviter* [Hobbies] *poetry, puzzles and books* [GA] *becoming born again January 7, 1961*

*I love poetry. I am eighty-seven years old and have arthritis in my hand so that I can no longer write. Here is my last thought. I hope you will accept it. I have more poems that I hope will someday be read. I have been a Christian since January 7, 1961 and can't live without the Lord.*

# Pendulums

shorter hours bring
longer miles
distant lights break through darkness
like egg shell cracks in plaster walls
white-striped seconds
breeze past
the cool wandering Sabinal river
bound
by lanky cypress trees
pendulums
to a lone wind traveling back to Utopia

Rodger Cunningham
*Atascosa, TX*

[Hometown] *Atascosa, TX* [Ed] *2 years college, majors in English and psychology* [Occ] *technical services manager (HVACR, electrical and plumbing trades)* [Hobbies] *puttering (that's a technical term)* [GA] *living this long*

*Born in December of 1950 in Hondo, TX raised in Utopia, TX until stricken with a serious illness that required experimental X-ray treatments in San Antonio, TX. It was that occurrence that influenced my family to relocate closer to the facility where I received my treatments. Both grandparents resided in Utopia and I loved the country life as much as I loved them, so I visited as often as I could. I was blessed with having grown up in the country and the city; something no doubt shaped how I perceived life and my environment. The formal education I've received as well as the practical knowledge I acquired meld together as curiosity and creativity in my thinking, my writing and my humor. I write to record the experiences, thoughts, and observations—at times in their entirety and often in phrases set aside to percolate on at a future time.*

## Inside

I smile all the time,
Do you see the pain?
Even though I laugh,
The darkness still remains.
How can you possibly see,
see right through my wall?
If so, then you hide it well
You act like you know nothing at all…
Do you really see it?
The hurt, sorrow, pointless pain of it all…
I don't, I can't, cry anymore,
My eyes are raw.
It eats me up inside
I wish I could describe it…
Some way you can understand…
Depression… that's it

Amanda Wisniewski Tolliver
*Angier, NC*

[Hometown] *Asheville* [Ed] *some college* [Occ] *state employee* [Hobbies] *writing, piano*

*I have always suffered from depression and I am a huge believer in being open about it because I feel that it may help others in the same situation and make an impact on someone's life.*

## Old Days

Old days
If we could go back, we'd wear coonskin hats,
cut our wood with a Daniel Boone ax,
carry our sacks on mule's back,
use old shack out back.
Old days
If we could go back we'd pick beans and eat chicken wings.
We'd raise fields of cotton,
in fields that are long forgotten.
We'd sit around the old cook stove
and listen for the rooster's crow.
Old days
If we could go back we'd use oil lamps and one-cent stamps,
eat flapjacks and black strap,
listen to old stories and fall asleep on the floor.

Elizabeth Bowman
*Clintwood, VA*

[Hometown] *Clintwood, VA* [Occ] *housewife* [Hobbies] *raising chickens, working outside, ginsing* [GA] *having a story published in hometown book*

*I am a housewife married fifty-one years.*

## Life

Life is full of
　　Pleasures and woes;
Onward it goes,
　　Skipping over our
　　　Troubles
Or bursting our dream's
　　　Bubbles.
It's made up of laughter
　　And tears,
Knowledge and fears;
　　Continuing all of our years.

Patricia Jo Long
*Terra Bella, CA*


## There Can Be Love

Why live in the dark
There can be love
I won't jump into the past
There can be love
Dreams can be love
There can be love

Jack Camp
*Boston, MA*

[Hometown] *Boston*  [Hobbies] *bowling, songwriter*

## Forgiveness' Reflection

You speak with conviction, expecting and wishing,
Thus, making things happen and come to fruition.
Indeed, you have power that soars like a tower,
Which brings forth new life as a warm summer shower.
Oh, your face how it glows as bright as pure snow,
To inspire and set forth a quick heart-pounding hope.
Smooth and subtle, clear unmuttle and tightly huddled,
Smiling giggles, warm with tickles, both big and little
Yea, what is the secret and how do you keep it,
The soul-saving salve of this daunting riddle?
The answer is simple, it is as simple as living.
It rests in your being when you are all-forgiving.
Even now being confronted both wounded, tormented,
By walls of isolation that seeks to cement ya.
Burdens crushing in pounds to keep you down,
With sharp piercing arrows which cut to the marrow,
Entrapping the heart in shadows of dark matter.
But with a power steadfast from a heart that is glad,
Which do not hold malice in neither future nor past,
With happiness you laugh through the good and bad.
Holding you to the path for life's very best.

Thomas L. Laidler
*Macomb, MI*

[Hometown] *Orlando, FL* [Ed] *high school, US Navy, ITT Institute (CAD)* [Occ] *USPS employee*
[Hobbies] *drawing, writing, musical instruments* [GA] *published author*

*I've always loved drawing and later in high school found a passion for writing to be able to convey positive and uplifting words of inspiration in various formats. I married my wife Madonna of thirty-five years and have two children. I'm a minister of my church and hope to continue writing in such a way to enrich peoples lives for the better.*

## It's Always Been You

I want something that's real
Something that's too good to be true
Something that's too good to lose
Something that goes both ways
I want to be a team not enemies
I want to fight and make up
I want to be mad and us still sleep along side one another
I want to sit down and *we both* say what's on our minds
I want to be on a whole other level than anyone else has before
I want us to be like no other couple
I don't want our relationship to be normal what is normal
You get me, I get you type of deal
I want to love again, to trust again, to have that happiness again
I want that feeling that nobody but you can bring
I want you

Destany Seirra Landman
*Warren, OH*

[Hometown] *Warren, OH*  [GA] *becoming a licensed massage therapist*

*My whole life I've searched for someone to love me like I would love them. But that person found me when I stopped searching. If it's not meant to be stop and take a step back and find yourself. Then and only then is when you leave yourself open to find what it is you seek.*

## A Tree in Memory

The wind blows, rustling the leaves of a tree
You spoke to me as we sat together on the grass
Why do I hear your voice now?

When the scorching sunlight almost burned my face,
you shifted the tree branches to shade and protect me.
Why do I feel your love now?

Your face, once obscure, sharpens slowly.
Only now do I feel gratitude for you.
You were so kind to me.

Have you forgotten me?
Our time together was short
Though the memory has lasted until now

A decade of time has passed
You would not recognize me
My face has changed too much
Why does this old memory of you
Cause me to be heartbroken now?

Myoung Soo Kim
*Fremont, CA*

[Hometown] *Fremont, CA* [Ed] *BS in pharmacy, EWHA Women University and finished pharmacy program UC in San Francisco* [Occ] *pharmacist in California* [Hobbies] *reading, writing, hiking* [GA] *published a fiction*

## Longshot

Standing on the other side of a
wing and a prayer
that you make it through the storm
over the bridge
down the river
courage to take the test
having the pride to let go
showing compassion when it wasn't deserved
earning back trust
be still and listen to the other side
because the grass is not always greener
be in it for the long haul or the hot days
working to mend the problem without pay
Taking unintentional actions
Just to chance the outcome of it all
trying to scratch an itch
that will not stop itching
Having the faith of a mustard seed
only to get it all over a white shirt
connections from old friends
going back to the way it was done
before updating began
Knowing the due date of understanding
that it must be handled
the hardness of it will make you weak in the knees

Lora Graham
*San Augustine, TX*

[Hometown] *Marianna, AR*  [Ed] *Stratford Career Institute*  [Occ] *care partner for Home Health*
[Hobbies] *songwriting, crochet, sewing, watching TV, movies*  [GA] *being able to write*

*I am Baptist being able to write. Trying to write my way through this last year and half and counting.*

## Shadows of Love

When I look at you, I see me
 What is this power you have over me, I think
 about you all the time, wishing and praying you
 were mine
You look at me and turn away, without ever having
 a word to say. I think I love you, I don't know
 yet, do you love me, want to make a bet
How can you see me, what can I do
 I really want to be with you. Time has passed
 and still no dice are we ever going to feel
 some rice
You get me so confused, till I can't think. I cry
 so much, till my eyes are pink
I see us together in our house one child,
 maybe two with love in our hearts, and
 smiles on our faces, there is no need
 to change places
I heard you got married the other day so I guess
 there is not much left to say

Rochelle Jones
*Country Club Hills, IL*

[Hometown] *Chicago, IL* [Ed] *BA in education and retired as a special education teacher* [Occ] *doing what I want to do*

*I was born in Chicago, IL. My father was a WWII vet and my mother was a businesswoman managing her father's many businesses. I had a sister and brother who are both deceased, and my father died when I was ten. I was baptized a Roman Catholic and still practice my religion to this day. I am married and have two sons, Antonio and Steven, whom I love with all my heart. I have three granddaughters who light up my life. I have training in teaching students with disabilities and working with adults with Alzheimer's.*

## A Poeter's Vow

My thoughts float upon the cloudless zephyr; across
The inner plains and meadows of my psyche; laden with moss
For, you, my reader shant never be left at a loss
The fields of thought are bestrewn with copses, words that emboss
Each line is written above and below with verbal artistry
Building each quatrain, framed like carpentry
Buttressing each thought with reinforced masonry
Avoiding truncation to spell out this baroque verbal pageantry
By planting the seeds of dreams in the mental fields
Ploughed and furrowed, borne by it yields
Produced on the pages, hence all books used as literary shields
For in the jousting of thoughts is the poeter's power to wield
The prowess of the poeter's trade is not an oddity
Nor has it ever been labeled an anomaly
Albeit, literature remains the world's greatest commodity

Dane R. Burgess
*Arlington, WA*

[Hometown] *Arlington* [Ed] *United States Navy veteran of 20 years* [Occ] *Department of Navy police sergeant* [Hobbies] *small scale farming* [GA] *my children*

## Cognizance

I have really lost mine
It is nowhere to be found
Scalpels could not cut as fine
No matter how well ground
I just cannot find mine
Having looked high and low
In the gas lamp's waning shine
Doubting all that I know
Today I shall regain mine
Always aware of the cost
To be the one to draw the line
Recovering all I have lost

Michael Landis
*Everett, WA*

[Hometown] *Everett, WA* [Ed] *high school* [Occ] *CNC machinist* [Hobbies] *poetry, video games*
[GA] *being a mentor*

*I am a fifty-five-year-old machinist who had always been inspired by quantum mechanics and science fiction, but I found myself writing about how awful we are to each other and to our world. I have been witness to a hurricane, several tornadoes, an erupting volcano, and have even fought forest fires in the conservation corps. These experiences have shown me that my true inspiration has been the human spirit of cooperation and support during times of tribulation.*

## Telegram from a Bottle

I am a bottle
Somewhat of a role model
Made of plastic I am
Though now a bit hostile
Thrown out to sea with a slam
I now float beside a clam
For you I am more than disgraced
So I write this telegram
From the world I was not erased
I was simply misplaced
Garbage at sea
Now I am called a waste
Trashing me
Cutting down a tree
Extinct soon the bees
Recycling me is the key
When will you learn
To have more concern?

Carolyn Croop
*Farmington, NY*

## Your Arms

Tho other arms have held me and lips have kissed me, too.
But in your arms my darling I know your love is true.
Since I've met you darling and you've proved your
love is true, the world has been my oyster and I owe it all to you.
The gifts you've given plenty and lovely as they are,
the love you give me sweetheart could reach beyond the stars.
The days are filled with sweetness never knowing
what you'll do, the nights are filled with wonders
as I spend them all with you.
Our love has been the binder that held us two as
one; my life would be so lonely if there was only one.
So hold our candle tightly and let our love flame burn,
until the candle's melted and our life on Earth is done.
The arms that held me tightly and never strayed away
still holds the woman in me, as we grow old and gray.
*For Gerry*

Willie Viola Bowden
*Lancaster, CA*

[Hometown] *Havre De Grace, MD* [Ed] *AV college* [Occ] *life skills coach* [Hobbies] *writing, gardening, traveling, and my grandchildren* [GA] *raising my children*

*I worked as a waitress for years before I became a life skills coach. I married young and my children have been my strength. My husband inspired much of my poetry. We now live in southern California an have ten grandchildren and five great-grandchildren. Retirement is lovely.*

## My Sanctuary

Looking back to the first day we met—
I knew as soon as I looked into your eyes
you would be my safe harbor. Such a
beautiful woman with gorgeous, big, blue
eyes that I could get lost in forever. I
have loved you through the good and bad
times as you have loved me. When I
hold you close I know you will forever be
my sanctuary, where my heart and soul
have only known peace and love. I will
forever carry you with me wherever I may
go. God blessed me with you and for that
I will forever be grateful. You are and will
always be my soulmate, my wife who has
touched my heart with love, understanding,
tenderness and joy. You are now and will
always be my sanctuary. I love you now and
for infinity.

Shannon L. O'Kelley
*Gordo, AL*

*Dedicated to Trish O'Kelley (October 2, 1959 - December 18, 2015). Trish is my sister's late wife who died from lung cancer. I tried to see my sister's, Lisa O'Kelley, love for Trish through her eyes. She will always be loved by our family.*

## Memories

Good, bad
Funny and sad.
Each snippet is a moment in time
That we will want to remember forever.
People come and go from our lives,
But we have the memories to remind us
Of the pain and joy.
The precious time spent with those we love
Become tales of elation to tell after they are gone.
We thrive for these moments,
These stories to tell,
So this together will live on forever.

Emily Gail Norton
*Mount Washington, KY*

[Hometown] *Mount Washington, KY* [Ed] *master's degree in teaching* [Occ] *special education teacher* [Hobbies] *writing, spending time with friends and family, listening to podcasts* [GA] *my first published poem*

*Writing has always been more than a hobby but a way to cope. I have written this poem in memory of my uncle, who recently passed away from cancer. It's one more way to keep his memory alive.*

## A Quest Fulfilled

He reached the summit of the mountain,
 Bidding farewell to the sun fading over the horizon.
He sat patiently for the moon to rise,
Waiting for it to be directly overhead,
And reaching out, touched it.

Mark Brainard Pinney
*Binghamton, NY*

[Hometown] *Deposit, NY* [Ed] *work experience* [Occ] *mental health counselor* [Hobbies] *reading, music, fishing* [GA] *my children*

*There's not much to tell. I have worked in Human Services all of my adult life. I have two adult children and three grandchildren. I am a widower. I have dabbled in poetry and the occasional short story since I was a teenager.*

# In My Backyard There Be Dragons

A dragonfly we call the Red Menace
Divebombed the pool time and time again.
Was he fishing for mosquito larva or
Staking out his territory?
Maybe it was a ritual known only to red dragonflies
His transparent cousins kept their distance
And never displayed their divebombing skills
In his presence.
He stayed only long enough to ensure that
His cousins knew he lived up to his name
Then darted in a red flash over the wall to
Inspect other pools he claimed as his own.
Petite Komodo comes out only in the midday sun.
He crawls majestically along the wall
Stopping now and then to huff and puff
Warning the grasshoppers, a dragon is on the hunt.
Ignoring his pretensions, a hummingbird
Inspects him up close from his rotating eyes
To his nipped-off tail, blowing his cover.
Exposed, he slinks off down the wall
To hide in the ivy to sulk alone in his shame.
In the face of a hummingbird Petite Komodo has
Been reduced to a lizard with a nipped-off tail once again.
In my backyard there be dragons.

Terry Underwood O'Banion
*Cathedral City, CA*

[Hometown] *Palm Springs, CA* [Ed] *PhD in higher education administration* [Occ] *professor of higher education* [Hobbies] *cooking* [GA] *breaking the poverty cycle for my children*

## Sister's for Life

A friend from long ago
We spent lots of hours at children's hospitals as you
Know, walking and talking about our kids. Not sure from
Day to day which one would go by the way.
A friend for life, sisters by sight
Walking and talking all night.
Through the hustle an bustle
Laughter and tears throughout the years
Walking and talking day and night.
In God's eyes in hindsight
Sisters by day and by night.

Lanaye K. Jewson and Laura Seidenkranz
Lena, WI

[Hometown] *Lena, WI* [Ed] *nursing* [Occ] *medical field* [Hobbies] *outdoors* [GA] *my children*

*To those who have children with a disability, this poem is for those who walk and talk day at night.*

## The Perfect Storm

The sound of falling raindrops
Softly fills the air
The sight of anxious fireflies
And June bugs everywhere
Far off into the distance
I hear the thunder crash
Rumbling through the valley
Then the lightning's sudden flash
I lay my head upon your chest
And gently call your name
I dream about the coming storm
Flowing through my veins
The hunger and the longing
Two bodies intertwined
The moment of belonging
Two hearts forever bind
Your touch is warm and tender
A tangled mass of sheets
The love I feel inside me
Two souls are now complete
And as I gaze into your eyes
My heart is sad no more
For the sweetest thing God ever made
Was create the perfect storm

Lesa D. Costa
*Redding, CA*

[GA] *my son*

## Seeing Joy

I saw a man with two young sons
on a bicycle built for three
they seemed to be having so much fun
that I could feel the jealousy
swell inside of me
as I sat in my car when they passed by
but I resisted the impulse to cry
for the joy of witnessing such a happy scene
which for me could only be a dream
because I was on my way home
where I lived…alone.

Donald Gene Millner
*Durham, NC*

[Hometown] *Durham, NC* [Ed] *associate, bachelor and master's degrees in electrical engineering; study toward a doctorate in education* [Occ] *retired engineering manager and training development manager* [Hobbies] *popular music history from the 1970s and 1980s* [GA] *my two children and four grandkids*

*Donald G. Millner is a retired engineer/engineering manager and training developer/training manager. He currently resides in Durham, NC and is enjoying a life of leisure as a parent and doting grandparent.*

## Try Our Lord God

Try our Lord God—the
Retirement Benefits
are FABULOUS!
(for the wages of sin is death, but the gift
of God is eternal life in Christ our Lord.
Don't be afraid of change or becoming more involved.
He is awesome, the God of all knowing, and He is the
Alpha and Omega. Our Mediator is glorious!

Ethelyn Barnes
*Kansas City, MO*

[Hometown] *Kansas City, MO* [Occ] *data transcriber* [Hobbies] *reading, writing, enjoying my family, helping others* [GA] *becoming a grandparent*

## The Game

For the love of the game I give my all
In the dark and shadows I promise to not fall
To continue the game is my main desire
To protect it and keep it is my fire
My motivation, the one thing I see with perfect vision
In patience, I'll hold close my main mission
The root of my love will never be abandoned
Of myself, progress and perfection is commanded
For my success in this partnership is seen in the light
However my work and improvements are made in the night

Elijah Will Cochran
*Absecon, NJ*

## A Colorful Journey

From the day you are born,
you begin a journey with family and friends
that is filled with adventures, sharing, and caring.

Each step you take gets you closer to your dream
and once you find it, your journey comes to an end
and fills your heart with hope and love.

Ariana Mary Holmes
*Thief River Falls, MN*

[Hometown] *Thief River Falls, MN* [Ed] *high school graduate* [Occ] *OAC, variety of jobs* [Hobbies] *reading, swimming, horses, and writing* [GA] *published author of poetry and a book called* Princess and the Zombie

*My name is Ariana Mary Holmes. I have lived in Thief River Falls, MN since and I was born. I am the youngest born of two children. I am autistic but it doesn't define me. I am a published author and my goal is to write another book. I get much encouragement from family and friends. I enjoy books, horses, swimming, and work three to four days a week.*

# From the Cliffs

From this rock lip I watch the sea
Beneath me, crashing over stone.
I smell the scent of salt wafting
Up to catch the wind and vanish.

My dark hair ruffles, twisting through
Wind and the barest of sea brine.
From the cliffs I turn, and am struck
By your embrace, fingers grasping.

I watch as you move close, kissing
My mouth, tasting the crisp air's salt.
Back to the liquid horizon
We look, waiting on the sun's drop.

Huddling close, we lay, gazing up
To the night sky: a brilliant moon,
Infinite stars, churning clouds, wisps.
From this rock lip we hear the sea.

Trevor Daniel Otis
*Constable, NY*

[Hometown] *Westville* [Ed] *AAS: computer graphics & design* [Occ] *associate at Walmart* [Hobbies] *videos games, reading, listening to music, walking* [GA] *publishing my book of poetry*

*I grew up on my family's dairy farm near the Canadian border, and got serious about writing poetry in college, when I took a course in creative writing. Three of my poems were printed in the campus literature/ art magazine. Since then I have written a book of poems entitled* Dream Deep: A Poetry Collection Based on Dreams.

## The Barrel

Within the barrel
The malt brews
Steeping, boiling,
And fermenting
To make the ale
That overflows and
Break the barrel
The pieces scattered
Like a broken vase
The water inside the
Coconut pure and refreshing
Made by the power of the sun
The green shrubs never
Withered. It's where the
Morning dew and the butterfly
Linger the flower
The source of everlasting love
Oh, within the barrel, the malt brews

Margareth Debrosse
*Valley Stream, NY*

[Hometown] *Valley Stream* [Ed] *college* [Occ] *nurse* [Hobbies] *writing poetry, reading, and singing* [GA] *becoming a published author*

*Margareth Debrosse was born on August 22 in Port-Au-Prince, Haiti, to immigrant Ulrick and Jeanne Debrosse. She came to USA in 1974 at the age of thirteen. She attended Lefferts Gardens Charter School in Brooklyn, NY. Then she attended Queens Borough Community College in Bayside, Queens. Then she attended Medgar Evers College where she completed her nursing career. Margareth Debrosse now resides in Valley Stream, NY, with husband Antoine Jean-Joseph. She is a mother of three children, son Reginald Debrosse; daughter Raquel; and son, Antoine Jr. She currently writes poetry for local websites and has received a plaque of honor and an award for outstanding poetry.*

## Brokenness

When you have been broken from the inside out and the outside in,
manifesting into a ball, you don't know how to begin. We are born to family; we don't know
how our story is going to be told. Is it a crime of passion? Is it father or mother hurting you, are
they taking out their pain on you?

Maybe a family member who has been violated, they bring a child to the world and seeing the
child growing remind her every day of the day when she was broken. Even if you give the child
away you suppressed memories of a pain you're trying to overcome.

Then comes the day it confronts you; here comes those memories rushing back in again. Do I
go back to the black hole I just came from? Brokenness follows us everywhere as part of the
human race that has experienced pain. In all events we are all in it together.

The anxiety quietly suppressing the memories. But reliving the pain will only keep you stuck
in cycle of mistrust in your daily lives. During a period of rebirth, use all the positive tools,
learn how to utilize them in our new beginnings, giving us strength, courage, and the power to
discover a newer version of you, how wonderful to see a new day indeed.

In life there are lessons to learn; just because we were knocked down doesn't mean we have
to stay down. From your brokenness you can mend those pieces and you can start over again
simply because life gives us second chances you'll see.

Nancy Garcia
*New York, NY*

[Hometown] *New York City*

## Golden Skies

The sunlight ripples through golden skies
crystal blue waters lie under rainbows on high
prism colors of red, yellow, violet, and green
spreads reflection like diamond glass beams
this brings me back to my vacation of memories
as I walked along the beach at Atlantic Ocean.
From a distance the lighthouse shines at night
protects sailors in storms by their guiding light
I watch the eagles spread their wings to fly
swooping down on the water to catch their prey
going back up high in the sky and soar away
when the morning comes at the break of dawn
thinking how many ships sail to the lands unknown
burning stars in the sky are a mystery to explore
loved picking up seashells along the sunny shore
nature is the miracles of our God's masterpiece
of crimson beauty of what this earth looks like,
so you know Heaven must be a glorious sight.

Nancy Lee Armstrong
*Pulaski, VA*

[Hometown] *Pulaski* [Ed] *diploma* [Occ] *housewife and a writer* [Hobbies] *love writing poetry* [GA] *Have a book published on Amazon, and I am in about 22 different books with my poems being published.*

*I am an inspired writer, I have poems listed on Allpoetry as Nanarm45. and a book published on Amazon. com titled: Most Precious Gift. I write about religion, nature, and many different subjects. I have one son Jeffery Armstrong who own his own Embroidery Co. My husband David works at a hardware store. I am also listed in many anthologies such as* Great Poems of Today, Timeless Voices, Grains of Sand, Circular Whispers *and lots of others. My goal is to spread God's word across the world and to inspire hope for others.*

## A Poem about a Poem

I thought that I might like to try,
A simple poem today;
I moved to the computer,
And began to type away.
It seems there is a deadline,
That I will try to meet;
I'll carefully choose the words I need,
To make my poem complete!
So let me think about some things,
That I may want to write;
Perhaps I'll use today's events,
Or maybe something bright!
There's structure in my phrases,
And it's great when things work out;
The poem will have the wording grouped,
To say what it's about.
For when I write my poetry,
I like the words to flow;
The verses will explain themselves,
My poem, in length, will grow.
And when at last I'm to the point,
My poetry is done;
I'll turn off my computer,
And do something else for fun!

Linda Mikula
*Youngstown, OH*

[Hometown] *Youngstown, OH* [Ed] *Chaney High School, Mahoning County Joint Vocational School, adult education, commercial art* [Occ] *assistant to executive director at Mahoning County Bar Association*
*My husband and I reside in Youngstown, OH and have two sons. I was influenced by my father's poetry. One of my poems won honorable mention in a national poets contest, and four poems were published by Eber & Wein. I'm also a fine artist and graphic illustrator, and have participated in three invitational shows at Pleiades Gallery of Contemporary Art in Chelsea, NYC. My art was selected as one of 137 winners in "Strokes of Genius 11," a national competition. Winners were chosen by guest juror, a nationally-celebrated artist Steven Assael; published in "The Best of Drawing."*

## What Would You Do?

I once asked the sky why do you cry?
It said *that's not me, that's you.*
You make the shower, you have the power
The strength lies completely with you.
I then asked a bird why do you sing?
It answered *why do you not?*
I wondered a minute; I wandered within it
And determined, I guess I forgot.
When a question remains, the song doesn't change.
So tell me, what will you do?
Despite your chagrin let us begin and tell me
What would you do?
Will you cry? Will you sing?
Will you chase a brass ring?
Or will you be happy with...
You being you?

Patrick Case
*West Allis, WI*

*I am a father and grandfather. Change can be difficult especially when lost between decision and emotion.
For Serenity.*

## My Nose

I'm glad my nose is on my face,
it has its own assigned space,
for if it were where it is not,
I'd dislike my nose a lot.
Imagine if my own nose
were somehow tucked between my toes,
that wouldn't be so very sweet,
for I'd be forced to smell my feet.
My nose would be a source of dread
if it were stuck upon my head.
It soon would drive me to despair,
forever tickled by my hair.
My nose, instead, through thick and thin,
remains between my eyes and chin,
not tucked in some other place,
it sits just right in upon my face!

Kim Jacqueline Klardie
*Turlock, CA*

*California State University Stanislaus Theater & Abstract Art. My greatest achievement is being a cast member and working with the Central Valley Touring Children's Theater. I am blessed with the thousands of children I come in contact with and the message our productions present. I also love the fan mail. How great is that! God is good...*

## Poppaw's Lap

Spent so much time
I can't even count the hours
Bouncing or rocking
Laughing and giggling
Singing along
And clapping my hands
It's precious memories
That I'll keep for a lifetime
Oh how I wish
I could go back to those days
Or turn the times
Where I wasn't too big
With my arms around him
And my head on his chest
I was safe
And I was free
Sitting right there
on Poppaw's knee
It's where I got my hat
Earned the title on the cap
I was Poppaw's little buddy
Oh how I miss you, Poppaw's lap

Joshua Adam Deweese
*Sophia, WV*

[Hometown] *Glen White, WV* [Ed] *some college* [Occ] *writer* [Hobbies] *writing* [GA] *got a poem published by this company*

*It's a poem about when I was little and got to spend a lot more time with my poppaw than I do now. He is like a father to me.*

## The Daily Grind

Another day with all these worries in my head
Should I get up or stay in bed?
In times when I feel down about the daily grind
I meditate to calm my mind.
When adversity feels like my middle name
I tough it out and just step up my game—no blame!
I can recall each challenge that I've muscled through
Glad for my faith and courage, too.
The daily grind might never stop, but that's okay
I'll overcome and face each day.
It's true, the daily grind may have no cure
But I know that I'll rise up—of this, I'm sure.

Nina M. Beck
*Redondo Beach, CA*

[Hometown] *Redondo Beach, CA* [Ed] *BA in music, The City College of The City University of New York* [Occ] *Library Messenger Clerk, Free-lance Jazz Pianist and Vocalist* [Hobbies] *personal finance; bridge; Scrabble; watching crime dramas and documentaries* [GA] *Winning the Metropolitan Junior Girls Golf Championship in 1973.*

*I'm a half-time library clerical worker, sixty-five, from Redondo Beach, CA, who is 1-1/2 years from retirement. Our 73 City of Los Angeles libraries were totally closed for over 3 months due to the COVID-19 pandemic, but became available in late June 2020 for "take out" only. It hasn't been easy for anyone during this time; but now, slowly, in mid-Spring 2021, libraries, restaurants, bars and other venues have started opening again. "The Daily Grind" represents the ways we can try to cope with and overcome the challenges we face in life.*

## What When Where Why How

These questions are asked but who has the answers?
We talk with a friend, neighbor, or maybe a relative,
but where is the answer?
The trees are green, yet tender.
They hang onto the branches as long as they can,
but to be aware of that strong, brisky wind.
Look up at the sky, in all the shades of blue;
all of a sudden you see black and gray.
Clouds are forming that could bring storms.
Rain, sleet, snow, we call rough weather.

Do we ask why?

Now, let the sunshine brighten up your day.
That will help in so many ways.
Watch plants, animals and even little kids.
They are all changing in their own special way.
These things can be unique, especially the kids.
They each touch your heart in so many ways.
We do not know what they might say or ask next.
So, stay alert and answer their questions
the best way you can.

Use the kids type of language, adjusting your words
so they know the meaning of what they've just heard.

Lola B. Clark
*Sanford, NC*

[Hometown] *Cumnock, NC* [Ed] *Sanford Central High, Sanford Business College* [Occ] *teller, Sanford Savings and Loan* [Hobbies] *poetry, jigsaw puzzles, word search books* [GA] *Editor's Choice Award, Outstanding Achievement in Poetry from the International Library of Poetry*
*The three hobbies listed I enjoy doing the jigsaw puzzles are time consuming and then the feeling of success is shared by having them framed, hanging on my walls or using as gifts to family and friends. My son, Joel, daughter-in-law, Heather, and my granddaughter, Mariella I truly adore always will be special to me.*

## The Final Verse

I don't understand prejudice
Or the ignorance of waging war
I disagree with omitting God
And the exploiting of the poor
I don't condone false accusations
Or bribing my fellow man
I don't validate people who steal
Or the taking of someone's land
I am against those who harm
The innocence of a child
Or waging bets on fighting dogs
After they have been riled
I think it's wrong to waste our money
On new ways to kill one another
There is only one race residing on Earth
They are called my sisters and brothers
I get angry viewing the destruction
Of the clear cutting of a forest
The erosion of once fertile land
Is now relegated to the poorest
I feel uneasy these times we live in
For better mostly worse
Only God knows of the day
When is read the final verse

Patricia Marie Batteate
*San Jose, CA*

[Hometown] *San Jose, CA*  [Ed] *LeHigh University*  [Occ] *engineer*  [Hobbies] *painting, writing poetry, gardening, inventing*

## Beyond the Screen

Purple and pink clouds color the sky.
Oceans of silver glass array the sea.
I just want something real, beyond a screen.
I want to smell the flowers and the crisp air,
And taste the lips of my lover's kiss.
I want to feel the warmth of arms wrapped around me,
And see the tops of the trees blow in the breeze.
No! I don't want another video chat!
I want to be under the stars and watch the moonlight
caress your cheek.
I just want something real beyond a video screen.
To be safe with God like Adam and Eve.
Far away from the virus and its deadly disease
where Love conquers evil
beyond the screen.

Colleen M. Thibault
*Beverly, MA*

[Hometown] *Beverly, MA* [Ed] *Bachelor of Art, English* [Occ] *transportation* [Hobbies] *writing, art, public speaking, roller-skating, hiking, reading, camping* [GA] *overcoming a head injury, graduating college, and buying my first home*

*For as long as I can remember I have been an emotionally deep thinking person. I have often felt misunderstood and been accused of caring way too much about things. I am happy to say that writing has been a way for me to express these deep thoughts and feelings. And when I write poetry people tell me I have the ability to write what they feel in my poems. It makes me feel good to know that I can do that for others, as well as for myself. I believe poetry is one of the most important forms of writing there is, because ultimately a poem is the writer's voice and our voice is what comes from our heart and our souls. And our heart is everything. It's what brings us all together in the good times and the bad. I will continue to write what is on my heart through poetry for as long as I am able. Thank you for being who you are.*

## My Son

No reason needed to love a son
When you're up, I'm full of pride
When you're down, I lift you up
When you're sad, I bring you down the stars
When you're far, you're closer to my heart
If you ever lack love, I'll love for both
If you ever cry, with a kiss your tears I'll wipe
Your hugs and kisses are tattooed in my heart
The moments we've lived together flashback in my mind
My love supply for you is endless
No distance, no circumstances will ever break us apart
For a mother/son's miracle was created by God

Juanita Aranda
*Palos Park, IL*

[Occ] *retired*

*My goal in life has been to raise my children with values and love for humanity.*

# My Light Shines from the Lantern in My Window

There is a lantern in the window
Shining out to the world
Lighting the way
A beacon in the night
Did I tell you I would leave a light on
to light your way to my door
Did you feel it in your being
That somewhere the light shines
for you
Searching but not knowing
Which direction to turn
How long will I light this lantern
in my wait for you
Until that day of your coming
and then every day after so that we will always
be in the light
Look to my window
Do you see the light
Walk forward

Lilly Whiteswan
*Madrid, NM*

[Hometown] *Madrid, NM* [Ed] *college* [Occ] *curandera* [Hobbies] *writing* [GA] *life*

*I live in a town in the mountains. Three kids, six grandkids. Writing all my life.*

## The In-Between Time

There is a time between dusk and dawn
When the night mist lays heavy upon the lawn
The early bird issues his reveille call
Time to get up one and all

I lay cozy and warm 'neath heated cover
Pondering the day and what I'll discover
My ears hear the joyful chorus of birds
Bringing in the daylight in their kind of words

The moon is taking the night and heading west
Her realm is elsewhere dressed in her best
The sun has yet to claim his throne
Heaven's light not yet home

It is the in-between time, a time of reflection
That I come before God in all of His perfection
Communing with Him my thoughts of choice
Quietly listening for the master's voice

The sun has arrived in all of his glory
Melting away the night mist, tucking away its story
That golden time of quiet revery
Will stay through the day a lovely memory

Nancy J. Medlin
*Chesapeake, VA*

[Hometown] *Chesapeake, VA* [Ed] *high school* [Occ] *homemaker* [Hobbies] *scrapbooking, writing poetry* [GA] *raising three godly daughters and enjoying three grandchildren*

*I have always loved the time between early morning dark and light and sunset and night. I call these times the in-between times. A time of quiet reflection, gathering yourself for the beginning and ending of the day. I've been writing poetry for about forty-five years and feel God has blessed me with this gift and I enjoy writing notes to others as a way of encouragement or comfort. I live in Chesapeake, VA and enjoy family, friends, church, Yahtzee, bunco and life in general.*

# Chronology

Once a time forgotten
Once when all life deemed
Days were for exploration
And anyone could dream
I stood in backyards flowing
With lawns grown green for mowing
With gardens ripe from sowing
Where all was what it seemed
And I drifted and I fluttered
In a wind still clean and warm
And I ran when someone uttered
Those words that carried harm
Now tired of profound answers
I look to walk with dancers
And honest kind freelancers
About whom joy does swarm
Then bring us some libation
Distraction for the mind
And start the celebration
Of all we'll leave behind
The signs of our accomplishments
The toil that they entailed
Our children and their children
Living proof that love prevailed

Dorinda Marie Palmisano
Massapequa, NY

[Hometown] *Massapequa* [Ed] *School of Visual Arts, Art Students' League* [Occ] *decorative artist and muralist* [Hobbies] *painting and writing* [GA] *my children*
*I am a happily married mother of two. Self-employed I worked for close to twenty years as a mural painter and decorative finisher. The love of poetry was given to me by my parents and I have written from childhood to present day. I reside close to the ocean and spend my time between my four wonderful grandchildren, my children, my husband, and my studio where I love painting and writing.*

## The Rancor

Tears flowing uncontrolled every day for months
Over unknown virus that plagued the world of humans
Peace suddenly truncated with bitter emotions unguarded
Darkness kicking out light in world unprepared
And here we are honoring layers of hatred in rancor!
Fathers abusing their trusting and dependent daughters
Gunmen shooting uncontrolled in marketplaces
Husbands killing wives out of frustrations
Teachers raping young girls left in their care
And here we are celebrating layers of deceit in rancor!
Natural calamities smiling on our destinies
Lawlessness causing lifelong tribulations
Humiliating experiences and never-ending pains
Kings and queens parading without adorned crowns
And here we are eulogizing layers of acrimony in rancor!
Wailings of death in decorated vicinities
Parents separated from children unprepared
Agony and anguish glaring sternly on blank faces
Joys cut short in speechless horizons
And here we are worshiping layers of envy in rancor!
That virus created colossal loses and mourning
Think of the plights of the untimely widows and orphans
Recall the innocent blood wasted in marketplaces
And figure out how love, peace and unity will work for us
To fight and destroy those layers of discord in rancor!

Cordelia Chimeziem Ekechi
*North Las Vegas, NV*

*My name is Cordelia Ekechi, a Nigerian by birth but a permanent resident of the United States of America. I've been married for thirty-seven years with children and grandchildren. I hold a master's degree in sociology and industrial relations from the University of Benin, Benin City Nigeria and have poetry, writing, drama, counseling, and motivational talks as my key hobbies. My philosophy is that life is simple if you understand its principles.*

## Our Orb

When you think you're Heaven bound—
Before you leave—just turn around
Look at our earthly orbit gem.
So far no one has found another one of them!

Our gem is Heaven here
The flora and fauna—all to endear.

Our gem has flaws, too, that are overridden
By the beauty of our gem.

So while you're here—make your choice to
Embrace our gem—remember—
So far no one has found another on of them!

Jean Hickman
Auburn, CA

[Hometown] *Auburn, CA in Sierra foothills* [Ed] *GED, music training* [Occ] *retired accountant* [GA] *proud mother of a son and daughter (deceased), both professionals, college grads*

*At ninety-seven I'm happy to be able to write poetry, go antiquing, cook a little, and, of course, enjoy our Gem.*

## Dead as Forgotten

Dead
As
I
Am
Quite
And
Gone
To
My
Grave
As
A
Ghostly
Spirit
Blows
A
Wind
Of
Smoke
Just
Remember
Me
As
I
Was
Alive

Trina Doneen Smith
*Tifton, GA*

[Hometown] *Tifton* [Occ] *retired* [Hobbies] *adult coloring, poetry writing, word puzzle, jigsaw puzzles, collecting celebrate pictures* [GA] *having all my poems published in a book.*
*That I am glad made it this far to have my poems published by Eber & Wein Publishing company and I hope one day I can get them all published in a book.*

## My Mom Ruby Lee

On July 8, 2020, the world as I have known my whole life
Took a long pause, the birds stopped singing, the sky's
Went from sunshine to clouds, because that's how
Everything seem to be in eye sight, although the world
Didn't stop, but my life did, with disbelief of the
News I had just received about my mom Ruby Lee.
I had no plan in place on how to move forward
Because she was always there, and now all I have are
Photos and voicemails, I'm very grateful to have them
But our rock, has been moved, our council is no longer
Available to hear my daily briefing, whether it's good
Or bad, she always had the solution. For 58 years, my
Mom was the best sculpture that God put together.
We were so blessed that God picked her, to be our mom
She was the sweetest, caring person I have ever known
Always smiling, always helping, and always available
Never wanted to be a burden to anyone, when most of the
Time we were the ones who were a burden to her
We have to go on now, and live the life she set in
Place for us, her job was well done, my mom should have
Written the book on being a mother, she was the greatest
Ever, I love you and miss you, it's still hard to let go
But I know I will see her again forever, in heaven,
She has a whole host of love ones ,angels, and Jesus
Himself with open arms, saying welcome home My
Child, your race is finish, time to enjoy forever love.

Bobby Louis Jarmon
*Forney, TX*

[Hometown] *Forney, TX* [Occ] *business owner* [Hobbies] *writing* [GA] *having the songs I wrote,*
*hearing them on the air*
*2020 has been a rough year for everybody. Loosing my mom hit home hard, but we have to keep on going and*
*think about the good times, and great times that are still to come.*

## Acceptance

As the blood drips
from the petals of your heart,
I sit and watch
you fall apart.
I twitch as you claw every stitch
trying to fix all that you've missed.
The demons you tried to cast away
are here to live, they're here to stay.
When there's no escape,
no other way,
your truth will be the only pay.
Because, honey,
you've lost the game.

Skyler Alexa Metviner
*Brookfield, CT*

[Hometown] *Brookfield, CT* [Ed] *Pace University, master's in literacy education* [Occ] *English teacher* [Hobbies] *painting, puzzling, and photography* [GA] *winning the Graduate of the Year award from Pace University in 2020*

*Greetings! I am an English teacher from Connecticut who graduated with a BA in adolescent English education and a MS in literacy education from Pace University. I use poetry as an outlet and a way to express myself. I aim to incorporate my love for poetry and creative writing in my classroom each and every day. I hope to one day soon publish my own book of poetry. I have been grateful for the support of my family, friends, colleagues, and publishing companies like Eber & Wein who help me continue to write and celebrate my poetry.*

## Eastern Dragon Breath

We breathe
We breathe the breath of truth
brought to light
against all forms of lynching ropes of slavery
We breathe
We breathe the breath of kindness
through yellow chrysanthemums
against anti-Asian and other hate-filled knuckles
We breathe the breath of artist's delight
thru rainbow-colored murals of intertwined hands
on walls of community buildings
We breathe
We breathe the breath of fiery blood giving justice
weighed against the violent shadows of black men
We breathe the breath of courage
that unseats the lies of fake elections
We breathe
We breathe the gentle breath of the wise humorous
eastern dragon
that will present soothing breath
to every single earthly child of God
Breathe...yes we breathe now.

Phyllis Jeanette Tyler
*Camarillo, CA*

[Hometown] *Sioux Falls, South Dakota* [Ed] *Morningside College, Wesley Seminary (MDiv) Claremont ST (DMin)* [Occ] *retired United Methodist clergy* [Hobbies] *walking, writing, ukulele, laughing, meditating, aging* [GA] *raising two sons, loving two husbands, savoring the moments*

*Inspiration for this poem came from the murder of George Floyd. I'm seventy-five years old, a white woman of South Dakota. Forty years as a United Methodist clergywoman I breathed against racial and gender discrimination. Now I garden, write, and meditate, laugh, and enjoy my Chinese-American husband, children, and grandchildren.*

## A Reader's Passion

Tonight the moon booms
in luxuriant lunar blooms,
with just a splash of lingering.
I imagine only foolish laughter happens
if you write with a reader's passion.
For every gave up gained is the exercise of change.
Your grassy, wet next step
is in perfect alive alignment.
Poetry is words of the moment,
like walking on a dirty carpet—
it stains crowded judgment, so lethargic.
For how few things
we have time to wait.
The water's dripping sixty degrees,
melting down our glacier gates.

Robert Mikolyski
*Old Town, ME*

[Hometown] *Old Town* [Ed] *associate's degree in video/radio productions* [Occ] *DSP, video editor, author* [Hobbies] *hiking, swimming, Penobscot theater, dating, posting nature therapy videos on Youtube* [GA] *surviving Lawrence, MA (a dangerous place to grow up)*

*Robert Mikolyski is a freelance video editor who lives in central Maine and works as a DSP for adults with disabilities. Bob has been featured in Eber & Wein Publishing's Best Poets of 2015 & 2020 and This Time Around, Safe Harbor. His poetry has circulated throughout Maine in 'The Poets Corner,' articles of the Eagle Magazine. He grew up in Lawrence, MA and went to Hesser College for video/radio production in Manchester, NH. After working for WMUR Ch-9 as an engineer, he became an auditor that traveled throughout New England counting super-centers. Today Bob enjoys hiking and video editing nature, promoting the Maine wilderness as therapy, even posting videos on Youtube called, Openfree poetry—After surviving two major surgeries and losing one hundred pounds, and reversing diabetes, a plant-based lifestyle transformed his health and inspired four poetry books.*

## For Another Day

which of us invented this red
woodpecker called heart
who keeps my longings
close from you, like a chart?
knock, knock, knock, knock,
beats in me without discern
ready to tear it to pieces
my daily return
oh, it's you who you want
to build a solid nest
to keep your flights for later
in my large chest!
a single fall occurs between us
and with an ecstatic delay
you give me a kind of
anesthesia for another day.

Bogdan Nicolae Groza
*Chicago, IL*

[Hometown] *Chicago* [Ed] *student, associate in art at Wright & Wilbur College, Chicago, IL* [Occ] *dietary aide* [Hobbies] *writing, hikes, movies* [GA] *In my native country, Romania, I won a few literary prizes and last year, in Chicago, one of my screenplays had advanced in quarter-final in a screenplay contest.*

*Poet, writer, and screenwriter. I emigrated to the USA seven years ago.*

# On the Road of Life

Walking down the road of life, gaining knowledge along the way.
Life is just a heartbeat given each and every day.

Taking in nature the sights and beauty, when we walk that day.
Thinking, my how time flies away.

Birds are carefree and have no worries you see.
God cares for them as He cares for you and me.

Take time my friends and heed His call.
All that is needed is acceptance and belief in Him.

Life will be the best it can be, happy, healthy and mostly worry-free.

One step at a time is all that it takes.
God gives us breath and ability to be strong.

Adventures never end and we are always on the way.
God given strength and directions each and every day.

Keeping us going as we walk along.

Barbara Amptmann
*Sacramento, CA*

## Old Oak

My family has been through many things in my years, but always remained strong like the "Old Oak."

Great-grandma always used to say, "To stay strong like an "Old Oak" tree."

Be able to bend in the wind but not break under the pressure of it all. It's tough at times. Lord willing we have all seemed to make it.

I look back at times and think how did my parents and those before them ever do it. How did they come this far? And then there is me, myself I somehow make life keep going on, being strong like the "Old Oak."

Passing down wisdom, a tradition, in a family is what makes us all be able to continue on in life, no matter what we go through and remain strong and resilient like an "Old Oak."

Vicki L. Clark
*Uhrichsville, OH*

[Hometown] *Bluffton, IN* [Ed] *high school graduate* [Occ] *housewife* [Hobbies] *reading, writing, latch hook, fishing, outdoor activities* [GA] *getting my poems published*

*I am an Indiana country girl, who grew up to marry an ex-biker from Ohio. We live in Ohio. My family has always been supportive of me. My old English teacher Mrs. Willy from high school told me I could be a writer if I chose to be, just go for it. My poem is inspired by my great-grandma's wisdom who passed away in 1997 a year after I graduated. She was in her late nineties. I love reading and writing. I have a few poems published but hope someday to have a whole book published.*

## Spring

A fresh new start is in the air
Open your eyes if you really care
This fresh new spring and blooming things
Can be a very special thing.
Let's play around like children do
Enjoy whatever this Springtime brings.
Be happy, have fun, let's play in the sun
This time of the year is so full of cheer
Easter egg hunts and families gather
Traditions are kept with baskets and laughter
The flowers are blooming, no storm clouds booming
Sweet smells fill the air; it's a treasure out there.
Song birds are singing and doing their nesting
Soon new life will be all around
Lift your hearts high and look to the sky
Rebirth has renewed us again.
Don't give up the hope—April is *no* joke
Just sometimes a little bit slow
Enjoy special time...don't linger behind
With this perfect time of the year
Be thankful and pray for all God has made
He has kept us through thick and through thin
Our blessings this spring will only begin
If with your whole *heart* you *believe*!

Martha A. Breakwell
*N. Belle Vernon, PA*

[Hometown] *N. Belle Vernon, PA* [Ed] *associate's in business* [Occ] *retired from executive administrative assistant positions* [Hobbies] *baking, flower and vegetable gardening, walking, reading* [GA] *being a published contemporary poet*

*After a seemingly long winter and lock downs, spring was so welcomed early with warm temperatures in our area. This set the wheels of my mind to bright spring days and the celebration of Easter and rebirth making me look at the world in new ways.*

## Down by the Lake

Looking out upon the lake
Nature is in full display
As the wind
Begins to blow
The gentle waves of water
Start to sway
It's a bit chilly
And it's early in the season
Which is the reason
There are few boats
In the water today
The rocks upon the shore
Are grayish
And very dour
Though the beach is quite pristine
No signs of litter
It's inviting and clean.

James Robert Nielsen
*Racine, WI*

[Hometown] *Racine, WI* [Ed] *associate degree from Gateway Technical Institute* [Occ] *retired surveyor's assistant* [Hobbies] *reading, watching lectures and interviews on YouTube, tai chi, painting, writing* [GA] *selected to the International Who's Who of Poetry in 2004*

*I'm sixty-three years old. In 2004 I was selected to the International Who's Who of Poetry. I'd taken up painting with watercolors a couple of months ago. Before getting into poetry seriously, I was into competitive chess; I was two-time Racine City Chess Champion. In 1985 I took sixth place in the Wisconsin State Chess Championship.*

## Blue Line to O'Hare

California
 I have to pull down your mask to kiss you
 Mind the gap, dear
Logan Square
 Doors open on the left at Logan Square
Belmont
 Remember the bad times to stop up the tears
Addison
 Our love is good, not right
Irving Park
 I'm trying not to crush your hand in mine
Montrose
 It's not goodbye.
 What do you know?
Jefferson Park
 Doors open on the left at Jefferson Park
 Harlem, Cumberland, Rosemont, O'Hare
Harlem
 There's a storm coming
Cumberland
 Cumberland, Rosemont, O'Hare
Rosemont
 I can't breathe. Why can't I breathe?
O'Hare.
O'Hare
 $2.50 for a goodbye and a cold seat on the train home

Greta Mae Geiser
*Chicago, IL*

[Hometown] *Minneapolis, MN* [Ed] *BFA in acting, Chicago College of Performing Arts* [Occ] *actor* [Hobbies] *costume design, exploring the city, reading*

*Greta Mae Geiser is an actor and playwright currently based in Chicago, IL. Poetry is the lifeblood of everything she creates, and she believes that there is prose to be found even in the mundane.*

## Intoxication

I'm a love drunk idiot
and I've come to terms with that.
Kaluha and coffee; you're the first
thing I see in the morning. Whiskey
hair disheveled, with a crooked
smile. Eyes still fogged with sleep;
what a sight for sore eyes, you are.
Salt, tequila, lime.
Hellfire soars through my veins as I'm
white girl wasted on you.
To be drunk on a person
is unexplainable;
a fuzzy feeling in the pit of my
stomach like how your tongue feels
after too many vodka sodas.
The world tilting and turning
with every blink of my amaretto
colored eyes. You sing to me
like late night karaoke. The hum
of our Suju soaked souls
vibrating our bodies to the
same frequency.

Jenni Schwartz
*Las Vegas, NV*

[Hometown] *Las Vegas, NV* [Ed] *Bachelor of Science, entertainment design* [Occ] *makeup artist with Mac Cosmetics* [Hobbies] *writing, roller skating, baking, and reading* [GA] *getting my first poem published in 2019 in the* Upon Arrival *anthology*

*I have been actively writing for as long as I can remember. Whether it's novels or poetry, I always have a project in the works. It's always been one of my most favorite creative outlets and I'm so excited to share my work with the world.*

## Lovers and Friends

We were reckless, my dear, in days of the past
What carefree moments, what hysterical laughs
That hidden cabin with no heat
Our jug of wine on a lover's seat
Up the coast and across the sea
No heavy worries, just you and me
We pinched our pennies and didn't care
We had each other and life to share
We cried and fought and had rough roads
But we bobbed above the heavy loads
We paused on the shores of Lake Louise
Danced to the tunes on a midnight breeze
Our travels together were so unique
On beaches with seashells to keep
The sun and sand and water flow in
You with your thoughts on ways to win
Life is so similar as we live and die
Only we capture as time goes by
Precious moments with the sand and the sea
All to share with the world and me
Now I look back upon those times
Those moments were the ties that binds
We look back upon those scenes
They are memories and seem like dreams

Charlotte C. McLaughlin
*Lakewood, CO*

[Hometown] *Wakefield, MI* [Ed] *Michigan State University* [Occ] *retired* [Hobbies] *crafts, writing, and poetry* [GA] *my wonderful long life with my husband*

*After a wonderful long life traveling with my husband and daughter, I find myself at the end of my years enjoying the writing that I have kept up over the years.*

## Messy Business

There are seasons in time
Forever reminding mortals
Life is but a messy moment
In the eternal scheme of things.
The genesis of mankind was a messy art.
God breathed His life into a lump of clay,
Called this artwork Adam
And gave this mortal a sense of the eternal.
Creativity is as messy as mud.
Mortality is mud-made magnificent.
And mortals—created in God's image—
Create grand messes, thinking they are gods.
Messy business—this art of living—
Building what rust and rot can take in a generation
Warehouses, Interstate highways, and rural dump heaps,
The paradoxical antithesis of creativity.
The letting go makes death a messy business.
Creative ways of parceling out material wealth
Takes détente and toilsome days of planning.
Surrendering to the ravages of mortal time
Creates, anew, some sense of the eternal.

Flesh and blood cannot inherit the Kingdom of Heaven.
In Christ man has passed from death to life.

Sherrie Morrison
*Lexington, SC*

*I was born a poet in Easter, NC seventy-six years ago. I have no memory of thinking other than in poetry, though not always in rhymes. Only in recent years have I begun to share. This is a poem from the year of COVID-19.*

## I Am Memory

I move among the living, but cast no shadow.
I am a memory.
How I look, how I was, floating free, yet bound,
soft, but forceful, loved, yet disdained.
I remain forever untouchable, lasting
a memory I am.
I drift through corridors of timeless places
looking far ahead at things that only have been
and some never were.
Dreams and not dreams,
hope and what remains without hope.
I am the shadow of life.
I am a memory, a memory I am.

Robert Gardner
*Rio Rancho, NM*

[Hometown] *Rio Rancho*  [Ed] *doctorate*  [Occ] *physician*  [Hobbies] *music, writing, language study*
[GA] *being alive*

## Texas Strong

As we waited here in Texas
We were not afraid of Harvey
Because Texas was strong
So as everyone prepared for
    the hardship
We were strong in the fight
And of being vigilant and
    defeating the storm
Of our strong and powerful God
who was here in the midst of
    His people
And as Texas we heard the cry of help
That reached out in the midst of
    trouble, pain and suffering
As we reached the unreached
With the helping hands and feet
Of our first responders, police
    officers, our fire fighters
And with many other teams of hope
And with the one who was there
In the midst of trouble
Jesus holding out His hands
To rescue us from the storm

Magdalena Charles
*Cuero, TX*

[Hometown] *Victoria, TX* [Ed] *daycare help in later years* [Occ] *retired, grandmother, great-grandmother* [Hobbies] *writing, painting, my short stories, writing poems and essays* [GA] *showing my paintings in art shows in Victoria, TX*

*My poem was inspired by so many things that were happening at that time. It was when we heard about Harvey, the storm. I remember my family and I were actually waiting for the storm to come through Victoria, TX. But as I waited I used my time to go volunteer at my church where we were donating water, food and other necessities to get people through the coming week. My Christian sisters also help in giving out meals to our Victoria residents. There were also many other people who helped in that area of preparing other teams to help with the affords of our city. Because it is a wonderful thing when God's love surrounds us through faith and hope. But I thank God for His care and protection.*

## Sinister Agenda

Ominous, foreboding
Coiled serpent lies in wait.
Lingering, looming
Cursed venom, my fate.
Stifled suffering
Within the quiet while others dream.
Haunting tormentor
Of my requiem of screams.
Echoing endlessly
Deafening my ears.
Facade fading
Take off the glasses, now I see clear.
Trap averted
Yet the mirage remains the same.
Enticingly lured
As it whispers my name.
Resisting fervently
Promises to good to be true.
Revealing agendas
As reality comes within view.
Plotting maniacally
to heighten my strife.
Shallow breathing
Valiantly fighting for life.
Choking violently
On the hemlock named pain.

Gabrielle Leva Nichols
*Saginaw, MI*

[Hometown] *Saginaw, MI* [Ed] *cosmetology, social work, psychology* [Occ] *retired* [Hobbies] *reading, writing poems and children's books, comic book collecting, Pomeranians* [GA] *being a mother and a wife. Gabrielle Nichols was born in January of 1973 in Michigan. She is of Greek and Native American descent. In 1996 she gave birth to her son, Austin. In September of 2015 Gabrielle married the love of her life, Edward Economous, in a traditional Greek Orthodox wedding. Her poetry is inspired by personal experiences and her observations of the human condition.*

## The Love of My Four-Legged Friend

I lost my Mr. he was my cat. He followed me around and sat in my lap. I miss him so much it tears me all up. I feel empty without his love. He was my cat I dearly loved. I miss my Mr. my four-legged friend. He was dedicated to me and loved me right to the end. My poor Mr. my four-legged friend. My love for my Mr. will never end. I can't wait to see him again. There is no dedicated love like this that I have ever seen. My heart is so broken, life isn't the same without you my four-legged friend.
I love you Mr. Mischief until I see you again.

Tracy E. Brown
*Kingsburg, CA*

[Hometown] *Kingsburg , CA* [Ed] *human resource admin.* [Occ] *human resource consultant, housekeeper* [Hobbies] *writing, drawing, crafts* [GA] *having four poems published*

*I've been happily married for twenty-eight years. I am a pet mom of six pit bulls, six cats (one cat is wild). I enjoy writing and drawing in my spare time. I love the beach and collecting sea shells. I also like helping the elderly. I enjoy spending time with my best friend when we can get together.*

## When the Dawn Became the Night

We wake to the sun.
What fun, fun, fun
We are warm,
Many of us think of being born.
Dawn is our beginning of today!
Then the news said, "No, you must not be in today's sun.
You must cover and not enjoy today, tomorrow, all year.
Our dawn is now something we must fear.
Stay inside, and hide, not to be seen."
What a life of night with no dawn.
We now live with no sun.
No fun, fun, fun.
When did our sun become the night?
Did we even get to fight?
I miss the dawn of each day.
I miss the sun and our human fun.
I can close my eyes and it is dark
But in my heart is a spark.
A spark of yesterday's dawn.

Phoebe C. Allex
*Las Vegas, NV*

[Ed] *professional educator and writer*

# I'm Outside, Looking In

I drifted off to sleep
While thinking of my family
I'm standing at the gate, looking in
At my loved ones in various scenes
My father fishing in a Golden River
With my uncles, his brothers
Having a good ole time
I'm outside, looking in
My mother back in Hawaii
Having a luau with her Ohana (family)
A glorious reunion going on
I'm outside, looking in
My son with his best friend, arm in arm
With the biggest grins, smiling at each other
Both totally content with one another
While, I am still outside, looking in
I awake with the start
My sobs are making my heart ache
I'm told to be patient, my time will come
I'm not done with you, just keep looking in

Jerry Wayne Yates
*Jacksonville, AL*

[Hometown] *Jacksonville, AL* [Ed] *auto mechanics, Navy food service* [Occ] *retired* [Hobbies] *coin detecting and collecting* [GA] *raising a wonderful son with manners, a heavenly angel*

*I am a simple man who enjoys nature to its fullest.*

## Another

Leaves changing colors
For many
A sign of change
Of chance
For me
It's a sign of another year gone
Time's running out
The symbol of another summer lost
The biting wind
Instead of the summer breeze
A harsh reality
A gut-wrenching loss
What am I doing with my life?
Do I have the time to figure it out?
Or will the leaves change
Before I can?
I'll probably run out of
Tomorrows
No time for evaluation
Keep on trucking
Till the colors drain
And everything falls
Another year . . .
Another dream . . .
Another tree . . .
Another failure . . .

Gratia Serpento
*Molalla, OR*

[Occ] *journalist* [Hobbies] *crocheting* [GA] *living through a pandemic and a fire evacuation in the same year and surviving*
*During the year 2020, Gratia Serpento lived through a pandemic and a fire evacuation. Those experiences fueled her creative writing passion. Because of the struggle, she ended up turning to poetry and finding a place of release, a place where she could let go of all the emotions in a civilized way. She lives in Oregon with her dictionary.*

## The Year 2020

It started off good, the year twenty-twenty,
 But it then brought something we didn't foresee!
COVID appeared and began to spread,
 Putting so many people into their sick bed.
"Keep your distance and wear your mask"
 Seemed like a very simple task!
But for some reason it didn't work that way,
 And a lot of family members had to hope and pray,
None of us, of course, enjoyed the pent up life,
 And seeing how stress lead to so much strife.
An evening cocktail gave many a welcome respite
 That helped to end the day in a positive light.
Short trips to neat places and watching *Schitt's Creek*,
 Also helped to keep things not so bleak.
Thankfully, vaccines became available to us,
 And we took ours without any fuss.
Now looking forward to being able to visit and see
 Our friends and all members of our family tree.
The future thus seems to be looking good
 And has already improved things in our neighborhood.
People seem to be less worried and in a better way,
 For all things to get even better is for what I pray.

Joseph Buczek
*Surfside Beach, SC*

[Hometown] *Johnstown, PA* [Ed] *studied mathematics and geodesy* [Occ] *retired general physical scientist, NOAA; retired USNR chief, aerographers mate; retired residential builder* [Hobbies] *golf, wood-working* [GA] *happily married*

## Tokes for Tokens

I'm not much of a gambler
But bet I have experience exchanging tokes for tokens
Secondhand smoke for oxygen I breathe when woke
Secondhand wind of weed for respiration from trees
Player two is my shadow that knows my every move
I don't like to gamble, but I take risks
Like hurting my back carrying more than I can lift
Or taking strides that were more than I bargained for
I put the chips on the table and roll the dice
But in exchange, all I get for my sacrifice
Is another cycle with a vice, sometimes
A personal demon that wants to cue conversation
Break the ice and play Russian roulette
Doubt in the chamber is the price
At times is additional stakes, a riskier hand to play
Especially when I go against them, they lay
As I hope to avoid chance of defeat, a bitter score
Counting on probability that I win the battle, the war
'Cause I've learned your demons will come to collect
Even when you try to counter them, deflect
Still, remember that they're the tokes to your tokens
The counterfeit bills to your authentic skills
You are priceless being who you are, scars and all
Your demons just want to see your downfall
Now, recollect yourself and claim your earnings
From the self-worth you've been yearning.

Julian Alwyn Wilson
*Amityville, NY*

[Hometown] *Bellmore*

*A thing that we don't like to admit to ourselves sometimes, is that we all have our personal demons—shadows on the inside that mess with our hearts and minds, that don't represent the core of who we are. They can hurt, but it's okay, because we can always rise above them and become who we wish to be in this world. We can count on our self-worth to remind us of this, and I believe that's a beautiful thing. Self-worth is something that we all have, too. As you read this, remind yourself of your self-worth and know that no painful situation or struggle is beyond your power to overcome. Trust in yourself and your inner power, and you can get through anything that comes your way. Peace and love.*

## Awesome Avenue

The pitch black in my pencil
is like a hockey puck
turning into a typing truck
on Awesome Avenue
built with macho math
Guilt is not the path

Grease is groovy peace
My pride proves to be perfect peace
Your ride record moves on respect road
to guide the Ford for the writers' guild gasoline
from the motor magazine and inspires the voter with a teen

Elect with no wrecked wheel
and we'll write what we feel
Driving is still the deal
on Awesome Avenue!

Walker Hayes
*Columbia, MO*

[Hometown] *Cleveland, OH* [Ed] *GED/vocational school* [Occ] *self-published writer* [Hobbies]
*listening to music on Youtube while reading poems* [GA] *writing the poem "Human Race 3.0" and
American Legion Award*

*I currently consider myself a different democrat and have the last ten years of my life but I've also considered
myself a liberal or libertarian, generally a late sixties to early seventies liberal or romantic individualist.*

## Girl in the Red Dress

A dance at the Grange on the tenth of June.
Her "Coming-Out-Dance" was approaching soon.
Everyone is going, mom, dad, and big sister, too.
She bought a red dress and red heals for shoes.

The satin dress shimmering all the way to the floor.
It enhanced her full breasts and her fanny more.
She was tall and lovely, auburn hair down her back.
Add crystal jewelry and "Evening in Paris" to that.

Entering the hall, she caused quite a stir.
She loved the feeling of all eyes on her.
The first hand she took brought blush to her face.
After a few more she knew her place.

A joyous evening and dances so many.
Drinks lined the bar but she didn't drink any.
Gentlemen tried every advance in the book.
Sis whispered, "Run like a fox, you have that look!"

The enchanting night hours passed way too fast.
She took off her heals to sit and rest at last.
Dad yelled out, "Get your shoes and get in the car!"
As he downed her last drink lined up on the bar.

Tess J. Wilke
*Durand, IL*

[Hometown] *Durand, IL* [Ed] *two years of college* [Occ] *retired — Honeywell-Aerospace* [Hobbies]
*watercolor, photography, reading (science& research), ordinance and marine rep.* [GA] *hiking the Grand
Canyon rim to rim, building our home, and raising six children*

## My Shopping Cart

L
O
N
G

L
I
S
T

My basket filled
Cash register
"No total"
"Really!"

"It's free!"

Smiles and sunshine
Moonbeams and melodies
Hugs and happiness
Raindrops and Rainbows
Love and laughter

The silver lining

All free!

Marilyn Peterson
*Cozad, NE*

[Hometown] *Cozad, NE* [Ed] *honorary doctorate in humane letters* [Occ] *university professor*
[Hobbies] *writing, music, painting, creating unique dinner parties* [GA] *delegate, First Amendment Congress/National Journalism Hall of Fame*
*I spend time observing others, noting how they live their lives, setting positive examples and thinking what can be done to create a happy day. My poem "My Shopping Cart," reflects my lifestyle, as I give to others. What I am sharing is available at no cost.*

## Jingle Jennie

Jingle Jennie
She is a honey
The best of the wild ones
you will ever see.

Biker Bob...Cowgirl Jill
Church bells ringing
Freaky lights...good night lights

Wrangler jeans, Ford machines
Sirens are blasting
Stars above...water below

Fender guitars...Oboe silent
Bike Mary...Cowboy Jamie
The moon lights...sun bright

Hippie Bill...Cat Amy
Tambourine the beat
Freaky lights...good night lights.

Jingle Jennie
She is a honey
The best of the wild ones
Your will ever see.

James Fred Brinkman
*Bismarck, ND*

[Hometown] *Palmyra, NE* [Ed] *guitar player* [Occ] *welder* [Hobbies] *fish, hunt, trap* [GA] *always play music all night and day*

## Meitzi

Shy Meitzi went a running
afraid of everything.
She bolts and hides at every noise—
a bell, a knock, or the tiniest thing.
She does like being petted
but is always quick to flee;
this means she hardly ever dares
come sit upon my knee.
We wanted so to soothe her;
it seemed a simple thing.
She's take off like as a furry blur,
which always left me wondering.
A new arrival, Mei Mei,
helped solve the mystery.
They play and romp about the room;
Meitzi's shyness now but history.
She likes this play and boldly ventures out;
these changes for all to see.
How fun cavorting with a friend,
Meitzi's new philosophy!

Nancy Lynn Mayer
*Freeland, WA*

## The Darkness Within

The dark night creeps up
Darker than ones before
The wind blows the window open
And I've shattered the mirror on the floor
I pick up a shard of glass
And slide it across my wrist
It does no damage and I say okay
But my mind screams deeper sharper
I run to my room
And find my blades
Race to the bathroom
Hoping the thoughts fade
I sit in the tub
Clothes still on
I roll up my sleeves
Now it's begun
A flash of silver
A gleam of red
The thoughts still rushing
Through my head
The thoughts have stopped
But my heart stopped too
Still bleeding out
Nothing left I can do

Rose Ellen Bingham
*New Market, MD*

[Hometown] *New Market, MD* [Ed] *incomplete high school* [Occ] *can't work* [Hobbies] *writing, reading, drawing* [GA] *self-publishing my own book of poems*
*The path of life has never been an easy one. Walking the road always felt like I was alone. Along the way friends came and went. There were occasions I barely made it out alive. But I'm still here and I'm using or trying to use my poetry to show others they aren't alone.*

## At Nana Jessie's Knee

Native voices
Soothe and calm
Laugh and tease
Stand ground to refuse the wrong
Slow talk that speaks the whole
Sends words into shared space
Words that circle the heart
Move with the spirit before they touch air
Words that share a more total logic
Create a more complete intelligence
Soul-saver words in calm and brave voices
Put me more whole again
Push me more strong again
Softer words that circle the heart
Swim through the spirit before being set free
Come from native voices
First heard at Nana Jessie's knee
Gazing up into her voice
Glowing and knowing home

Pamela Lynn Stiles
*Baltimore, MD*

[Hometown] *Baltimore* [Occ] *non-profit warehouse worker* [Hobbies] *bad poems and blurry photography* [GA] *I saved Dirty Eddie from being run over by a bus.*

*Love to swim. Hate to get wet.*

### Pretty Blue Bird

Birds sing while I
Sit under a tree
Thinking of a long life
Journey that awaits for me.
Blue skies fade my last goodbyes
I make my last promise;
I say I love you my pretty blue bird now fly
home fly fly fly home
I will see you in the spring once again
My pretty blue bird

Tisha Marie Campbell
*Joplin, MO*

[Hometown] *Joplin, MO* [Hobbies] *painting, poetry, and singing* [GA] *singing solo at NEO College*

## Love and Light

Illuminating brightly like a maroon glow from the heavens
A sacred glow only visible to the divine eye
Open and vulnerable yet healed completely
Filled with warmth and vitality for a life worth living
Stored in a chest worth every breath
The heart grows stronger every day
As it recharges from love in every way
Negative cords are cut and forever kept away

Natasha Monique Shultis
*Kerhonkson, NY*

[Hometown] *Washington, NJ* [Ed] *associate's degree in human services, degree in nursing* [Occ] *LPN*
[Hobbies] *watching movies, listening to music, reading, writing poems* [GA] *graduating nursing school
and raising my 2 beautiful children*

*I wrote this poem during my spiritual awaking; it is about how I learned to love myself and keep myself in a
high vibration.*

## Ache

And so
what I really want, more than anything
(anything in the world)
Anything, is to have you
with me, just me, by myself
Alone, just me
and you
so I can hear your sounds
and smell your scent
and sing my songs with you
And be pretty and lovely and wispy and fragile
so that you would love me and hate to leave,
hate to stay away, hate to say goodbye
Just you and me, alone
And no one would hear or see or find us
No one would care or notice or wonder
and no one would understand
how it feels to be really and truly and utterly
alone

Elaine Carron
*Leland, NC*

## Concrete Finisher

It's another hot day and once again
we're getting ready for some concrete.
A driveway extension it's not a hard pour only stretching out about 40 feet.
Finally done with the digging, break out the hammers and nail bags get ready to set forms.
Once that's done time to throw in and tie steel until you can't feel your arms.
With all this work already done there's still a lot more, after all it's only been half a day.
We're all caught up time for a quick break, breaks almost over 'cause the truck's on its way.
As the truck starts to pour, they pull their rakes and we follow behind with the straight edge.
Hold on we forgot to pull up this inside stake, quick somebody pass me a sledge.
The truck's finally emptied and now it's about time for me to pass the bull float.
Boss can you give me a minute, I'm thirsty; at least give me a chance to wet my throat.
Done with the floating and edging I'm all caught up but, soon it will be ready for a trowel.
Or maybe not, concrete is still pretty wet looks like I might be here for a while.
With the edges nice and open, it laid down good and it's about ready for a broom.
Boss said he'll pick me up at 7AM tomorrow morning, to get some rest and be ready to resume.

Louis Mejia
*Monroe, LA*

[Occ] *concrete finisher* [Hobbies] *writer*

*Another day of finishing concrete. It's hard work but for some reason I like it!*

## Space and Time

We are enveloped in a small space,
here in our time on Earth.
During our time we are laced
with opportunities of worth.

Space and time
go hand in hand.
We are unique beings of a different kind.
Created by our God, who helps us understand.

We were by Him and for Him.
How else could it be explained?
In the beginning we were made by Jesus, without sin.
A beautiful creation on Earth through time, proclaimed.

Through this, in conclusion.
Dear Lord, utilize our time, help us to find
in our search for a solution
by being a light in our own space through time.

Cinda M. Carter
*St. Louis, MO*

[Hometown] *New Haven, IL* [Ed] *graduation diploma, flora diploma* [Occ] *retired* [Hobbies] *flowers* [GA] *having three books published*

*My desire is that all come to know Jesus as Lord and Savior. I reach out through poems that will either inspire others and encourage them by sharing with them a part of my life, through what I have learned through the scriptures. I know it has changed my life for the good. Praise the Lord!*

## Opportunity Knocks

Not aware globally about the news
Adults don't have time to give all the clues
Only beware school for all its rules
Creeps up on you this stage of stardom
Goes to show this lack of participation
What does it take today to motivate
Why don't we find time to inspire
May influence some claustrophobia
Teachers deal every day with arachnophobia
Authority seeks to reveal the matter
Puberty fails to hear the banter

Elizabeth Efstathakis
*Forest Hills, NY*

[Hometown] *Forest Hills* [Ed] *BA psychology, Queens College* [Occ] *customer service representative*
[Hobbies] *tennis and piano*

## The Easter That Was

The world took a deep breath, paused and then stood
still. As isolation and despair, like never known
before, covered our land. Some mysterious force spread
droplets of evil upon humanity and brought our land to
the brink and in a blink of eye one by one we fell.
This curse had no knowledge of our stamina and, for so
many, our faith in God but nor did it care. Our
dedicated doctors, nurses, first responders, parents,
caregivers and children all pitched in to help.
Little by little we started the process of standing up
to this unwanted monster that crept into our lives.
Only to fall to our knees in prayer after each life was
lost or saved whichever the case.
We have not won the battle for the moment, nor can we
claim absolute victory, but we will win the fight. And
as the sun comes up over the horizon on Easter Sunday
we can rest in the assurance that our God cares.

Bobbie Tyler Hill
*Vestavia Hills, AL*

[Hometown] *Vestavia Hills, AL* [Ed] *administrative assistant field but now retired* [Occ] *retired*
[Hobbies] *writing poetry, enjoying my four grandchildren* [GA] *my two sons (Mike and Kelly Scott)*

*The strength and resilience of the American people has been on full display during the COVID-19 outbreak. We have risen to the occasion and to some have individually faced the fight of our lives. Through it all our sheer determination and lust for life has held us together and for me, my faith in God. My poem was written in April of 2020 as America was shutting down businesses, schools, and churches. It is dedicated to those who deserve to be thanked and those who have lost a loved one, or perhaps for you.*

## Keeping in Touch

With cookies in the oven
as Christmastime draws near
I take a moment to reflect
on those whom I hold dear
It's amazing how the years fly by
while trying to stay in touch
Sure wish we had more time
for fellowship and such
If you do not hear from me
please know how much I care
I may not get to visit
but my heart is always there
If you don't get a card or call
I've not forgotten you
There's only so much time
and oh so much to do
So have a Merry Christmas
And hold your loved ones tight
Say your prayers and hug your dreams
Before you say goodnight

Teresa Abbott
*Aberdeen, OH*

[Hometown] *Lynx, OH* [Ed] *leadership training and college courses* [Occ] *retired* [Hobbies] *reading in the winter and boating in the summer* [GA] *accepting and following Jesus Christ as my Savior*

*I have two sons and three grandchildren whom I love very much. In the work force area of my life, I worked with direct sales for thirty-eight years. I retired after battling stage IV cancer. God has allowed me another opportunity to live so I can better serve Him. I discovered how much I loved writing poems just a few years ago. I love life!*

## Back Then

Long ago in the shadows
Where we once lived
We were young
Invincible it seemed
Smooth skinned, full of dreams
Wishing on stars or wishbones
Even though sometimes hungry
For bread or fame maybe
Mirrored images of who we once were
Altered now by time
In the procession of wrinkles
Looking back, things looked good
Maybe better than they were
Time changes perspective you know
Looking behind is easier than looking ahead
The outcome still glowing or glaring
Time altered
Look behind you may learn for tomorrow, or
Let go, lest you drown in the past
it takes courage to decide
Are you brave

Judy Rasmussen
*Twin Falls, ID*

## I Didn't Realize

Sad enough to understand for not crying over it the full terms.
Not knowing the value of being around you.
Knowing the loyalty that I had grown so beautiful into a form of trust we both learn from each other how to live daily.

Theo Tor Carter
*Pittsburg, PA*

[Hometown] *Pittsburgh, PA* [Ed] *general studies* [Occ] *housekeeping* [Hobbies] *cooking, music, shopping, and reading* [GA] *being able to vote at 18 years old*

*My name is Theo Carter and I am from Pittsburgh, PA where I have lived most of my life. I'm currently employed at a local animal shelter where I do housekeeping for two days—Thursday and Fridays. My birthday is April 24th and zodiac sign is Taurus the bull that I am open-minded, down to earth, and yes I am stubborn.*

## Crawl

On my hands and knees I crawl
through the blindness
and the blackness
and the darkest dusk
weakly feeling my way along
manic movement, lost in circles
A rasping grasp at innocence
a semblance of knowing beyond the veil
while roaming lost in endless tale
a dark and weary raven's call
a praying caw
hungry for the carrion
of this sacred body's holy communion
Tender touches of tainted rapture
our Elysium scorned with
lusus naturae
and those that stalk the night
hungry
hopeless
harrowed
I open my eyes
and breathe in deeply
and count the floorboards beneath me
and try to remember where I am

Kaz Nerys Flowers
*Fairmont, WV*

[Hometown] *Weston, WV* [Occ] *caretaker* [Hobbies] *D&D, creative writing* [GA] *seeing my poetry published*

*The greatest creative blessing I ever received was playing D&D again. I made a character, a seventeen-year-old boy, and I decided that he was very creative and emotional. He wrote his feelings in a poetry journal, and I wanted to write a few poems from his perspective. Four months later, this journal has over a hundred poems in it. I used to go entire years not being able to write a single word, and now I spend hours a day writing stories and poetry. This poem is for you, Corvus, and your path to understanding your own power.*

## Telephone

The phone rang for a minute.
Hello! Who is there?
A voice answered "Lincoln."
Lincoln who?
The five-dollar monster.
It was the ultimate enjoyment demolishing your salary.
Pennies for you and five more for the monster.
Bullying the office perks was the biggest incentive.
The office filled with heightened racism effortlessly.
Taking your flowers became routinely bias.
It was essential to shred out the staff.
A write-up here and a warning later.
Today you are in; tomorrow you are out.
You are the clown for any day I choose.
Removing the access card got you barred out for good.
Listen up! return at $8.00 wage.
Or your life will be a living hell.
A minute pass in silence
Monster—*I Quit*
Goodbye
Call disconnected....

Monique Susan Murray
*Weymouth, MA*

[Hometown] *Weymouth, MA* [Ed] *Bachelor of Art in global affairs, minor in Italian studies* [Occ] *founder and CEO of Nokamo Apparel LLC.* [Hobbies] *I love to dine-in at various local restaurants.* [GA] *completing my degree was one of the greatest achievements. It set me up for success providing the tools I needed to create and build my own business. My poem was inspired from the hardships employees undergo experiencing workplace discrimination.*

## My Time Clock in Life

My time clock is ticking away, what
I do will be etched in my time clock today.
What will I talk about has my mind in whirl.
Why not talk about my childhood growing up
in country on our large daily farm.

At the barn there stood Mahogany Sweetheart.
Looking down in her box for her corn on the cob.
I guess I will saddle her up for a ride on farm.
Sugar Babe was prancing as some colts often do.
Looking for his lump sugar I held in my hand.

Off I go down memory lane always stopping at
the grape harbor to pick a pod of grapes.
They tasted so yummy for Sweetheart and me.
Why not stop at chicken coop to check on Cluck
to see if she has laid her big brown egg today.
In distance there set daddy on Farmall tractor.

While tying Sweetheart to tractor wheel, I said, "Daddy
I came out to help you bail the hay." What was I doing
that hot summer day driving tractor to bring in the hay.
Looking back at Daddy who had a grin on his face and
he said, "You know Helen this in the load of hay we have
been looking for last load of day."

Helen Wilson
*West Alexander, PA*

[Hometown] *West Alexander, PA* [Ed] *nurse* [Occ] *retired age 90* [Hobbies] *play guitar, mandolin, travel, cruises, writing poetry* [GA] *marrying Robert in 1954 and having five-generation family*
*I'm retired after ninety years and this is what I know. Our lifetime here on Earth is very short. Teaching, writing and living close to God our Father and His Son Jesus Christ is what I live close to. Marrying my husband Robert in 1954 and our five-generation family keeps me really busy. My mother Margaret taught me to love poetry. What inspired me to write this poem was my father Melvin who taught me to love our country we call America.*

## For Elizabeth

When I first asked God for a little girl
I never guessed the happiness you'd bring
The sweetness, love, and laughter in your eyes
Such endless joy from such a tiny thing
My friends warned me that it would be different
That life would change so much in many ways
How daughters wrap us dads around their fingers
And make our hearts melt with a single gaze
What they didn't tell me was how special
The moments we share together would be
Just walking place to place while holding hands
The simple pleasure of your company
I still recall your first stumbling footsteps
The tuck-ins every night to calm your fears
And when Mom got your hair cut short and grownup
I smiled for you to help me hide my tears
All the years that I dreamed of a daughter
Never expecting those dreams to come true
When I asked God to make a little girl
He made a miracle and gave me you

Anthony Charles Busillo II
*Harrisburg, PA*

[Hometown] *Harrisburg, PA* [Ed] *BA/MS University of Pennsylvania, JD Temple University (Beasley School of Law)* [Occ] *attorney* [Hobbies] *chess, bocce, trivia, playing keyboard, and writing poetry* [GA] *being appointed General Counsel for the Pennsylvania State Lodge of the Fraternal Order of Police and serving two terms as chair of the Pennsylvania Bar Association's Lavor and Employment Law Section*

*This poem was written as a surprise gift for Elizabeth's eighth birthday. After everyone had left, I asked Liz if it was fun. Liz said yes, but also asked me if I had forgotten something...her gift? I replied, "Oh my gosh, I forgot. Sorry, here it is," and handed her the poem, which was printed on parchment paper and set in a gold wooden frame. I'll never forget the moment when, after reading it, Liz looked up at me and smiling said, "Daddy, this is the bestest present ever." It almost brought tears to my eyes.*

## Fly with Me

I take your hand our eyes now meet, so
Hold on tight, come fly with me.
This night belongs to you and I,
Just two more stars in the midnight sky.
So high above the Earth are we, we ride
These winds of destiny.
Moonlight shines upon your face, this
Angel whom I can't replace.
Come close my love, I'll keep you safe,
These memories now yours to take.
Now back to Earth, feel gravity,
Till next time, love, you fly with me.

Matt T. Zubiller
*Glen Cove, NY*

## Fortitude

Two naval officers were cast into choppy waters
When their PT boat was sunk
Then a 3 hour swim in shark infested sea
One pulled the injured one with his teeth
TO a possibly unsafe nearby island
Four nights he swam out hoping for help
Then sent out a coconut with a "help" message
They were rescued
John Fitzgerald Kennedy: *Deas gratias*

Margaret Coralie Pearce
*Englewood, CO*

## "...for They Shall Not Perish..."

"Marash City or Kermanigeh, moon goddess of my Cilicia!
Until 1080 'twas my ancestors' hometown of 3000 years.
November 1895—a missal and candle in my childish hands
My parents, Vartavar and Trvanda Pamboukian/Maljian,
Chiropractors, on their knees reciting their rosary...
When a vile mob roared: 'Open the doors, pig infidels!'
With frenzied banging in unison...A sudden lightning
Of an axe yataghan high in the air struck a blow,
And my father's skull rolled into my legs...As if,
on a football field...I screamed: 'ba...ba...baba...'
Fell on my father's body...A moment of bloody terror
Where human memory banishing with poignant madness,
Truth from Hell, no longer a dream but now a *reality*!
Then Father Muret urged my mother to send me to Rome.
1915 genocide eve Fr Pascal Maljian returned home
Falsely accused of distributing food to deportees of
Zeitoun; I was imprisoned along with Cardinal Tappouni.
During my 1916 mission, Marash's court found me *guilty*.
Aleppo's supreme court sentenced me to die by hanging!
Seeing immoral actions of criminal guards to clergy and
The cries and crawling of innocents begging to be shot,
Afraid to commit suicide, lost their mind, found peace.
November 11, 1918 *armistice day*, prison doors opened,
And we dashed out to an uncertain freedom.
1928 Rome awards me 'Monsignor' for apostolic mission
June 16, 1976 he entered into eternal rest in Bronx, NY.

Rose M. Akian
*Belleville, NJ*

*Since the onset of the COVID-19 pandemic over a year ago, I've been reflecting on my life and memories of my childhood. Part of that reminiscing also includes the trauma my uncle endured during his earlier years.*

## The Dungeon

A dungeon
Of darkness
Of madness
Terror and humiliation
Swarm the soul
Pain and agony
Take over the body
Torture continues
The heart is strong
The heart can take it all
Stubbornness and pride
Create a monster within
The dungeon has no power
The dungeon will lose this battle
She laughs to herself
This pain will end
The body may suffer
But the heart will live forever
Free of all sorrow and fear

Candyce Therrien
*Denver, CO*

[Hometown] *Denver*  [Occ] *information technology*  [Hobbies] *crafting, writing, fundraisers, billiards*
[GA] *starting home business*

*Life is a struggle; it's how you choose to handle it, determines the outcome.*

# The Wrong Exit

Busted windows, sticky doors
Plaster ceiling, squeaky floors
Poor lit room, home to some
Sleepless nights, no way fun
Monthly cost, weekly rent
Hard-earned funds, poorly spent
Comforts little, amenities few
Torn-up curtains, brick wall view
Fortunes gone, or never made
Occupants visit, history stayed
Passing people, future guest
Check in/out, a moment's rest
Faint lit sign "vacancy"
Desperation the reality
How did stopping come to this
The exit sign you wish you'd missed

Paul L. Lewis Sr.
*Spring Hill, KS*

[Hometown] *Sumter, SC* [Ed] *aviation mechanic* [Occ] *retired navy* [Hobbies] *bowling, helping others in need when asked* [GA] *raising two wonderful men*

*I often write poems to help others who need words of inspiration to get them past whatever problems they may face in life. If it helps them even a little bit then I've done my job as a poet.*

## Words Matter

There are sticks and stones
And there are words
Words that never...
But often do.

Words do matter
The hurts are real
A label attached
Can push us out.

Away from the rights
Due to all mankind
A much more lasting hurt
Than sticks and stones.

Robert B. Aukerman
*Centennial, CO*

[Hometown] *Centennial, CO* [Ed] *social work* [Occ] *Public Health and Human Services Administration* [Hobbies] *reading, gardening, fishing* [GA] *maintaining my family*

*People are more important than things. This is the principle I was raised with and have tried to live by. Poetry enables me to look forward and back, inward and out. It enables me to seek this principle as an essential part of my being. Poetry also provides perspective to trials in my life and a respite from the purely rational approach to both positive and negative events. Poetry is in my soul.*

## Football Blues

Each weekend there is a game or two,
The season is going strong.
To be with my husband
I just tag along.
He rushes me through dinner
So we'll be there on time.
Just to have the perfect seats
Right on the fifty yard line.
Bundled in layers of clothing
From my head down to my toes.
I shiver for two hours
Till the starting whistle blows.
Still as often as I've seen it
I don't understand the game.
Center, tackle, quarterback
They all look the same!
It really is a mystery
What happens to the ball?
I see it, then it disappears
And men run till they fall!
So why are people cheering?
I'd love to join right in.
Won't someone please tell me
Did we lose or win?

Joan Patterson Yeck
*Moosic, PA*

[Hometown] *Moosic, PA* [Ed] *Mercidian School of Nursing* [Occ] *homemaker/retired rehab nurse*
[Hobbies] *reading, writing poetry, playing accordian, water aerobics, walking* [GA] *my children and
grandchildren*
*I enjoy writing poetry for and about my family and everyday situations and events. Since I was a majorette
in high school and attended every football game, I thought I should know something about the game but I
don't! It was fun to write something humorous about what I don't know about the game. During this past
year with the pandemic, writing and reading poetry has been a comfort to me.*

## Swans on the Pond

Peaceful is the view that morning reaches out to
Find, out on the waters are two swans joined
In heart and mind. They float on, and
Elegance marks them in their pace.
Exquisitely arrayed, they tie their neck and
Face. Their silky wings do but help enhance
The breath capturing sight that leaves a
Viewer in a trance. Silent bells pronounce their
Every motion. One gives a whisper, the other
Reacts upon the notion. Oh, one can't help but
See the bond of the two white swans
Floating on the pond.

Geisha Battle
*Chester, VA*

[Hometown] *Chester, VA* [Hobbies] *poetry* [GA] *Best Poets of 2018,* Best Poets of 2019, Best Poets
of 2020

## Cupboards Filled With Love

For years my cupboards have always been stuffed
    Right up to the brim;
Most often when the mood hits,
    I try cleaning out some of them.

Upon the first day I do really good,
    Discarding stuff we don't need;
About the second day or so,
    My sentiment takes over the lead.

There's all those little outfits,
    From when my babies were born;
They looked so beautiful in them;
    And the clothes aren't all that worn.

I'm keeping them for the grandkids,
    In case I should ever have any;
Along with the rattles and Fischer-Price toys,
    And let me tell you…there are plenty.

As I was digging on the fifth day
    And had cleared one shelf above;
The rest I left upon deciding,
    My cupboards are filled with love!

Patricia (Zeigler) Bossard
*Montesano, WA*

[Hometown] *Montesano, WA* [Ed] *high school* [Occ] *farming, retired school janitor* [Hobbies] *river floating, horse riding, ice skating, wild berry picking, reading, writing music and dancing* [GA] *my three sons My Great Depression era parents Frank and Rachel Zeigler raised my sister Leta and me on our dairy farm in the Wynooche Valley near Montesano, Washington. They taught us "Don't throw anything away, you might need it!" My husband Jerry and I welcomes our sons Jerrod, Kevin and Arnie on that farm. I took many photos and collected postcards, etc. when we traveled. Grandchildren did arrive after writing this poem; Summer, Benjamin, Lilly, Faith, Ella and Finn. Now, there's special mementos about them to keep. Some people call it hoarding…I call it "Cupboards Filled With Love!"*

## Ole Linda

We've made it through all kinds of shit. Come on, cuz!
You can pull through this. I know it's hard, I feel upset.
You're all alone in your body's crypt.
You fight, ole Linda, you still have time.
We've got trips to take and smiles to have.
You've always held on through thin and through thick.
You come on, ole Linda, out of the thick of this.
Your children need you and the rest of the fam.
We're pulling for you; you're in our prayers.
Come on now, cuz, don't go out like this
unless it's too hard and you just can't take it.
It's easy for me to pray that you pull on through,
but, cuz, I ain't there, so I can't attest to—
what you're seeing, hearing, feeling, or
what else is on you?
Whatever path you choose,
I know the Lord has you.
My sweet cuz, ole Linda,
my heart is with you.

Keely Lynette Gibson
*Detroit, MI*

[Hometown] *Detroit* [Ed] *Master of Fine Arts in creative writing/poetry* [Occ] *rater* [Hobbies]
*cooking, baking, flowers & plants, writing* [GA] *motherhood*

*I wrote this poem for my favorite cousin who was in a coma after a tragic automobile accident. I love my
younger cousin and am praying for her daily. She's pulling through and is recovering slowly.*

## Reunions

They like, yet, they don't like each other.
Disagree who is wrong or is right.
They smile, say hello, they hug and they laugh.
Congenial opposed to a fight.
The thoughts of each other, live inside the
mind, things you can't say face to face.
They talk in a circle, words go round and round,
and they stay in a very safe place.
As time passes by, they can't look in the
eyes of the one they don't want to see.
They go on, day to day, month to month, year to
year, don't fold, stay as straight as can be.
They live in the middle of the false and the true.
Put on a display, they fool others, too.
Just bad things remembered, good things forgot.
Condemning is easy, forgiveness is not.
There's too much at stake to make a mistake.
Must keep waters calm and do no harm.
So, at all cost, to keep the peace and not
cause any strife.
Resist emotions that cause explosions
and accept, each must live their own life.

Marie Klein
*Staten Island, NY*

[Hometown] *Brooklyn, NY* [Ed] *high school graduate* [Occ] *retired crossing guard, aerobics teacher* [Hobbies] *drawing, painting pictures, interior home decoration, collect coins, reading, writing* [GA] *being a mom of 4, 2 daughters and 2 sons*
*Born October 14th (Libra), in Bensonhurst, Brooklyn, NY. Had a happy childhood. Through school years I studied Italian, typing, dictation, played violin, sang and danced in festival. Played volley ball, ran races, and twirled a baton. Married at eighteen years. Had two daughters. Divorced after six years. We remarried others. I had two sons. He, one son and three daughters; they've all grown now and have families. Through all these years, I always worked. Our blended families get together on many special occasions, mixed with happiness, hurt and drama. With this in mind, I write my poem.*

## Red Head Bird

Looking up in a nearby tree
There I heard watching me
A red head bird
Not by accident you're following me
At my home in the biggest tree
Then far away gone off to the park
A clear revelation started passionately
Red head authority
As bird represent spirit
In a boardwalk park on the river
Stillness and quietness guided me here
Poetry and God mended together
Downloading thoughts released atmosphere heaven
Freely given sitting on a bench hill
Where a red head bird appeared

Carolyn Annette Stovall
*Tampa, FL*

[Hometown] *Tampa, FL* [Ed] *certified medical abstractor/coder* [Occ] *medical coder* [Hobbies] *poetry writing* [GA] *author of several published poems*

*I believe poetry is a gift of spoken words that heals a broken soul. So release and let go.*

## Hindsight

What if I could blend it all together?
These days outweigh the pain
In a place it doesn't get better
Quite the view in hindsight
Every night is my favorite night
Every now and then, I question
If I could do it all again…

But when you blend it all together
I sip my wine and think this
Is what forever
Is supposed to feel like

All the bad
Doesn't stand a chance
All we have
Comes alive when we dance
When we cry
When all the moments move to our mind
What a beautiful hindsight
Every night was my favorite night
You know, every now and then
I question, if I could do it all again
But I sip my wine, in good time we find
This is what forever feels like

Katie E. Dunkelberger
*Oceanside, CA*

[Hometown] *Elizabethtown, PA* [GA] *serving 8 years in marine corps and having my first son*
*Honestly, I don't write much anymore. In the past two years, a lot has changed in my life. I used to spend*
*moments thinking of poetic lines to describe that given moment. Now I find myself writing less and being*
*more present. So when I sat down to write the full version of this poem I realized how beautiful the past*
*was—the good, bad, happy and sad. Every night, even the hard ones, became my favorite night. And when*
*I sat there blending all the moments together leading up to the present, a sense of peace came over me…it was*
*sort of what I imagined "forever" felt like.*

## Pulling Beauty out of Ashes

How can it be after suffering love's latent lashes
The phoenix appears, pulling beauty out of ashes?
Yet here you are, with deep set scars but open heart
Exposing your soul for kiss's cure from dragon's mark
Let my pressed lips serve best to seal all we feel
Lancelot and Guinevere knew their love burned real
If we say it out loud, it won't make it sound proud
Passion's persistence gives consent of what's allowed
So love me, fiercely, between sheets of fated flames
The intensity of our heat burns off slated shame
Please, leave sweet searing memories upon my skin
Brand me with your scent, possess me with life within
Hold me, mold me, into an angel of the night
Spread my wings, let me fly with your melded delight
Let your touch flavor my flesh with the salt of lust
As I cry out wanting love, from the only one I trust
Poetry in motion, a paragon's rhythmic ballet
I am yours, you are mine, in love's sensual Palais
For the spirit of the phoenix rises in your eyes
Pulling beauty out of ashes as sunrise descries

Cherie Leigh Sumner
*Denver, NC*

*My name is Cherie Leigh Sumner, but I use my pen name of just Cherie Leigh for my books. I am an author, writer and artist. I am obsessed with passionate love poetry.*

337

## Jupiter with Saturn a Great Conjunction

The seasons change during each year,
But in some, astronomers find things to cheer.
The year 2020 brought something new,
It was a conjunction that was historical, too!
Maximum Conjunction was on display.
This time the winter solstice was the day.
Here we are after the great event, but the planets
Are still close as toward the horizon they descend.
Looking in the direction of the southwest
Is where we saw the conjunction at its best.
The last time these planets were seen this close
Man believed the Earth to be the center post.
Man was at the center of the universe,
Our thinking was that around us all things traversed.
Things were really different back then.
The 1200s saw the idea of knowledge expand.
There in Timbuktu, a university arose anew.
But history is in the past so let's see what's new.
We see images in the sky today,
And think in the past it was the same way.
Jupiter and Saturn appeared close in the sky.
The ancients believed this was magical.
They saw something which they tried to describe.
Perhaps it was the star of Bethlehem they surmised.
A great event that we celebrate today.
Since their time some have seen it that way!

Clarence G. Underwood
*Esparto, CA*

[Hometown] *East Coast* [Ed] *college degree* [Occ] *retired* [Hobbies] *reading, writing, astronomy, and chess* [GA] *having and maintaining a family*
*As we look to the heavens let us not forget our place of birth. We are the people of Earth. As a man of this planet I understand that life is finite. Although it is long lived, the planet is also finite. Our recent history suggest that while mankind has evolved, we still lack a basic understanding and the compassion which we subscribe to mankind. Let us go forward and work towards loving one another and ourselves!*

## Covid—We All Went Numb

Covid—All who were alive during Covid.
As a person, family members, we are patients, we are caregivers.
What is going on the stores are closed, we must cover up our faces/identity our love ones we
no longer can be seen in hospital/home cares. I no longer can hug my family members?
Months go by and our soul and identity go numb.
EMT, ER staff alongside hospital staff.
Running to help, we are needed every place, no available coworkers to be found no supplies to
be found. Family members calling we cannot speak to them, patients asking for love ones.
So many patients coming for help never stopping. Medical staff are human need breaks,
We need hugs to cover our tears.
 Months go by our soul and identity go numb.

Mary Bantz
*Hicksville, NY*

[Hometown] *East Meadow* [Occ] *unit clerk emergency room* [Hobbies] *great out doors and fresh air*
[GA] *to work side a great bunch of people that work together during the worse of times and teach each
other and learn from each other every day*

*This poem it for all my coworkers in the emergency room, for all medical staff in the hospital, all patients and
family members who had to live and die Covid 2019. All who lived/worked "MSSN."*

## Than You for Your Service

You fought for freedom and the red, white and blue.
You suffered for your country and the ones you love, too.
You traveled across the seas to far-off distant lands
And put the symbol of freedom into outstretched hands.

Your country didn't always recognize your vows
To uphold the values that freedom allows.
But you took up the call and made it your purpose
And we all thank you for your service.

The wounds you suffered are reminders for us all
Of your sacrifice and courage when you answered the call.
The price you paid for freedom doesn't come wrapped in a bow
But the gifts that freedom brings to us is worth more than you know.

So thank you for your service from all of us to all of you.
You represent the best that our country can produce.
Wherever you may go and whatever you may do,
We will always appreciate your service and will always honor you.

Lloyd Hammond
*Beaver, OH*

## Prometheus

I sustain on ten second moments
where I forget you've gone.
Briefly able to feel full again
before grief plucks the piece from my chest.
Like a slice of ultraviolet emanating through the curtains
you expose just enough.
Peeking through the cracks I gaze in on your afflictions
hoping to extinguish its intensity.
Melted cornea pools at my cupids bow
as I am devoured by curiosity.
Never considering forever until now.
I burn harnessing your fiery aura.

Hannah L. Betancourt
*Forest Grove, OR*

[Hometown] *Forest Grove, OR* [Ed] *associates in applied science* [Occ] *administrative assistant* [Hobbies] *writing, cooking, making people laugh* [GA] *having my first poem published in 1999 at the age of 8*

*I was born and raised in a small rural town where I spent much of my childhood outdoors cultivating my love for animals and plants. Living in the lush pacific northwest provides endless imagery and inspiration for my writing. Poetry has always been a source of comfort and expression for me, especially during these trying times. I aspire to be a well known poet and a motivator to others to follow their writing dreams. We are all more alike than not, so always choose love.*

## Going Home

The past fades behind you
Your future straight ahead
Many reasons you can't stay here
Isn't that what you said
So far you will travel
To get your life right
That's why you're driving
To Colorado all night
You swear to God
You'll get it right this time
And you're ready and willing
To spend your last dime
Deep in your heart
You know this is best
Keep with you good memories
And throw out the rest
Going to Colorado
Your destiny ahead
The past far behind now
It was just a dead-end
Many friends that you know
They just can't understand
When fate comes calling
It changes a man
Quit your job and sold all your stuff
Truth be told though those things
Anymore didn't mean very much
Why is life so hard you're thinking
As you drive down the road
Might as well be towards Heaven
Sure feels like you're going home
May truth, beauty and goodness
In your life may you find
Remember to keep love in your heart
And let your light shine

Judy Russell
*Big Bear City, CA*

## God—Universal—Presence

Omnipotent divine grace
How great thou art.
God's universal presence
God's unlimited power, here, there, and everywhere.
Your light of love, shine in every direction, brilliant light of love
here, there and everywhere
Holy light of love
brilliant bright and beautiful, dew drops of sweetness, here, there
and everywhere. Pathways, lighten with love
Road's lighten with love
your love is higher than the highest mountain, deeper than the deep blue sea
extremely sentimental.
Rush of love flowing here, there and everywhere. Genuine, heavenly divine.
God's love flying on the wings of the wind, sweet breezes blow, here, there
and everywhere. God's love is sweeter than honey
cascade of sweetness here, there, and everywhere. Pure love, true love.
Amazing grace how great Thou art
echo of melodious
How sweet it is.
Iridescent of beauty
Great, grand here, there, and everywhere.
Extraordinary remarkable profusion of beauty, brilliant
light of love. Exceeding wonderful
Exhibition of joy, exceedingly of joy in my soul. Mighty, mighty
tender. Profuse of beauty.
God painted the rainbow in the sky where the bald eagles
fly and in every nation, God creation.

Mae Nell James
*Dearborn, MI*

[Hometown] *West Point* [Ed] *inspiration writer* [Hobbies] *variation* [GA] *writer*
*My faith in God and my testimony in Jesus Christ has inspired me to give inspiration to all who read my poems about our Father, Son, and Holy Spirit. He is the light of the world. Picturesque of beauty, God wants us to put love where hate used to be and to give a brilliant view of beauty in the light of love. To open our heart let sweet breezes into the world, everyday for love, forever love. Display of beauty and to let our brilliant light of love shine bright.*

## Memory of Scotland

I hear the waves crashing on rocks below
And smell the ocean's salty air
And I'm in Scotland just once more
I'm young and free and have no care
The highlands beckon me on again
Those misty mountains of ancient lore
I hear the pipes of Scot clansmen
I feel the chill of highland winds once more
The medieval streets of old town
In the Edinburgh I know
Have seen me before in past days gone
And yet their histories with me show
That I'm not free of past old time
When the bells of old St. Giles did chime
My memory jogs of the breezy walk
On top Lions Head in Old Queens Park
Tasting fish and chips in paper bags
The smell of pubs in memory lags
The castle on high rock stood still
Overlooking Princes Street Garden
And off in the distance Carlton Hill
Where I walked alone very often
Scotland haunts my memories still
The clouds and snowy days do fill
My mind with lovely memories
Of youth, of love, and mysteries

T. H. Henning
*Haymarket, VA*

[Hometown] *Haymarket, VA* [Ed] *BA, Med Penn State University* [Occ] *retired IBM* [Hobbies] *writing, reading*
*T. H. Henning is a veteran of the US Air Force. This poem was inspired by the three years he spent in Scotland. He earned BA and Med degrees from Penn State University and completed a certificate of attendance at Cambridge University, England. Although he authored six books—*Memoirs of a Defense Contractor, The Scotland Spy, Web Based Corporate Institutes, Legend of the Chinese Spy, Anaria: A Collection of Poems, *and* Ballad for Those Lost at Sea*—his greatest achievement was marrying his wife, Helen, the birth of their son, Zach, his wife Autumn, and having a beautiful granddaughter, Makena.*

## My Dream

This child, -----
This sister, mother, wife,
Envisions a world
Without sorrow nor strife;
Where lamb and lion,
Stranger and kin,
Abide side by side,
Friendly, peacefully, within.
Seasons, sunsets beautifying,
Flora, fauna multiplying.
Water, food a-plenty;
Not a cupboard empty;
Where enmity ne'er exists.
Lo, respect and honor persist.
E'er patriotism, worship owned;
Yes, wisdom, talents honed.
Will such happiness sublime
Be enjoyed beyond this rhyme?
Will our Earth e'er dwell in peace?
Will inhumanity ne'er cease?
This child believes it will.
The "good books" teach us still,
To trust, honor and obey.
Our "Compass" has shown us the way.

Rosemarr Greathouse
*Carbondale, CO*

[Hometown] *Blanding, UT* [Ed] *junior, BYU* [Occ] *housewife* [Hobbies] *music (piano, organ, vocal) art, poetry* [GA] *wifehood and motherhood*
*Rosemarr Burtenshaw Greathouse, 81, eldest of 6 children. Music, art, poetry, dance, hard work central to upbringing, Blanding, UT. Piano/vocal performances, 4-sisters' quartet, BYU acapella choir, Southern California Mormon Choir; accompanied vocalists, instrumentalists, choirs, stage productions; painted scenery, posters, invitations; produced greeting cards, composed songs, poems;; married Hugh E. Greathouse while at BYU. Also resided in Guadalajara, Mexico, Arcadia, California, (35 years), where he completed USC Medical School, internship/residency, neurosurgical practice with South California Permanente Medical Group at Carbondale, CO 2005. Five children, seventeen grandchildren, seventeen great-grandchildren, our greatest accomplishments! Thank you for this much-appreciated opportunity.*

## Inspire Anyway

If you work hard and give your best to inspire others, you might be accused of competing
*Work hard and inspire anyway*
If you share your work often to inspire others to create their own ideas, you might be accused of being arrogant
*Continue to share your work and inspire anyway*
If you advocate for honoring learning styles in children and adults to inspire uniqueness, you might be accused of not being a team player,
*Advocate and inspire anyway*
If you generate ideas to inspire change and learning, they might be resisted and suppressed only to resurface as another's idea
*Generate and inspire anyway*
If you have a passion for life and learning and inspire a passion in others, you might be termed boastful
*Stay passionate and inspire anyway*
If you bring different knowledge to the table to inspire research and new ideas, you might be made fun of and laughed at
*Bring your knowledge and inspire anyway*
If you speak your truth and use your voice to inspire change, you might be accused of being difficult to work with
*Speak your truth and inspire anyway*
If you bring your experience to the table to inspire not only diversity in race but in ideas, you might be accused of being conceited
*Bring your experience and inspire anyway*
If you introduce new initiatives to inspire growth, you might be accused of not being a team player
*Initiate and inspire anyway*
You see in the end, it is not about who likes or dislikes you, as this is out of your control.
Instead, it is about how much your work, passion and presence have impacted and inspired others and systems with ideas that weren't there before.
Even if your impact is never given credit,
*Inspire anyway*

Cherry-Anne Gildharry
*New Braunfels, TX*
*This poem was inspired by Mother Teresa's Poem, "Anyway." I am a district math instructional coach who is extremely passionate about education. This poem was written to inspire others who face adversity and are falsely accused when they share their ideas and work. In addition, it was also written to inspire others to keep on creating and sharing their ideas even when these are suppressed, but then resurface as new ideas by the monopolies in education.*

## Heart Is Pure

Thinking quietly one evening how family have left
For a better home so glorious—and you my husband
Thinking of your pure heart—my beloved husband
You left too soon here one day, gone the next
You were a beautiful person—showing your kindness
Always willing to teach and help those you could
My beloved husband with the pure heart
You listened and loved me so much but
You kept a secret to leave me—my beloved husband
Your heart was so pure—when the time came
Father showed you the vail and off you went
Your pure heart and the love we had for each other
My beloved husband you will never be forgotten
Because of your pure heart I am a better person
Taking the knowledge you taught me to
Have my own pure heart

Shirlene D. Williams
*Las Vegas, NV*

[Hometown] *Adelanto* [Occ] *management assistant and pharmacy technician* [Hobbies] *writing, playing piano, shopping, and going to yard and estate sales* [GA] *having children, seeing grand and great-grandchildren; made it to retirement*

## It's About Time

Thank you Lord I'm free
like a butterfly flipping in the wind
from flower to flower
I can come and go as I please
no more the way it used to be
no more abuse from people
that I thought loved me
I was abused so much
I thought abuse was love
no more touching me
and hitting me
I was so afraid I ran away
She controlled where I went
what I did
who I talked to
from age eleven to age twenty-eight
she said if you don't work
you don't eat
I worked sixteen hours a day
then I came home and cleaned for hours
I was so afraid
when I saw her, my body shook
I was afraid to speak I vomited
God took her away;
now I'm free to do as I please.

Sheila Evans
*Forest City, NC*
[Hometown] *Chicago, IL* [Ed] *medical* [Occ] *med tech* [Hobbies] *poetry, all kinds of crafts* [GA] *my children, two boys—I was told I would never have kids*
*I've live in Forest City, NC since 2004. I went to Camden Central High, then Elmhurst in Illinois for nurses training, then Harry S. Truman for certification. I worked at Cook County hospital. Married, he died, one child from that. Married again twenty-four years, one child from that. Was in a bad accident. Went to Tennessee Tech to start over. I worked as a sitter from hospice sixteen years here in NC. Was hit by a dump truck in 2015. Now I do all kinds of crafts. I love to write poetry. My greatest achievement is my kids. They're good kids and I'm proud of both of them.*

# Index of Poets